atlantis

the truth

the lost wisdom of our
forgotten ancestors

ian lawton

Rational Spirituality Press

First published in 2020 by Rational Spirituality Press.
Previous versions of this book were published in 2003 under the title *Genesis Unveiled* and in 2010 under the title *The History of the Soul*.

All enquiries to be directed to www.rspress.org.

A CIP catalogue record for this title is available from the British Library.

ISBN 978-0-9928163-6-0

Cover design by Ian Lawton.
Cover photograph by Elena Schweitzer, licensed by dreamstime.com.
Author photograph by Simon Howson-Green.

Introducing the 'Prehistoric Truth' series

This series of books – summaries of each of which can be found in the closing pages – deals with Giza, Atlantis and Mesopotamia respectively, and its title requires a little explanation. First, I chose the word *prehistoric* simply because *historic* alone would convey a false context. Yet all three do at least partly cover the period of humanity's development *after* written records came into being.

Second, and perhaps rather more contentious, is the choice of the word *truth* in the title both of the series and of the books themselves. This originally sprang from the fact that the first volume was named *Giza: The Truth* by Virgin Books some twenty years ago. But the continued creation and dissemination of wild, alternative theories about ancient human history and prehistory in the interim has led me to the conclusion that, just as in modern politics and life in general, there's so much 'fake news' around that a dose of reality is more than ever required.

Of course that doesn't, however, mean I believe myself to have a monopoly on truth in these matters. All I strive to do is research and write with the maximum integrity and scholarship of which I'm capable, and to present both sides of the coin where necessary and possible, so readers can make up their own minds about the validity or otherwise of my conclusions. Basically I'm just trying to reintroduce a little dose of sanity and discrimination into the various debates, so that people with little time to properly research these matters for themselves aren't led completely astray by outlandish ideas that have little basis in reality.

There is, after all, more than enough that we still don't properly understand about human prehistory, and new discoveries are being made all the time by professional historians and archaeologists. So we hardly need to invent apparent 'mysteries' that have little foundation... however much the human mind may be fascinated by such things.

To the perceptive eye the depth of their degeneration was clear enough, but to those whose judgment of true happiness is defective they seemed, in their pursuit of unbridled ambition and power, to be at the height of their fame and fortune.

Plato, Critias, on the fall of the divine Atlanteans

CONTENTS

PART TWO: CORROBORATION

LIST OF FIGURES

LIST OF PLATES

These are located at the end of the book.

ACKNOWLEDGEMENTS

Much of the material in this work comes from the original manuscript of *Genesis Unveiled*. Therefore it continues to owe a great deal to the assistance of those close friends and colleagues mentioned first time round: Flavio Barbiero, Nigel Blair, Michael Brass, Michael Carmichael, Simon Cox, David Elkington, Garret Fagan, Mark Foster, Nigel Foster, Adrian Gilbert, Paul Heinrich, Robin Crookshank Hilton, Edmund Marriage, Crichton Miller, Lynn Picknett, Clive Prince, Colin Reader, Nigel Skinner-Simpson, Danielle Stordeur, Greg Taylor, Marcus Williamson and all the staff at the British Library.

In addition when I was revising it as *The History of the Soul* Andrew Collins apprised me of various new research in the area of catastrophes in particular. Finally for this latest version my former co-author on *Giza: The Truth*, Chris Ogilvie-Herald, pointed me towards various research papers about Gobekli Tepe; and I have found the reviews of the work of a plethora of alternative authors penned by the American researcher Jason Colavito to be absolutely invaluable – he too seems determined to get behind all the hype and inject a little groundedness and basic scholarship into the whole alternative field.

PREFACE

In the Western world we're pretty familiar with the book of Genesis from the Old Testament. How God created the world in six days, and rested on the seventh. How he created the first man, Adam, and then his companion Eve. How Adam's descendants acted as patriarchs overseeing human affairs up to the time of the great flood, which God sent to destroy humankind. How Noah was spared in the ark and went on to father the new human race.

Over the last few centuries, spurred on by Darwin and the breakthroughs of scientists in all fields who've followed in his footsteps, we've increasingly been told to reject all of this as nothing more than a fable constructed to foster a religious outlook in simple people – and it's probably not unreasonable that any traditionalist who still insists the world was created in 4004 BCE receives pretty short shrift.

Yet many *post-flood* biblical traditions originally dismissed as mere stories were validated in the late nineteenth century when Mesopotamian cities mentioned in the Old Testament – for example Nineveh, Erech and Ur – were unearthed by intrepid explorers such as Sir Austen Henry Layard and Sir Leonard Woolley.[1] Similarly the discovery of Troy by Heinrich Schliemann, and of the Minoan civilisation in Knossos on Crete by Sir Arthur Evans, proved that settlements had existed at both sites since around 3000 BCE, forcing a similar revision of orthodox thinking about certain Greek traditions. These wonderful breakthroughs came from the dedication and bloody-mindedness of pioneers who refused to accept the conventional wisdom. In that time it has also become clear that reports of a catastrophic flood exist not just in the Bible but also in sacred texts from all around the world.[2] Meanwhile various researchers have attempted to show that these are backed up by geological evidence, to such an extent that in recent decades the idea has received widespread publicity and a fair degree of acceptance.

As a result of all this in the mid-1990s, in my formative years as a writer and researcher, I became fascinated by the possibility that the sparse and enigmatic record of a widespread *pre-flood* culture in the early chapters of Genesis might also contain some element of truth. So I set myself the challenge of unearthing as many of the ancient texts and indigenous traditions from around the world as I could, to find out what the rest of our ancestors might have to say about any early race of people on our planet who were wiped out by some sort of major catastrophe.

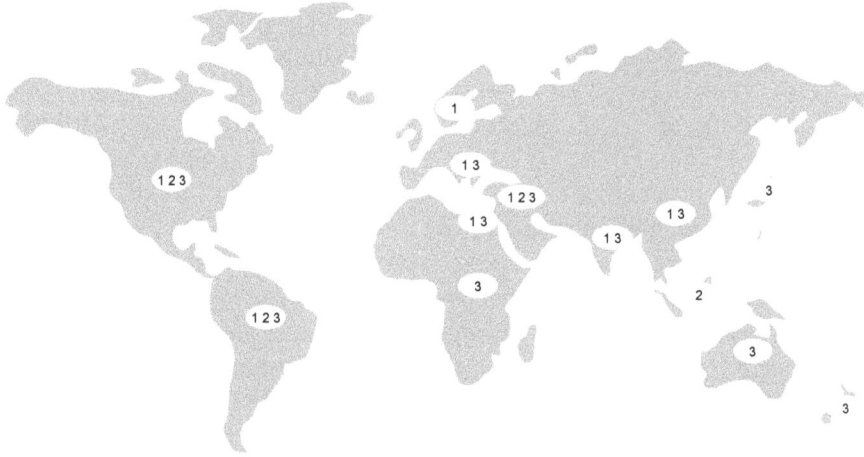

1 A golden age followed by debasement and destruction
2 Multiple attempts to create a successful human race
3 The world created from the void by the supreme deity

Figure 1: The Common Themes in Ancient Texts Around the World

Most of my original research was undertaken in the days before the internet made it so incredibly easy, and I was often spending weeks at a time in the British Library poring over obscure anthropological studies and other rare manuscripts. But I became increasingly enthralled as I discovered that various ancient cultures right across the globe preserve a tradition of a forgotten race that was originally highly spiritual but degenerated until it was wiped out. As can be seen from Figure 1 these traditions are far more widespread than is sometimes recognised. Were all these too just simple fables put together by relatively primitive, superstitious cultures, or did they contain some grain of truth? Intuitively I felt the latter might just be true.

Having said that, in any study of this kind we must proceed with extreme caution. Nowhere was this brought home to me more than by the issue of the so-called 'King Lists' from Ancient Mesopotamia, Egypt and China, which acted as the forerunners for the biblical list of pre-flood patriarchs.[3] Originally I was excited by these as potential proof of a pre-catastrophe civilisation – until, that is, I was confronted by the cold, hard scholarship of Garrett Fagan, professor of ancient history at Penn State University:[4]

> In every instance, to my knowledge, the lists start out with the gods. The lists then function to show (a) the antiquity of the regime or culture that composed them and (b) that regime or culture's direct connection with the gods. It is much harder to challenge a divinely ordained system than an admittedly human one.

It seems obvious once pointed out that many of the messages found in the ancient texts and traditions are explainable in sociological terms, especially when acting to reinforce the rule of the prevailing politico-religious hierarchy. Allied to this it's clear that many of the versions of sacred texts that have survived have been repeatedly edited over time by different sets of cultural leaders with just such motives, making it much harder to see through the fog and establish the nature of the original underlying message.

Then, of course, there's the whole issue of symbolism in what is commonly termed 'mythology'. In the first of his four-volume masterwork *The Masks of God,* published between 1959 and 1968, that most respected of experts in this field, Joseph Campbell, describes how any would-be interpreter is walking something of a tight-rope:[5]

> It must be conceded, as a basic principle of our natural history of the gods and heroes, that whenever a myth has been taken literally its sense has been perverted; but also, reciprocally, that whenever it has been dismissed as a mere priestly fraud or sign of inferior intelligence, truth has slipped out the other door.

To some degree Campbell developed the work of his equally eminent predecessor Carl Gustav Jung, who prefaced the English version of his *Psychology and Alchemy,* first published in 1953, with the following overview:[6]

> Some thirty-five years ago I noticed to my amazement that European and American men and women coming to me for psychological advice were producing in their dreams and fantasies symbols similar to, and often identical with, the symbols found in the mystery religions of

antiquity, in mythology, folklore, fairytales, and the apparently meaningless formulations of such esoteric cults as alchemy... From long and careful comparison and analysis of these products of the unconscious I was led to postulate a 'collective unconscious', a source of energy and insight in the depth of the human psyche which has operated in and through man from the earliest periods of which we have records.

There can be little doubt that Jung's symbols, or archetypes, are the key to unlocking the hidden meaning of much of the body of myth from around the world that our ancestors have left as their legacy. This is one of the main reasons why the most sacred texts and traditions of all ancient cultures can appear so enigmatic and obscure to the uninitiated – because to a large extent the archetypes, whether in picture or textual form, are not designed to speak to the logical left brain, but rather to the intuitive right brain that's the link to both the personal and the collective unconscious. Nowhere is this more clearly demonstrated than in the texts of the Ancient Egyptians, whose hieroglyphic symbols often had multiple and subtly different meanings appreciated only by those fully initiated into their mystery.

It is also the case that the earliest texts and traditions of our ancient cultures tended to be handed down orally, even after they'd also been recorded in writing. Indeed we often find important philosophical concepts embedded within a story format, not only so they could be more easily memorised and would be entertaining to relate, but also so that they might better penetrate the non-logical, subconscious mind. This allowed them to survive over centuries or millennia, even if the real understanding of their symbolic message was lost on most of the audience. In addition, of course, couching such traditions in symbolism and archetype was particularly useful when, as has happened throughout history, esoteric sects were trying to maintain them under threat from a dominant religious orthodoxy.

The foregoing analysis is fine as a general summary of the modern approach to mythology. But are there any grey areas, even concerning the time *before* the flood, where it would be right to debate whether something more than just symbolism and myth underlies the relevant texts and traditions? Might they have some basis in fact that, albeit perhaps in only the broadest of senses, can act as a pointer to real historical events? My research led me to believe these grey areas did exist, particularly in the passages I repeatedly encountered that appeared to describe a veiled history of humankind only hinted at in Genesis.

Not only that, but several other themes were continually cropping up too, in particular those dealing with the 'creation of humankind' and the 'origins of the world'. Again their spread is shown in Figure 1. In my view many orthodox scholars tend to oversimplify these aspects of the traditions of our most celebrated historical civilisations by concentrating on the anthropomorphic qualities of the various well-known gods that take centre stage. By contrast I became increasingly convinced that, when properly interpreted using the nascent spiritual and esoteric worldview I was starting to develop, these consistent themes revealed their originators to be anything but intellectual dwarfs trying to concoct a simplistic philosophical framework with which to make sense of the world around them. It seemed to me they had a highly sophisticated worldview, and probably a common source of spiritual wisdom on which to draw.

We are now some two decades on, but the reason I'm rewriting and republishing this work is that I continue to believe that a proper appreciation of the legacy left by our forebears across the globe, and a reappraisal of the consistent elements of their worldview from a *spiritual* perspective, is long overdue. This just may take us closer to uncovering the underlying messages in their texts and traditions than we've ever been before – and may also lead us, at last, to a true understanding of the legend of the lost civilisation of 'Atlantis' that has so beguiled us ever since Plato first mentioned it.

Nevertheless this work couldn't stand up to scrutiny if it relied solely on the reinterpretation of ancient texts and traditions. In support, first we can turn to archaeology, where a mounting body of *orthodox* artifactual evidence increasingly suggests that modern humans have been around in highly cultured form for rather longer than has hitherto been accepted. Second we can bring in the geological evidence that in the relatively recent past our planet has been rocked by at least one major catastrophe, which could easily have wiped out all traces of any advanced culture that prospered beforehand. Some of the older material in this area has proved to be of little value, but important new research keeps catastrophe theory very much alive and kicking.

The number of alternative researchers who have put forward unconventional views of the history of our planet, and of human life thereon, has proliferated dramatically in the last half century. Indeed, as we'll see later, several of these are the very authors who inspired me to begin my own quest. But it wasn't long before I found out that unfortunately many of them can be somewhat lacking in scholarship. Even when I was conducting the original research for this book my experience with my first book *Giza: The Truth* – first published in 1999 but now the first volume in this newly-published 'Prehistoric Truth' series – had already taught me not to take anything written by alternative authors on trust. Instead one must always go to the primary source to check out their references and interpretations. In doing so I also learned that some of them aren't averse to *deliberate* misinterpretation and even falsification of supposed evidence.

A case in point was when I became hugely excited by New-York journalist Zecharia Sitchin's apparent revelations about the Mesopotamian texts that predate the Old Testament and, it turned out, provided the antecedents for biblical themes such as the story of the flood and its hero. Not only did he claim to be one of the few scholars in the world able to interpret their complex cuneiform scripts but, far more exciting, he announced that that they described how humankind had been genetically created by a race of extraterrestrials called the 'Anunnaki' from a planet called 'Nibiru'. These revelations initially came in 1976 with his first book, *The Twelfth Planet*, but over the next few decades they were augmented by a number of follow-ups in his 'Earth Chronicles' series. By the time I was introduced to his work by a girlfriend in the mid-1990s, like so many other people I'd already developed the inner sense that not everything about our orthodox, materialistic view of life on Earth was to be trusted – and that there must be something *more*. To a complete novice like me, Sitchin's revelations were like manna from heaven, the answer to all my doubts, the key to the alternative history that so many of us suspected must exist. The problem came when I decided to do something that most casual readers don't have the time or energy to do. I checked out the Mesopotamian texts for myself.

It didn't take long to obtain translations by orthodox scholars, and to realise that something was very, very wrong. Not only did Sitchin not have any proper endnote references in his books – something that should perhaps have been a dead giveaway even to a novice researcher like me – but also the references within the text were often sporadic and incomplete. This meant that tracking down passages in texts he claimed to quote from proved close to impossible in some cases. Undaunted, I began to list all of the older Sumerian and later Akkadian texts I could locate in the translations made by orthodox scholars, and to summarise their contents. I then made a case study of Sitchin's claims concerning the word *shem*, which he insists really means 'sky rocket' even though experts are agreed that it's mainly used to denote 'name' or 'reputation'. It was then, when I also consulted those few scholars who had been prepared to devote precious time to commenting on Sitchin's work, that the true extent of his falsification was revealed. For a start he was very far from the sort of linguistic expert he claimed, instead randomly mixing up Akkadian and Sumerian script to suit his wild interpretations and showing almost total grammatical ignorance into the bargain. Worse still he would sometimes leave out interim lines or phrases in his extracts, with no ellipses to show that he'd done so, which when reinstated from orthodox translations rendered his interpretations completely untenable. This could only imply one thing: the deliberate and conscious falsification of evidence on his part.

At the end of this somewhat painful process I collated my research into a number of papers published on my website, which have now become the third volume in the 'Prehistoric Truth' series, *Mesopotamia: The Truth*.[7] But the reason I include all this here is because it's highly instructive. We have to adopt the highest levels of discernment when reading, writing and researching alternative history, and if we don't we might as well be indulging in complete fantasy. Entertaining fantasy, perhaps, but fantasy nonetheless.

I hope it's fair to say, without sounding too arrogant, that *Giza: The Truth* gave me certain credentials as an independent and discerning author who isn't afraid to admit when orthodox scholars have got it right – which remains, in my experience, the majority of the time. They are by no means infallible, any more than any of the rest of us, and of course we can all be selective in what we research and present, even if only as a result of entirely subconscious bias. But by and large they haven't achieved what they have by being narrow-minded imbeciles. Of course some leading alternative researchers are masters of rabble-rousing, and their followers love to hear them pouring vitriol on anything to do with the orthodoxy. But For many years I've felt that it's time for a new, more scholarly approach to alternative history to come to the fore. An approach that has the independence and freedom to question aspects of the orthodoxy that possibly deserve re-evaluation, but without blatant disrespect. An approach, too, that doesn't gloss over or remain ignorant of orthodox arguments, but instead faces them head on.

One key aspect of all this is that I and my co-author on *Giza: The Truth*, Chris Ogilvie-Herald, felt that up to that point there'd been an almost complete lack of peer review and constructive criticism among the 'club' of leading alternative authors. So after it's first edition came out I began to take issue with them – not because I liked the sound of my own voice or had a point to prove, but in the genuine hope that highlighting those theories that were clearly nonsensical or lacked coherence would actually advance, at least in some small way, the alternative movement's general cause and credibility. I carried on in the same vein in this second book when it was first published as *Genesis Unveiled* in 2003. Of course I understand that there are commercial considerations for modern authors under pressure from hard-pressed publishers, but surely the constant underlying aim should be to move together towards a better understanding of the enigmas of our past, and to share this research in an honest and responsible way with the general public. What is more there are a hard core of real enigmas that remain largely untouched by orthodox scholars but do deserve serious study, without us needing to fabricate all sorts of weird and wonderful nonsense.

In particular when postulating a 'forgotten', 'lost' or 'hidden' former race of people on Earth, some alternative researchers have demonstrated a disturbing lack of understanding of orthodox arguments in three main areas. The first is human evolution, where certain of them provide supposed evidence of *extreme* antiquity for modern *Homo sapiens*. Not only is this evidence fatally flawed anyway, but they also fail to place it in any philosophically or scientifically logical context. Meanwhile others propose that extraterrestrial intervention is the only answer to supposed evolutionary enigmas they appear not to have fully investigated. The second is the role not just of symbolism but also of *context* in myth. So some of them, for example, produce entirely literal translations of specific texts with no regard for the context of similar themes in other cultures. The third is the dating of monuments from our earliest historical civilisations, where again the significant body of *contextual* evidence archaeologists have painstakingly amassed is often disregarded. Nowhere is this latter phenomenon better demonstrated than in attempts to ascribe a far earlier date to the Great Pyramid and Sphinx, a subject covered in detail *Giza: The Truth* that we'll also touch on in Part 2.

Other alternative researchers take a different tack and, even if they accept the orthodox view of human evolution and of the dating of ancient monuments, suggest the level of technology displayed by these early civilisations couldn't possibly have 'developed overnight' – some even arguing that highly advanced technology must have been handed down by survivors from Atlantis or introduced by extraterrestrial visitors. Yet they fail to properly appreciate just how much can be achieved by a civilisation like that of the Ancient Egyptians with superb organisation and focus, but not necessarily high levels of technology in the modern sense of the word. When we understand that there's a development period in the archaeological record of these civilisations that such researchers tend to ignore, and we remind ourselves of how rapidly our modern Western world has developed in only a handful of centuries, these arguments just don't stand up.

By contrast, rather than using the argument that the supposedly advanced technology of our earliest historical civilisations *implies* that previous counterparts must have existed, I'd argue there's prima facie textual as well as indirect archaeological evidence of an extensive pre-catastrophe civilisation – although to me there's nothing even remotely conclusive to suggest they were technologically advanced. They might have constructed settlements of considerable size, but not necessarily with huge structures, advanced techniques or even durable materials. If located in the right areas of the globe, and not competing for scarce resources, they might have developed a high state of culture – but one based primarily on inter-group cooperation and trade, knowledge development and education. We always tend to assume others must be like ourselves, and we're only too aware of how aggressive and war-mongering we can be, even in the modern world. But what if originally they were nothing like us? What if they lived lives of peaceful cooperation and harmony, both with nature and each other, for many millennia – until, like us, they became slaves to the great god of material progress.

Above all, instead of extrapolating the supposed *technical* knowledge of our post-catastrophe ancestors back to their pre-catastrophe forebears, we should arguably concentrate on tracing the roots of their *spiritual* knowledge. Although other commentators have explored the symbolism and esoteric wisdom displayed by our earliest historical civilisations, they often seem to fall short of being able to put this into any meaningful metaphysical context. So we will re-examine what really underlies the consistent motifs found in the creation of humankind and origins of the world traditions from around the globe, and consider the possibility that they might display a profound spiritual wisdom. We will then use this as the key to unlock their hidden messages regarding our forgotten, pre-catastrophe race. It is their original *spiritual* advancement in a 'golden age', their subsequent debasement through concentration on the material world and forgetting of their spiritual roots, and their consequent destruction, that appears to shine through loud and clear. Is this just another socio-political, religious or psychological construct – or does it carry an echo of real events?

All in all, then, when I *do* depart from orthodox opinion and postulate that a culturally advanced but non-technological civilisation may indeed have emerged on our planet tens of thousands of years ago, I do so with some hope that it will be seen to be more than just wild speculation and fantasy.

Ian Lawton
July 2020

A NOTE ON CHANGES

The differences between this work and the original, *Genesis Unveiled*, are widespread and not just cosmetic. Although the basic arguments and chapter structure presented in Part 1 remain broadly similar, in Part 2 whole chapters and sections have been removed, added or renamed. Moreover *every* chapter has been edited and in most cases substantially rewritten. For more details see my website.[8]

A NOTE ON THE DEFINITION OF CULTURE

Because the word *culture* can be used in many different contexts, and its specific meaning in particular instances is of vital importance to the arguments in this work, I intend to use four broad definitions thereof:

- *Primitive culture* includes language, cooperation, the use of fire and a degree of ritualistic behaviour, for example in simple burials. It is typified by early hunter-gatherer cultures.
- *Culture proper* includes artistic expression in sculptures and paintings sometimes of high complexity, as well as in music. It is

typified by, for example, the Cro-Magnon culture of Southern Europe.

- *Advanced culture* includes the development of permanent and sizeable settlements; large-scale agriculture with grain cultivation and possibly animal husbandry; trading and ocean navigation; and an advanced understanding of astronomy. It is typified by, for example, the city-states of Ancient Mesopotamia – although note that certain aspects such as building in stone, metalworking and writing needn't *necessarily* be included in this stage.

- *Technologically advanced culture* includes the use of sources of power for lighting, heating and tools, of powered vehicles for terrestrial, aerial and even space travel, and all the other developments that typify our modern society.

A NOTE ON STYLE

Comments in square brackets in quotes are mine, for clarification, while ellipses are used to indicate the omission of intervening words, sentences or paragraphs that are repetitive or irrelevant. Italics in quotes are mine unless otherwise stated.

PART ONE

REVELATIONS

1

MYTHS IN THE MAKING

We face a formidable task in attempting to identify genuine historical pointers in the body of ancient texts and traditions from around the world that are broadly categorised as 'mythical' by the established orthodoxy. Researching opinions across the whole spectrum of mythical analysis, from those of learned specialist scholars to those of the more outrageous alternative researchers, it soon becomes clear that *everyone* is heavily influenced by their own largely subjective judgments regarding what's possible as history and what's not, and whether or not they contain any genuine spiritual messages.

This work starts with the premise that the scholarly consensus about these texts and traditions may have been developed under an unduly restrictive paradigm, both from a historical and a spiritual perspective, and that there *are* some aspects of the ancient texts and traditions that are worthy of reappraisal. Of course many alternative researchers have uttered similar sentiments before but unfortunately, as noted in the Preface, many of them have proved to have a somewhat inadequate understanding of the body of orthodox opinion they seek to overthrow. To overcome this deficiency we should attempt to lay out the foundation of the orthodox position before putting forward alternatives. So let's begin by considering the fundamentals of the consensus attitude toward mythology that currently prevails.

A BRIEF HISTORY OF COMPARATIVE MYTHOLOGY

A variety of definitions of *myth* have been attempted with varying degrees of usefulness. But broadly speaking the modern consensus distinguishes between historical or canonical records on the one hand, and myths, legends and folklore on the other. Within this framework, myths are normally held to deal with important metaphysical concepts such as the origins of the world and of humankind, and to involve gods or supernatural beings. Legends by contrast tend to involve human heroes, usually on great quests of one sort or another, while folklore is pretty much dismissed as localised superstitions of minimal significance. Even these broad categorisations suffer from myriad weaknesses – for example, many legends contain important motifs also found in myths, so to exclude them from this study where relevant would be a nonsense. In any case I advocate the use of the more generalised but less pejorative terms *texts* and *traditions* – the latter usually referring to information handed down orally in indigenous tribes until anthropologists recorded it – because they don't have the unhelpful connotations of words such as *myths* and *legends*.

So, accepting a relatively broad definition of the term, let's look at the history of what's been referred to as the 'science of myth'.[1] A number of important contributions are worth noting, starting in 1856 with that of the man regarded as the founder of the discipline of comparative mythology, Max Müller. In his *Essays on Comparative Mythology* he proposed that all myth was an attempt to explain natural phenomena. This was closely followed by the work of Daniel G Brinton, who brought in the burgeoning study of the New World alongside that of the Old; of Adolf Bastion, who attempted to introduce psychological factors into the study of 'constants' in mythology; and of Edward Burnett Tylor, who used similar methods to analyse animistic motifs. In the late nineteenth century Bronislaw Malinowski kept the psychological theme to the fore in his study of various surviving indigenous cultures, while in 1890 Sir James George Frazer published the first two volumes of what would eventually become his twelve-volume *The Golden Bough,* a landmark work that introduced the importance of the cyclical nature of life as an underlying mythical motif.

In 1889 Leo Frobenius presented a counterargument to the psychological school, positing that a primitive cultural continuum once existed around the equator, so that any similarities in myths result more from transoceanic diffusion than from parallel development. In part this is exactly the view this work seeks to re-establish, except removing the word *primitive* from the mix, because the focus in the twentieth century has remained resolutely on psychological interpretations, often underpinned by an atheistic perspective that sees psychology and spirituality as stark alternatives rather than as possibly complementary to each other. The most celebrated proponent of this 'psycho-materialist' position was Sigmund Freud, with his emphasis on sexual and relational tensions in the make-up of myth. One notable exception, however, was his collaborator-turned-opponent Carl Jung, whose concept of archetypes we discussed in the Preface. He was one of the few influential figures in the formative years of psychiatry who was hugely interested in all things metaphysical and, although not exactly explicit on the matter, always allowed plenty of room for spiritual interpretations of his work.

Overlapping with Jung, three of the giants of modern mythology took the arguments forward in the 1950s and subsequent decades. We have already mentioned Joseph Campbell, whose *Masks of God* represents the apogee of general studies of the subject. It contains an incredible breadth and depth of knowledge of myth from all over the world and all ages, combined with detailed and erudite commentary. Mircea Eliade has also made a huge contribution to the study of comparative religion and mythology in a number of works, including *Myth and Reality*, *The Sacred and the Profane*, *Shamanism* and *Patterns in Comparative Religion*. Likewise Claude Levi-Strauss, who has especially attempted to analyse the contradictions and opposites so often found in myth, in works such as *Myth and Meaning* and *The Way of the Masks*.

THE DEVELOPMENT OF MYTH

Any summary of the orthodox approach to the analysis of myth should arguably use Campbell's *Masks* as its primary reference. Although certain aspects have been questioned by some of his successors, it remains the definitive study to this day. The basic starting point is that myths in their purest form evolved primarily because of certain psychological features of the human makeup.[2] Campbell begins by discussing the differences between 'innate' stimuli built into all humans and those that are 'impressed' by cultural influences. This can be best be understood if looked at from the context of the three basic stages of human growth:

- At the beginning we have the psychological trauma of birth, of switching from the safety and warmth of the womb to the unpredictability of life outside it. Psycho-materialists suggest this innate experience underlies the recurrent mythic theme of the search for nirvana, which they insist is actually only a desire to return to the womb. Then during childhood individual, selfish desires – for sustenance, warmth, and affection – predominate, and most are seen as being satisfied by the mother. Again psycho-materialists suggest this is the cause of the massive importance attached to the mother figure in myth.

- As we move into adulthood the self-oriented behaviour of childhood has to be re-engineered into a sense of social responsibility, especially in more primitive cultures where the group has to work together just to survive. There can be little doubt that much early myth sprang up to assist this process, because it's the 'sacred lore' into which young adults are initiated even in modern tribal cultures that helps prevent them from disintegrating. These stimuli are culturally impressed and will vary from one group to another.

- Finally with the onset of old age we find ourselves orienting once again toward the individual, universal and innate in our contemplation of death. This stimulus lies at the very heart of legends involving the hero's quest for immortality that so predominate in one form or another.

Campbell continues by describing how, as primitive humans evolved, they became increasingly interested in their surroundings. Prosaically they needed to understand how changes in weather and climate, for example, would affect them from the practical perspective of food, shelter and basic survival. But they also began to wonder about their underlying workings from a more abstract or philosophical perspective. For the first time our ancestors started to ask fundamental questions about how the earth, sun, moon, plants, animals – indeed humankind itself – originated, and they tended toward supernatural explanations involving supernatural beings. Of course psycho-materialists tend to leave it at that, without questioning whether some underlying element of this supposedly primitive philosophy actually derives from innate stimuli – which themselves derive from a universal consciousness, as Jung suggested, and therefore have genuine spiritual significance. But this is an argument we must leave to one side for now.

Campbell concludes that the aspect of their surroundings that most impressed itself on early humans was the extent to which all of nature is cyclical. They noticed the cycles of the sun and moon, of the seasons, of plant life – all of which implied a continuous cycle of birth, growth, death and rebirth. They also recognised the impact the cycles of the moon had, for example, on female menstruation and on the tides; and they became intrigued by the opposing forces that so often predominate in myth – of night versus day, dark versus light, male versus female, life versus death and so on. These, he says, are the underlying factors that led to the sun and moon in particular playing such a decisive and enduring role in myth. Moreover it was this impetus that led to the more detailed study of the stars and planets, and this in turn would lead eventually to the all-pervasive mythic theme in all advanced cultures that saw the Earth as a mirror of what was happening in the skies – that is, 'as above, so below'.

This is necessarily an extremely brief survey of the major psychological stimuli that are thought to underpin much of mythology, although it should provide a sufficient backdrop for the analysis to follow. But to complete this backdrop we should consider, again in highly summarised form, the orthodox view of the differing mythological motifs of our various, earliest-known cultures.

To begin with, says Campbell, two major cultural variants developed.[3] On the one hand the primitive planter culture of the equatorial zone depended primarily on protoagriculture and harvesting natural crops, so communities were relatively settled. The emphasis of worship was on Mother Earth as a provider, the culture was typically matriarchal and the serpent was the dominant animal symbol – its ability to periodically shed its skin being representative of death, rebirth and renewal. By contrast the hunter-gatherer culture of the less temperate zones to the north was typically more patriarchal, given their dependence on their menfolk to hunt and kill game, and the dominant animal symbol was the bull.

According to the orthodoxy a combination of these two cultural influences prevailed until civilisation proper emerged in Sumer in the latter half of the fifth millennium BCE. The new city-states, with their hierarchies of kings, priests, merchants and peasants, required an entirely new form of control – indeed needed to create 'order out of chaos', another fundamental theme of myth. This is how Campbell describes the huge impact this had on the development of mythology:[4]

> The new inspiration of civilised life was based, first, on the discovery, through long and meticulous, carefully checked and rechecked observations, that there were, besides the sun and moon, five other

visible or barely visible heavenly spheres (to wit, Mercury, Venus, Mars, Jupiter and Saturn) which moved in established courses, according to established laws, along the ways followed by the sun and moon, among the fixed stars; and then, second, on the almost insane, playful, yet potentially terrible notion that the laws governing the movements of the seven heavenly spheres should in some mystical way be the same as those governing the life and thought of men on Earth. The whole city, not simply the temple area, was now conceived as an imitation on Earth of the cosmic order, a sociological 'middle cosmos', or mesocosm, established by priestcraft between the macrocosm of the universe and the microcosm of the individual, making visible the one essential form of all. The king was the centre, as a human representative of the power made celestially manifest either in the sun or in the moon, according to the focus of the local cult; the walled city was organised architecturally in the design of a quartered circle (like the circles designed on the ceramic ware of the period just preceding), centred around the pivotal sanctum of the palace or ziggurat (as the ceramic designs around the cross, rosette, or swastika); and there was a mathematically structured calendar to regulate the seasons of the city's life according to the passages of the sun and moon among the stars – as well as a highly developed system of liturgical arts, including music, the art rendering audible to human ears the world-ordering harmony of the celestial spheres.

As for the effect this had on the symbolism of these new civilisations, Campbell adds:[5]

The impression one gets from these is of a considerable hodge-podge of differing mythologies being coordinated, synthesised and syncretised by the new professional priesthoods. And how could the situation have been otherwise, when it was the serpent of the jungle and the bull of the steppes that were being brought together? They were soon to become melted and fused – recompounded – in such weird chimeric creatures as the bull-horned serpents, fish-tailed bulls, and lion-headed eagles that from now on would constitute the typical apparitions of an extremely sophisticated new world of myth.

THE FUNCTION OF MYTH

To complete our necessarily brief introduction to the orthodox view of mythology, let's finally see what Campbell has to say about the function of myth, and the closely associated activity that puts it into practice – ritual:[6]

Functioning as [an innate] 'way', mythology and ritual conduce to a transformation of the individual, disengaging him from his local, historical conditions and leading him toward some kind of ineffable experience. Functioning as an [impressed] 'ethnic idea', on the other hand, the image binds the individual to his family's system of historically conditioned sentiments, activities and beliefs, as a functioning member of a sociological organism. This antinomy is fundamental to our subject, and every failure to recognise it leads not only to unnecessary argument, but also to a misunderstanding – one way or the other – of the force of the mythological symbol itself, which is, precisely, to render an experience of the ineffable through the local and concrete, and thus, paradoxically, to amplify the force and appeal of the forms even while carrying the mind beyond them. The distinctive challenge of mythology lies in its power to effect this dual end; and not to recognise this fact is to miss the whole point and mystery of our science.

Campbell's writings are underpinned by a fundamental spirituality, albeit that he seems to have held the broadly agnostic view that all spirituality is a search for an 'unknown force' that is, itself, 'unknowable'.[7] But despite his erudition and undoubted influence, most orthodox scholars still tend to adopt a broadly psycho-materialist and non-spiritual view of myth.

CONCLUSION

Mythology is fickle. Every single ancient text or tradition handed down to us from every part of the world has had a multitude of influences brought to bear on its composition. These include psychological, cultural, political, religious and philosophical influences, as well 'historiographical' ones – those deriving from attempts to record actual historic events – with which we're most concerned. One of the simplest and most poignant examples of editing for political and religious purposes, which sometimes comes as a great surprise to those brought up in a Christian environment, is that there are actually two separate Hebrew words that are translated as 'God' in English versions of the Old Testament: one is Yahweh, a *singular* proper name, while the other is Elohim, a *plural* collective term. Broadly speaking these two words derive from two separate sources known as the Yahwist and Elohist texts. For an accurate translation the latter word would have to be rendered as gods plural, but this would of course contradict the basic monotheism of Christianity. So the simple removal of the *s* at the end is one of the finest examples of expedient editing of older texts that we have.

To make matters worse it's often difficult to distinguish between the different influences in any given text. We will find, for example, that the traditions of indigenous peoples across the globe contain much that's obviously conditioned by local sociological factors, along with much that's quite clearly allegorical. Does this mean it will be impossible or pointless to attempt to discern any historiographical material they might contain? Not necessarily, but we must tread extremely carefully in attempting to find it.

Another general factor we'll have to consider is the way in which traditions that were originally firmly founded on historical fact can be distorted by the passage of time and by geographic diffusion. Campbell himself uses the term 'regressed mythology', and discusses an example of this by tracing certain distorted aspects of the tenth-century *Tales of the Arabian Nights* back to the now-proven custom of ritual regicide that prevailed in many early cultures:[8]

> So, from what we now know, it can be said with perfect assurance that in the earliest period of the hieratic city state the king and his court were ritually immolated at the expiration of a span of years determined by the relationship of the planets in the heavens to the moon; and that our legend of Kash is, therefore, certainly an echo from that very deep well of the past, romantically reflected in a late story-teller's art.

Such a statement does of course support the case for a historical re-evaluation of certain aspects of supposed mythology. But before we become too complacent let's look at the other side of the coin. Here he is discussing the 'great traditional books' of history:[9]

> The world is full, also, of great traditional books tracing the history of man (but focussed narrowly on the local group) from the age of mythological beginnings, through periods of increasing plausibility, to a time almost within memory, when the chronicles begin to carry the record, with a show of rational factuality, to the present. Furthermore, just as all primitive mythologies serve to validate the customs, systems of sentiments, and political aims of their respective local groups, so do these great traditional books. On the surface they may appear to have been composed as conscientious history. In depth they reveal themselves to have been conceived as myths: poetic readings of the

mystery of life from a certain interested point of view. But to read a poem as a chronicle of fact is – to say the least – to miss the point. To say a little more, it is to prove oneself a dolt. And to add to this, the men who put these books together were not dolts but knew precisely what they were doing – as the evidence of their manner of work reveals at every turn.

Strong words that are hard to disagree with, except perhaps in their somewhat uncompromising emphasis. Of course such records were comprehensively and skilfully edited to fulfil all sorts of purposes, and so will never represent strict and detailed chronicles of history. Yet can anyone sensibly dispute that there are grey areas too, ones that *may* carry a germ of underlying factuality in *certain* aspects? It is the possibility that such a germ resides in the passages describing an advanced culture, which existed before and was wiped out by a great catastrophe, that we'll examine in the next chapter.

2

DEBASEMENT & DESTRUCTION

THE PRE-FLOOD PATRIARCHS

The book of Genesis forms part of the Torah or Pentateuch, the first five books of the biblical Old Testament traditionally attributed to Moses. Scholars still don't know the true identity of the original authors, but we do have access to several early Hebrew and Aramaic forerunners that were in circulation in the first half of the first millennium BCE.[1] Our focus is on the early chapters of Genesis that deal with the period between the creation of humankind and its destruction in the flood. As we saw in the Preface, while the former is clearly fanciful, the latter is now seen by many as the point at which myth turns into reality – this because, apart from the geological evidence we'll consider in Part 2, similar catastrophe traditions exist all over the world.[2] So what are we to make of the biblical account of what happened in between, which suggests that humans lived in relatively civilised circumstances for a long time *before* the flood?

Ten pre-flood patriarchs are listed in Genesis 5. They are Adam, Seth, Enos, Cainan, Mahalaleel, Jared, Enoch, Methuselah, Lamech and Noah, and they're given lifespans of anywhere from 365 to 969 years. Even though these are clearly unrealistic, some alternative researchers suggest this list offers proof of a pre-catastrophe civilisation. However we saw in the Preface that such King Lists were used as a political tool, and cannot be relied upon to support the case for such a civilisation. Nevertheless there's a great deal of other textual support, as we're about to find out.

THE NEPHILIM REAPPRAISED

The first place we find such evidence is in the celebrated and rather more intriguing account of life before the flood in Genesis 6:

1. And it came to pass, when men began to multiply on the face of the Earth, and daughters were born unto them,

2. That the sons of God saw the daughters of men that they were fair; and they took them wives of all which they chose.

3. And the Lord said, My spirit shall not always strive with man, for that he also is flesh: yet his days shall be an hundred and twenty years.[3]

4. There were giants in the Earth in those days; and also after that, when the sons of God came in unto the daughters of men, and they bare children to them, the same became mighty men which were of old, men of renown.

5. And God saw that the wickedness of man was great in the Earth, and that every imagination of the thoughts of his heart was only evil continually.

6. And it repented the Lord that he had made man on the Earth, and it grieved him at his heart.

7. And the Lord said, I will destroy man whom I have created from the face of the Earth; both man, and beast, and the creeping thing, and the fowls of the air; for it repenteth me that I have made them.

8. But Noah found grace in the eyes of the Lord.

Who were these 'sons of God' and their 'giant' offspring? Are they mere fictional creations of an earlier age, or was there really a race of culturally advanced humans who lived in a remote time before a great catastrophe wiped them out? The Hebrew word for these giants is 'Nephilim'. Meanwhile their progenitors, the 'sons of God', are usually referred to as 'fallen angels', but also sometimes as 'Watchers' because of the way they're described in the equally celebrated *Book of Enoch* – a text that holds many clues to their identity, as we'll shortly see. Perhaps more than any other biblical characters apart from Jesus himself, these enigmatic figures have fired the imagination of a whole host of theologians, artists and poets down through the ages – as well as, more recently, a host of alternative researchers. Two main, modern schools of thought stand out, and we should consider any shortcomings in their arguments before attempting to correct them. It is also instructive at this point to get a feel for the full extent to which their hugely popular proponents have misled their massive worldwide readerships.

THE ANCIENT ASTRONAUT SCHOOL

Although a number of lesser-known writers had gone down this road in the preceding decades, it was Swiss hotelier Erich von Däniken who really captured the public's imagination in 1969 when *Chariots of the Gods* was published for the first time in English. It perfectly reflected the anti-Establishment spirit of the age, and became a huge overnight success. He didn't specifically mention the Nephilim, but he certainly examined some of the relevant Enochian and Mesopotamian literature, provocatively asking: 'Does not this seriously pose the question whether the human race is not an act of deliberate breeding by unknown beings from outer space?'[4]

Sadly there are obvious flaws in his work. An obvious example is his suggestion that one part of the infamous 'Nazca lines' in Peru, an enigma he admittedly did much to put on the map, is 'reminiscent of the aircraft parking bays of a modern airport'. Even the most casual researcher can easily discover these are drawings of various animals and insects, and he must surely have known that his cut-down picture of the 'parking bays' is in fact a depiction of the tail feathers of a huge bird. Admittedly these pebble sculptures laid out on a wide expanse of flat desert plain can only really be appreciated from the air, and their construction – presumably from scale drawings – as a tribal offering to the gods is a wonderful piece of ingenuity. But aircraft runways they most certainly are not. Meanwhile other questions such 'why should ancient gods be associated with the stars?' only serve to demonstrate his lack of understanding of myth and symbolism.[5]

After a few sequels von Däniken disappeared for many years, amid typical allegations of a conspiracy to silence him – although as we'll see in chapter 11 he's actually made a return in the last decade with multiple extra offerings in a similar vein. But the public imagination had been fired. Into the fray stepped journalist Zecharia Sitchin, who as we saw in the Preface rocketed to fame in 1976 with *The Twelfth Planet,* then followed it up with a number of sequels in his *Earth Chronicles* series. He *was* intrigued by the Nephilim specifically, proposing that they were a race of beings originating from an undiscovered planet in our solar system who came to Earth and genetically engineered the human race.[6] This latter aspect gave rise to that special breed within the Ancient Astronaut school known as 'Interventionists'. Perhaps unsurprisingly, he too attracted a huge, worldwide army of fanatical supporters who, even after his death in 2010, continue to regard him with total reverence.

Let us be clear that both of these alternative pioneers should be commended for introducing huge numbers of people to ancient texts, monuments, artwork and artifacts of which they might otherwise have remained largely ignorant. I very much include myself in this group, because von Däniken captured my imagination as a teenager. Nevertheless as I showed in the Preface, when referring to my work in Volume 3 of the 'Prehistoric Truth' series, *Mesopotamia: The Truth*, Sitchin's scholarship proved no more reliable – to such an extent that his interpretations of Ancient Mesopotamian texts can really only be viewed as entertaining fiction. Moreover it seems to me inescapable that both men were, at least some of the time, *consciously* distorting the supposed evidence they presented. Unfortunately, as we'll see in Part 2, this hasn't stopped others from following their lead and using their work to develop further ill-founded theories.[7]

Does that mean that the Ancient Astronaut or even Interventionist hypotheses are inherently implausible? In my opinion, no, not given the overwhelming likelihood that many extraterrestrial civilisations exist in other parts of our galaxy, let alone least universe, some of whom may well be advanced enough to have achieved interplanetary travel – although whether or not we're currently being visited by same isn't a question I feel qualified to answer, never having properly researched it. What is clear, however, is that the supposed textual and physical evidence used to support the idea that they've visited Earth in the remote past has been thoroughly misinterpreted and distorted.

Of course none of this would matter much were it not for the fact that Sitchin's theories in particular tend to suggest that, as humanity, we're under the control of an extraterrestrial master race rather than masters of our *own* fate, which in my view is a thoroughly pernicious and destructive concept. Added to which such obvious shortfalls in scholarship have provided an easy target for the scholarly establishment, and helped to blacken the name of alternative research in general.

THE REDATING MOVEMENT

The prime movers of this second alternative school are the authors Graham Hancock, Robert Bauval, John Anthony West and, more recently, Robert Schoch. From the mid-1990s they began to use much of the same evidence of supposedly advanced technology and so on first brought to our attention by von Däniken, Sitchin and others to postulate the existence of an advanced pre-catastrophe civilisation – although *not* one of extraterrestrial origin. Crucial to much of their work was a revision of the age of the Great Sphinx of Giza. However, while their arguments in this respect are undoubtedly more scholarly than their predecessors, and while there's a very small possibility that this monument may indeed be older than orthodox scholars allow, it's almost certainly not of the antiquity they suggest. Of course I too am postulating a forgotten pre-catastrophe race but, as indicated in the Preface, *without* the emphasis on high technology and on the redating of known monuments – for which, so far at least, no convincing evidence has been produced. We will return to these issues in Part 2.[8]

One author who has done more than most to bring a reasonable standard of scholarship to the alternative movement is Andrew Collins. In his 1996 work *From the Ashes of Angels* he suggests that the Watchers and Nephilim were post-catastrophe remnants of an advanced Egyptian culture who then migrated around 9000 BCE and introduced 'civilisation' to areas of Anatolia and Kurdistan, from where they spread in due course into Mesopotamia and, again, Egypt. He argues that these people were of different physical appearance to their Near Eastern subjects, being taller, with elongated heads, emasculated white faces, narrow slit-like eyes and long white hair – although exactly where this racial type is supposed to have originated is never made clear. He further suggests they were primarily a shamanic people that identified with the vulture, serpent and goat and wore long robes made of feathers. Moreover that the cause of their supposed fall and subsequent demonisation was that certain of their number left their isolated enclave in the Kurdish mountains to live among the indigenous people of the surrounding plains, where they took wives and taught the more advanced aspects of their culture.

Unfortunately there are a number of potential problems with this 'out of Egypt' hypothesis. The first is that Collins' postulation of the migration of an Egyptian 'elder culture' was originally founded on the mistaken redating of the age of the Sphinx already discussed. The second is that the texts clearly state that the Watchers and Nephilim lived *before* the flood. He attempts to overcome this by postulating *two* floods – a devastating global event around 10,500 BCE that caused the migration out of Egypt and another more localised one around 5000 BCE, which is the one Noah survived – although he admits there's little evidence for the latter.[9]

In fact in 2015, long after this book was originally published as *Genesis Unveiled*, Hancock released a new addition to his corpus called *Magicians of the Gods: the Forgotten Wisdom of Earth's Lost Civilisation*. Given that he was well aware of my original book, about which we corresponded and which in any case sold pretty well, it's interesting to note that he chose an almost identical sub-title to mine, with just two words changed around. Nor do the similarities end there, because in many ways he follows a similar line of reasoning to mine – albeit that to some extent he was only expanding on ideas first expounded in his 1995 best-seller, *Fingerprints of the Gods*. He also follows a similar line to Collins in proposing two catastrophes, although for him the second one came only 1000 years after the first. Meanwhile his forgotten race were apparently white men with red beards who ended up in the Caucasus after the first catastrophe, from where they attempted to reintroduce civilisation to other survivors before being wiped out by the second. In any case it still contains the usual redating and other arguments that I don't support.

Perhaps the greatest shortcoming of all of these alternative theories, however, is their failure to acknowledge the clear existence in the Near Eastern traditions, and in all the others from around the world, of the theme of the *debasement* of a forgotten race that resulted in its destruction. Arguably it's this key facet that lies at the heart of a proper understanding of the fallen angels or Nephilim.

A TALE OF TWO CITIES

One clue to what's going on in Genesis 6 lies in a less frequently discussed preceding passage. The first two chapters describe God's creation of the world, of all animals and of Adam and Eve, while the third deals with their 'first fall' having tasted the forbidden fruit in Eden, and their expulsion therefrom. The early part of the fourth chapter commences with the birth of their first two sons, Cain the farmer and Abel the shepherd, and describes how the former slew the latter in a jealous rage, for which he was rejected by God and banished to the 'land of Nod', east of Eden. Then we get to the heart of the matter, because the remainder of the chapter is devoted to a genealogy of *Cain's* descendants who, although their lifespans are not given, are named as Enoch, Irad, Mehujael, Methusael, Lamech and his sons Jabal, Jubal and Tubalcain. We are also told briefly that Cain built a city that he named after his son Enoch and that Lamech, like his forefather, was guilty of murder – although these two are clearly not meant to be the same as the celebrated patriarchs descended from Adam's third son Seth, as listed above from Genesis 5.

So here we have another line of pre-flood ancestors who appear to have coexisted with the line descending from Adam via Seth. What is more while Seth's line was regarded as God-fearing and righteous, Cain's was damned as evil and murderous. In his *Ancient History of the Jews* the first-century historian Flavius Josephus provides more useful details, describing how Cain 'built a city named Nod' and 'only aimed to procure every thing that was for his own bodily pleasure', becoming 'a great leader of men into wicked courses'.[10] Even more intriguingly, we find that:

> He also introduced a change in that way of simplicity wherein men had lived before; and was the author of measures and weights. And whereas they lived innocently and generously while they knew nothing of such arts, he changed the world into cunning craftiness.

Saint Augustine's fourth-century biblical commentary, *The City of God*, gives us a further insight into the sparse Genesis narrative:[11]

> When the human race, in the exercise of this freedom of will, increased and advanced, there arose a mixture and confusion of the two cities by their participation in a common iniquity. And this calamity, as well as the first [fall], was occasioned by woman, though not in the same way; for these women were not themselves betrayed, neither did they persuade the men to sin, but having belonged to the earthly city and society of the earthly, they had been of corrupt manners from the first, and were loved for their bodily beauty by the sons of God, or the citizens of the other city which sojourns in this world.

So God's wrath and his decision to destroy humankind in Genesis 6 appears to have arisen because a highly spiritual and simple race, here represented by the 'other city' containing Seth's descendants, was gradually perverted and swallowed up by a far more materialistic and decadent race, the descendants of Cain residing in their 'earthly city'. So can we shed any more light on the underlying causes and significance of this 'second fall' – and on why the composers-cum-editors of the Old Testament decided to so massively condense the more comprehensive source material available to them?

ENOCHIAN CONFUSION

To answer these questions we should turn to the aforementioned *Book of Enoch*, which contains far fuller details of the passage in Genesis 6.

28

Although it's attributed to the enigmatic pre-flood patriarch it's impossible for scholars to say with any certainty when it was originally compiled, albeit that a version of it was undoubtedly regarded as part of the genuine divine revelation of early Judaism.[12] But its existence was clearly something of an embarrassment to the founders of the Christian Church because, along with other lesser-known texts from that time that have been discovered in the modern era, it describes a messiah figure who acts in very similar ways to Jesus, but clearly predates or at least isn't the same person as him. This of course casts huge doubt on their insistence that he was the uniquely divine 'saviour of humankind'.

So, instead of being given canonical status when the Old Testament was compiled in its current form in the fourth century, this text was rejected as part of the Apocrypha – meaning 'of questionable authenticity', although whether they understood the irony that the original Greek word means 'something that's hidden' is unclear. As a result of this deliberate prejudice it remained almost unknown in the West for nearly fifteen hundred years until three manuscripts were discovered in Ethiopia in 1773 by James Bruce. Like his more famous ancestor Robert he was a leading Scottish Freemason, and had almost certainly gone looking for it deliberately because it plays a huge part in Masonic tradition. But even then the main public copy lay forgotten in the Bodleian Library in Oxford until 1821, when Archbishop Richard Laurence translated it into English for the first time – at which point this long-hidden text caused an immediate sensation. Since then a different version of the text has been found in Slavonic Russia.[13]

So what are the explosive secrets that have generated so much controversy? Because it's so important the most relevant verses are reproduced in full, starting with the seventh chapter:[14]

> 1. It happened after the sons of men had multiplied in those days, that daughters were born to them, elegant and beautiful.
> 2. And when the angels, the sons of heaven, beheld them, they became enamoured of them, saying to each other, Come, let's select for ourselves wives from the progeny of men, and let's beget children...
> 9. These are the names of their chiefs: Samyaza, who was their leader, Urakabarameel, Akibeel, Tamiel, Ramuel, Danel, Azkeel, Saraknyal, Asael, Armers, Batraal, Anane, Zavebe, Samsaveel, Ertael, Turel, Yomyael, Arazyal. These were the prefects of the two hundred angels, and the remainder were all with them.

10. Then they took wives, each choosing for himself; whom they began to approach, and with whom they cohabited; teaching them sorcery, incantations, and the dividing of roots and trees.

11. And the women conceiving brought forth giants,

12. Whose stature was each three hundred cubits. These devoured all which the labour of men produced; until it became impossible to feed them;

13. When they turned themselves against men, in order to devour them;

14. And began to injure birds, beasts, reptiles, and fishes, to eat their flesh one after another, and to drink their blood.

15. Then the Earth reproved the unrighteous.

The eighth chapter then continues the theme:[15]

1. Moreover Azazyel taught men to make swords, knives, shields, breastplates, the fabrication of mirrors, and the workmanship of bracelets and ornaments, the use of paint, the beautifying of the eyebrows, the use of stones of every valuable and select kind, and of all sorts of dyes, so that the world became altered.

2. Impiety increased; fornication multiplied; and they transgressed and corrupted all their ways.

3. Amazarak taught all the sorcerers, and dividers of roots:

4. Armers taught the solution of sorcery;

5. Barkayal taught the observers of the stars;

6. Akibeel taught signs;

7. Tamiel taught astronomy;

8. And Asaradel taught the motion of the moon.

9. And men, being destroyed, cried out; and their voice reached to heaven.

There are sufficient similarities between this and Genesis 6 that there can be little doubt they share a common origin, except this time those who err are described as 'angels' or 'sons of heaven' rather than 'sons of God'. But before we consider any new spiritual interpretation of these passages, let's pause to consider the more prosaic possibilities. Could they simply be in the King List mould, attempting to tie Judaic bloodlines back to great antiquity and to a divine source? Surely not, because then it would be counterproductive to include such a strong debasement theme. Alternatively do they act as nothing more than a general warning that materialism and sin will be heavily punished? Again surely not, because this time attributing the debased behaviour to the sons of God or angels would make no sense.

Theological commentators down the ages have interpreted these passages as meaning that the angels, who were normally incorporeal beings, took some sort of temporary physical form in order to consort with the daughters of men. But this is hardly the most logical of interpretations. So what's the alternative?

DISENTANGLING TWO THEMES

A strong argument can be made that these passages contain two separate themes that have been distorted, condensed and interwoven – and that only when they're disentangled can we can gain a proper perspective.

First we have in both Enoch 7 and 8 a description of the angels teaching sorcery, divination and astronomy to their human counterparts, which can arguably be seen as a perfectly constructive development, even if here it's confused with other less savoury practices. The same argument could be made concerning Josephus' description of Cain introducing the use of 'measures and weights'. All this seems to fit perfectly with the positive theme of 'divine beings' who teach the 'arts of civilisation' and reveal various other 'secret' knowledge to humankind, which is widespread in other traditions that we'll consider in the next chapter. But remember, unlike with Collins' suggestion of the rebuilding of civilisation after the great flood as above, all this is clearly happening *before* it. This, then, is civilisation being introduced to the Earth for the first time. If we consider a typical, modern, spiritual worldview, is it too far fetched to suggest that at some point in the distant past, once our species was sufficiently evolved, highly aware souls were finally able to incarnate on Earth with the specific objective of introducing a hitherto unknown degree of spiritual understanding, culture and civilisation?[16] Indeed in the next few chapters we'll encounter the suggestion that this process produced a 'golden race' with a high degree of spiritual awareness, although this aspect is largely omitted from the biblical and Enochian literature. So there's a strong argument that this theme of education or 'knowledge transfer' should actually be seen in an entirely positive light.

Second, of course, in both Enoch 7 and 8 there's a clear echo of the debasement theme in the biblical commentaries, this time with rampant materialism joined by excessive fornication, greed, cannibalism and impiety of all kinds. Furthermore it seems this was tied into the loss of the spiritual worldview with which the golden race had originally been imbued, to such an extent that only a few remembered, appreciated and honoured the real truth about their spiritual roots. Indeed the fact that the race who fell from grace are so often seen as somehow angelic surely reflects the very spirituality they originally possessed.

HERMETIC PROPHECIES

The *Hermetica* are a body of texts dating to the second century although, just as with *The Book of Enoch*, the suggestion that they contain divine revelations made to the Greek god of wisdom Hermes – the equivalent of the Egyptian Thoth and arguably of Enoch too – has led some commentators both ancient and modern to argue for their far greater antiquity. They are of Greco-Egyptian origin and separated into two broad categories, the 'philosophical' and the 'popular' or 'technical' treatises. Although certain texts appear to contain elements of both, broadly speaking the latter include astrological, alchemical and magical works.[17] However it's the philosophical texts that are of most interest to us, comprising the 17 treatises of the Greek *Corpus Hermeticum* plus the Latin *Asclepius*.[18]

Unfortunately there are considerable inconsistencies between the various texts, and these must surely have arisen not just through their repeated editing in antiquity but also because of a somewhat haphazard approach to their compilation as one body of work. In particular it seems likely that the versions we now have were based on shorter works that were repeatedly added to in the form of commentary. However in general they do contain some wonderful glimpses of metaphysical wisdom.

That having been said they make only a brief reference to our current theme, the idea that a loss of spiritual roots led to a previous catastrophe:[19] 'Choosing the lesser [path] has been humankind's destruction.' But they're worth introducing at this point because they also contain an intriguing prediction of a supposed repeat performance at some point in the future:[20]

> They will not cherish this entire world, a work of god beyond compare, a glorious construction, a bounty composed of images in multiform variety... They will prefer shadows to light, and they will find death more expedient than life. No one will look up to heaven. The reverent will be thought mad, the irreverent wise; the lunatic will be thought

brave, and the scoundrel will be taken for a decent person. Soul and all teachings about soul (that soul began as immortal or else expects to attain immortality) as I revealed them to you will be considered not simply laughable but even illusory.

Is this not, to some extent at least, exactly the state of affairs produced by our increasingly materialist preoccupation over the last century or so?

GNOSTIC ABOMINATIONS

Staying with the Near East, rather more significant support for our interpretation of the biblical and Enochian texts is provided by the Gnostics. They were a separate sect with roots in both Judaism and Christianity who broke away to plough a lone furrow. The largest source of their traditions is a cache of scrolls found buried in a jar in Nag Hammadi, Upper Egypt, in 1945. It comprises 52 tractates written in Coptic script – Egyptian written in the Greek alphabet – although they're clearly translations from Greek originals. The texts as we have them date to the middle of the fourth century.[21] They are similar to the *Hermetica* in that as a body of literature they contain many inconsistencies, and the close link between the two is proved by the fact that the Gnostic texts include four Hermetic tractates.[22]

But this is about as far as the comparisons with the *Hermetica* go because, as much as the two are often spoken about in the same reverential tones, the Gnostic texts are arguably far less sophisticated. They are dominated by the idea that one particular 'lesser god' created the physical world and everything in it because of his arrogant assumption that he was the ultimate creative power, and due to his ignorance of the true power above him.[23] Accordingly they regard the entire physical world as a mistake and an abomination that should never have arisen, and unfortunately this oppressively negative view pervades the whole Gnostic corpus.[24] As a result their entire focus is on the achievement of 'gnosis' – the Greek word for knowledge – in order to escape the bonds of the physical. By contrast a typical, modern, spiritual worldview would tend to see incarnation into the Earth plane as an interesting experience that many souls choose to have.

In any case the most important Gnostic passage for our current purposes comes from the *Apocryphon of John*, which describes the behaviour of the fallen angels thus:[25]

They brought gold and silver and a gift and copper and iron and metal and all kinds of things. And they steered the people who had followed them into great troubles, by leading them astray with many deceptions. They became old without having enjoyment. They died, not having found truth and without knowing the God of truth. And thus the whole creation became enslaved forever, from the foundation of the world until now. And they took women and begot children out of the darkness according to the likeness of their spirit. And they closed their hearts, and they hardened themselves through the hardness of the counterfeit spirit until now.

It is quite clear from this that once again our two themes have been mixed up. The entirely constructive knowledge transfer process is only hinted at in the first sentence, with the golden race omitted, as is usual with Judaeo-Christian material. Meanwhile the theme of debasement is described as prevailing 'right from the outset until now', but this is hardly surprising given the Gnostic view of the entire physical world. Perhaps rather more interesting is this text's explicit assertion that the account of the flood in Genesis is wrong, and that there were multiple survivors:[26]

It is not as Moses said, 'They hid themselves in an ark', but they hid themselves in a place, not only Noah but also many other people from the immovable race.

However it could easily be argued that this was just the Gnostics' way of proving that their entire lineage, the 'immovable race', had survived even the flood itself.

THE NOISE OF HUMANKIND

The most obvious place to continue our quest is Ancient Mesopotamia, originally located between the Tigris and Euphrates rivers in what's now Iraq. The Sumerian civilisation first developed here in the latter half of the fifth millennium BCE, more than a thousand years before the dynastic era commenced in Ancient Egypt at the beginning of the third millennium BCE, and it revolved around city-states with advanced religious, political and legal systems. The Sumerians dominated the region for several millennia, but increasing political upheaval meant their power was eventually usurped, first by the Akkadians in about 2300 BCE, and more conclusively by the Assyrians who established their capital at Babylon in about 1750 BCE.

Apart from biblical references this Mesopotamian civilisation remained largely unknown until the middle of the nineteenth century, when the diligent efforts of numerous explorers and archaeologists – Paul Emil Botta, Sir Austen Henry Layard, Stephen Langdon and Sir Leonard Woolley notable among them – led to the ruins of cities such as Eridu, Nippur, Lagash, Uruk, Shuruppak, Ashur, Ur, Babylon and Nineveh being unearthed from beneath the desert sands that had smothered them for millennia. Not only did these excavations confirm that a number of biblical sites previously thought to be fictitious were real, but they also revealed a multitude of fragments of delicate clay tablets inscribed with a variety of scripts.

With incredible dedication scholars including Sir Henry Rawlinson, Edward Hincks and Julius Oppert set about the painstaking task of not only reassembling but also deciphering them. In terms of writing the earliest used was Sumerian pictographic script, which then developed into Sumerian and finally Akkadian cuneiform, the latter named after their distinctive wedge-shaped characters. Now a huge variety of texts are available to us, including historical and administrative ones such as votive inscriptions detailing a ruler's major achievements, law codes, court decisions and royal letters. But for our purposes the literary texts are far more fascinating. As per the convention they're divided into the myths of the gods and the legends of the epic heroes, and in reflecting the warrior-like nature of a patriarchal society they're full of descriptions of ferocious battles – although they do have a more subtle side as well.[27]

They contain a plethora of gods, referred to collectively as the Anunnaki or sometimes Igigi. The chief members of the original Sumerian pantheon were An (Anu in Akkadian texts), residing in heaven; Enlil (Ellil), the chief god of the earth often portrayed especially in later texts as somewhat harsh on humankind, who is associated with air; Enki (Ea), who is usually represented as the god who brought civilisation to humankind and is associated with water; Ninhursag (Ninmah), the earth mother goddess; Inanna (Ishtar), the goddess of love; Nanna (Sin), the moon god; Utu (Shamash), the sun god; Ninurta (Ningirsu), the war god; Ishkur (Adad), the storm god; and Nergal (Erra), the plague god and ruler of the underworld with his consort Ereshkigal. But as in many other ancient cultures these names changed over time, so that in later Akkadian texts in particular we often find localised gods elevated to the main pantheon in certain areas. A case in point is the relatively late emergence of the pre-eminent Babylonian god Marduk.[28]

Perhaps the most stunning discovery of all was that some of these texts were the clear precursors for key passages in the biblical Genesis, especially the three main compositions that include the flood tradition. The most detailed is the Akkadian *Atrahasis*, named after its flood hero, the oldest version of which is thought to date to around 1700 BCE. It contains themes repeated throughout Mesopotamian literature and is comprised of three tablets:

- The first describes how the gods rebelled against their excessive workload in digging and maintaining the irrigation canals that were so fundamental to the area, how they asked that humans be created to assist them, and how their request was granted. This all takes place in a clearly mythical epoch that has little relevance to the current enquiry, although we'll return to it in chapter 7.

- The second reports how the new creations proliferate, but Enlil protests that 'the noise of humankind has become too much', so he sends first a plague of sickness, then a drought – towards the end of which the people are so hungry they resort to cannibalism – and then, when neither appears to work properly, he decides to destroy humankind in its entirety with a flood.

- The third describes how Enki warns Atrahasis of the impending disaster and how to survive it; the deluge itself; and finally the argument and subsequent rapprochement between Enlil and Enki when the former finds out that Atrahasis and his family have survived.[29] It is only the second tablet that interests us here, but even then there's precious little information about life before the flood. The only message we find repeatedly in these texts is that it was sent because humankind made too much *noise*. Is this some distorted echo of the idea that humankind was becoming more degenerate?

The next text that contains a description of the flood is the *Eridu Genesis* and, although the earliest version found is thought to date to only around 1600 BCE, it's written in Sumerian script and is therefore likely to be of earlier provenance. The tablets that survive are far more fragmented and as a result shorter than *Atrahasis* but its tone is quite similar, with the hero here called Ziusudra.[30] Again, however, little survives about life before the flood other than a brief description of the building of the early cities of Eridu, Bad-Tibira, Larak, Sippar and Shuruppak, as if they'd been constructed *before* the flood. This suggests either that this aspect of the account is fictitious, or that the flood described is only a local and relatively recent event that has perhaps been confused with a more widespread, earlier event. Incidentally, the global spread of flood traditions militates against any suggestion that this is a satisfactory explanation for them all.[31]

The third main text to mention the flood in any detail is the Akkadian *Epic of Gilgamesh*, which is thought to represent a lengthy composite of a number of Sumerian originals. The flood story is recounted to the hero Gilgamesh by its main survivor, this time called Utnapishtim, in the first part of the eleventh tablet. But again, although it's broadly consistent with the other accounts, it contains little information about what happened before.[32]

So far then, apart from a clear flood tradition, the better-known Mesopotamian texts have added little to our body of evidence. But important additional information is contained in one of the lesser-known Akkadian compositions entitled *Erra and Ishum*. Although this only dates to around the eighth century BCE it's thought to be based on far older traditions, and the version we have appears to be mainly politically inspired, reflecting the instability of the time. It mostly consists of a series of rhetorical, warmongering speeches by Erra, the god of the underworld and of plagues, and by his rival, the chief Babylonian deity Marduk, interspersed with placatory comments by the lesser-known deity Ishum. Yet it also contains clear echoes of the Judaeo-Christian fallen angels with its brief reference to the seven 'divine sages' sent by Enki to teach the 'arts of civilisation' to humankind before the flood.[33] Intriguingly, after it they anger Enki in some way – although here his place is usurped by Marduk – and as a result are banished back to the 'Apsu' from which they originally came.[34] Although the idea of banishment is a negative one, in general even in this relatively late text the sages are described in a positive light. Indeed their place of banishment is described as 'a domain of sweet, fresh water beneath the earth', and remember this is also their place of origin.[35] Surely this suggests that the late Mesopotamian texts started the process of confusion that their later Judaeo-Christian counterparts thoroughly completed – that of merging the two originally separate themes of knowledge transfer, and of debasement and punishment.

We also find in this text clear echoes of *Atrahasis* in that once again plagues and a flood are sent against humans, but this time there's far greater emphasis on them not revering their gods. The events are somewhat jumbled but we're told that: 'The people abandoned justice and took to atrocities. They deserted righteousness and planned wickedness.'[36] Erra also declares that he'll 'make their words wicked, and they'll forget their god, will speak great insolence to their goddess', and that 'the belt of god and man is loosened and can't be retied'.[37] These passages provide far more support for our theme of debasement and destruction — while several others deal with the more prosaic phenomenon of the flood itself, with one again suggesting that, instead of just one survivor and his family, Erra 'left a remnant'.[38]

THE EYE OF RE

Let us now turn to the wealth of Ancient Egyptian literature that has been bequeathed to us. This comprises literally thousands of inscriptions inside burial chambers and on sarcophagi, temple walls and stone steles, as well as on clay tablets and later papyri. The subject is rendered more complex because, although early Sumerian pictographic script is difficult to interpret, Egyptian hieroglyphs are arguably even worse — despite the popular fascination with them and the massive amount of time devoted to their study in the last two centuries.[39] So although scholars have made commendable attempts to provide translations for us they can still only guess at the significance of some of the enigmas, and nowhere is an appreciation of symbolism more crucial.

The Ancient Egyptian pantheon includes Nun, the primeval waters; Ra or Re, the sun god; Ptah, also known as Amon and Atum, the creator god and his sister and spouse Sekhmet, goddess of war and destruction; Shu, the air god and his spouse Tefnut, the goddess of water; Geb, the earth god and his spouse Nut, the sky goddess; Osiris, the god of the underworld, his spouse Isis and their son Horus; Seth and his spouse Nepthys; Thoth, the god of wisdom; and Ma'at, the goddess of truth and justice. As for the texts a number of compositions were clearly of great importance, including what are now known as *The Book of What is in the Duat*, *The Book of Gates*, *The Book of the Dead* and *various Pyramid Texts* and *Coffin Texts*.[40] Some of these date at least as far back as the end of the Fifth Dynasty around 2350 BCE. But many other lesser-known texts are referenced by commentators and, to make matters worse, they often describe various Ancient Egyptian traditions without even identifying the relevant source.

One celebrated composition that's highly pertinent for our current purposes is *The Story of Re*:[41]

> Then Re took on the shape of a man and became the first Pharaoh, ruling over the whole country for thousands and thousands of years, and giving such harvests that for ever afterwards the Egyptians spoke of the good things 'which happened in the time of Re'.
>
> But, being in the form of a man, Re grew old. In time men no longer feared him or obeyed his laws. They laughed at him, saying: 'Look at Re! His bones are like silver, his flesh like gold, his hair is the colour of lapis lazuli!'
>
> Re was angry when he heard this, and he was more angry still at the evil deeds which men were doing in disobedience to his laws. So he called together the gods whom he had made – Shu and Tefnut and Geb and Nut – and he also summoned Nun. Soon the gods gathered about Re in his Secret Place, and the goddesses also. But mankind knew nothing of what was happening, and continued to jeer at Re and to break his commandments. Then Re spoke to Nun before the assembled gods: 'Eldest of the gods, you who made me; and you gods whom I have made: look upon mankind who came into being at a glance of my Eye. See how men plot against me; hear what they say of me; tell me what I should do to them. For I will not destroy mankind until I have heard what you advise.'
>
> Then Nun said: 'My son Re, the god greater than he who made him and mightier than those whom he has created, turn your mighty Eye upon them and send destruction upon them in the form of your daughter, the goddess Sekhmet.'
>
> Re answered: 'Even now fear is falling upon them and they are fleeing into the desert and hiding themselves in the mountains in terror at the sound of my voice.'
>
> 'Send against them the glance of your Eye in the form of Sekhmet!' cried all the other gods and goddesses, bowing before Re until their foreheads touched the ground.

This is clearly the theme of debasement and destruction rearing its head again. Having said that we should note that the destruction subsequently wrought by Sekhmet is only described as being local to Egypt. Not only that but a flood is only mentioned as part of a ruse involving beer, adopted by Re to stop her before everyone was wiped out.

THE VEDIC ASURAS

If we now move further east and turn our attention to India, we find in its earliest texts an intriguingly similar theme of debasement. According to the orthodox view a sophisticated civilisation suddenly emerged in Northwest India in the middle of the third millennium BCE. The two most celebrated sites of this high Indus culture are at Harappa, on the River Ravi in the Punjab, and at Mohenjo-daro, on the Indus in Sind.

Although they'd developed a script that appears on their stamp seals, for example, it has yet to be deciphered and we have no real written texts from this period. But we do know from the cultural remains that, while they exhibit a degree of Western influence from Mesopotamia, they also exhibit clear strains of an indigenous culture that's assumed to have already developed in India by this time – perhaps in the east in the Ganges delta and Bengal areas, or perhaps in the Dravidian south. This indigenous culture appears to have been more spiritually advanced than any other of the time, arguably including that of the Egyptians whose Old Kingdom dynasties were by now in full flower. This is no more clearly demonstrated than in the meditative Yogic poses found for the first time in this era, again on various stamp seals.[42]

The two main cities seem to have remained largely unchanged for something like a thousand years. At this point they were overcome and destroyed by the incursion of largely nomadic Aryan or Indo-European warriors from the West, who had mastered the art of horsemanship and developed the wheeled chariot. According to the orthodoxy this marks the start of the so-called Vedic Age, around 1500 BCE, which represents something of an enigma. This is the era of the first written Sanskrit records of India, by far the most important of which are the *Vedas*. Joseph Campbell and other Western scholars – presumably allowing their arguments to be dominated by the essentially negative and regressive influence of the invaders – have suggested that the Vedic religion was largely exoteric, and that the indigenous traits were not re-established until some five hundred years later in the Brahmanic Age.[43]

Other commentators disagree with this view, however, instead arguing that the *Vedas* represent the earliest written embodiment of a largely indigenous and highly esoteric Eastern philosophy, which had probably been passed down verbally for many millennia beforehand. In fact in their 1995 study *In Search of the Cradle of Civilisation* Georg Feuerstein,

Subhash Kak and David Frawley go as far as to suggest that the Vedic Age should be properly dated to 3000 BCE or even earlier, and that the 'Aryan invasion' never happened. They also present a strong case for the level of metaphysical sophistication of the *Vedas*.[44] In part they were taking their lead from Ganga Prasad, whose *Fountainhead of Religion* was first published in 1927. He argued that the *Vedas* influenced the development of all the other major religions, which only emerged *after* them:[45]

> We have seen that the principles of Mahommedanism and Christianity are derived from Judaism, those of Christianity being partly traceable also to Buddhism, that the doctrines of Judaism can be deduced from Zoroastrianism, and further that both Zoroastrianism and Buddhism are directly traceable to the Vedic religion. Can we similarly trace the teachings of the Vedas to any other religion? No; for history does not know of any older or prior religion.

This is not intended to be a definitive study of comparative religion, and the whole question of the interplays between the three most ancient historical civilisations of India, Egypt and Mesopotamia is infinitely complex. Nevertheless the point seems to be well made that we find in the *Vedas* a level of esoteric sophistication that seems highly unlikely to have derived from either of the other two. So it must either be indigenous or the legacy of a more universal, possibly even pre-catastrophe, wisdom. We will return to this possibility in chapter 8.

The Sanskrit word *veda* means knowledge or wisdom, and there are four main such texts: the *Rig Veda*, *Yajur Veda*, *Sama Veda* and *Atharva Veda*. As with most Indian literature they're extremely lengthy, to the point that English translations provide only excerpts – although that didn't deter the Brahman priests who held such enormous influence from memorising them word for word, as their forebears would have done when there were no written records. But from around the start of the first millennium BCE various commentaries known as the *Brahmanas* were developed to help explain their contents.

So much for the background. We find in the *Vedas* that the major gods such as Indra, Varuna, Agni, Savitri, Rudra and Shiva are all originally described as Asuras, and that this term translates as 'breather or giver of life', or alternatively 'spiritual, signifying the divine, in opposition to human nature'.[46] But the tradition of the Asuras is more complex than this, because scholars are united in suggesting that in later texts the term also came to be associated with demons or devas, the enemies of the true gods.[47] This must surely be seen as related to the fallen angel motif we've already encountered, but can we shed any light on what caused this fall in Vedic tradition? Prasad's commentaries on the Asuras are highly illuminating in this respect:[48]

> In later Sanskrit the word has come to be used in a bad sense being a synonym of Rakshasa, an evil being. The idea then is 'one who takes pleasure in, or enjoys, his present life disregarding the next or future life; one who only cares for his body and not for the spirit.'

Of course the suggestion here is that the Asuras' context changes according to the age of the texts in which they appear, and not that the change describes genuine events in remote antiquity. Still it seems likely that this is an oversimplification. For example in one hymn from the highly celebrated *Rig Veda* entitled 'Indra Lures Agni from Vrtra', the nature of the Asuras and of their relationship to the various gods is already unclear.[49] It even seems to be attempting to describe the conflict between two sets of gods, in which the 'good' set 'has the sacrifice' and has 'regained the power of kingship', while the 'bad' set have 'lost their magic powers'. It also makes a brief reference to Varuna 'letting the waters flow', which could be indicative of an original destruction theme related to these events.

We must always remember the rules of engagement when dealing with all these texts, and it would clearly be foolish to attempt too literal an interpretation of this enigmatic book. But arguably there are echoes of the fallen angel and debasement theme in the Vedic traditions of the Asuras. What is more this suggestion is strengthened by the fact that later Indian traditions clearly support the idea of an original golden race, as we'll see in chapter 4. Meanwhile there's a flood tradition in India too in which the survivor, Manu, is told to build a boat by a magic fish.[50]

KARMIC REBOOT?

We won't be investigating the potential nature of the catastrophe until Part 2. But whether it resulted from huge earthquakes and volcanic eruptions, or a comet or asteroid impact, or a combination of the two, it was surely just a natural phenomenon. Indeed the idea that it was divinely inspired is preposterous to the rational mind. Or is it? Perhaps it's not that simple? Here we need to delve a little into the underpinnings of what I've been referring to as a 'typical, modern, spiritual worldview', certain of whose broad characteristics I've already described several times in this chapter – and to compare this with more traditional religious approaches.

Broadly speaking under the monotheistic religions that predominate in the West – that's Christianity, Judaism and Islam – 'God' tends to be seen as an all-powerful individual who is separate from and external to each of us, and is able to exert total control over our destinies. Indeed Campbell sees the 'mythic dissociation' of God and humans as underlying the theme of the first fall in Genesis 3, when Adam and Eve eat the forbidden fruit of the 'tree of the knowledge of good and evil' at the serpent's suggestion, as a result of which they're banished them from Eden.[51] Unfortunately it would appear that this idea of a separate God was deliberately invented and introduced at a relatively late stage, along with the idea of punishment in hell, as an essentially political control mechanism designed to keep the common people in their place.

By contrast many modern spiritual seekers adopt the far older and broadly Eastern view that essentially 'we're all *part of* God', or even go as far as my preferred suggestion that 'every single one of us is a god in our own right'. Certainly the concept of the 'holographic soul' that I first developed back in 2007 was always designed to show that our soul energy or consciousness, as well as being a full holographic representation of a far greater, more divine consciousness, also has an individual aspect whose aim is to *experience* what it's like to incarnate in this Earth reality of ours – which I propose, is just one of many realities that our greater consciousness can project aspects of itself into.[52] In my more spiritual books I refer to this greater or higher consciousness as our 'supersoul', and emphasise that it's clearly still an individuated consciousness in its own right – and therefore not to be confused with 'source' or 'universal consciousness', whatever that might be. Indeed I also emphasise that our supersoul level of consciousness is so divine and wise that there's little point in speculating what other forms of consciousness might lie beyond it. This isn't intended as a detailed treatise on the ideas that underlie what I refer to as 'Supersoul Spirituality'.[53] But the key point here is that the idea of a separated, even vindictive deity who decides to destroy the human race because of its shortcomings is anathema to such a worldview.

But what if collectively our higher selves, who reside in a variety of planes of consciousness or awareness that we might broadly associate with the concept of the 'afterlife' – about which I've written elsewhere –

are able to oversee what happens on our planet?[54] What if, even though we have individual free will while engaged in this reality, a collective decision is sometimes made at a higher level to intervene and change the broad course of events on Earth? So if at some point in our history we did go somewhat off the rails, forgetting our true spiritual nature and immersing ourselves in materialism and greed, might there not have been an agreement at a higher level that action was called for to redress the balance? Perhaps even drastic action, such as a massive clear-out of the human population so that we could start again with a clean slate?

As for this perhaps being a 'karmic reboot', this concept generally is much misunderstood and often associated with ideas of punishment and even retribution, but its true sense is simply 'action and reaction'. In this context I would propose that under two of the key precepts of Supersoul Spirituality – that is, the supremacy of the well-known 'law of attraction', and the fact that time doesn't really exist as a continuous flow but instead can best be thought of as 'a discrete series of now-moments' – we as individuals can undertake a karmic reboot in any given now-moment, and wipe out any link with previous actions, as long as we're able to completely reset our beliefs and expectations. This is immensely hard in practice, and it usually takes some 'time' to change ourselves and adopt a completely different path. But it's theoretically true – and of course what can be achieved at the individual level can also be achieved at the collective level, if there is unanimous agreement.

It is now universally accepted that serious natural disasters have repeatedly ravaged the Earth. For example, as we'll discuss further in Part 2, a massive comet impact wiped out the dinosaurs – and such events are relatively commonplace although of varying scale. This raises the question of whether all the major ones have been 'karmically driven'? I am not in a position to judge definitively, except in as much as my understanding is that everything seems to have an underlying spiritual dynamic – whether it's an individual or a more collective experience, and even if we don't always understand what this dynamic is at the time.

There is of course an alternative, psycho-materialist interpretation for all this – which is that even if the flood catastrophe did occur and did wipe out the bulk of the human population, the simplistic reaction of the survivors would be to assume their forebears had done something wrong for the gods to want to inflict such serious punishment. This would indeed be plausible were it not for the more general context of the various worldwide texts and traditions. As we'll see in chapter 4 many of them contain descriptions of the original golden race that are full of spiritual insight. Then in chapters 7 and 8 we'll find that this tends to be coupled with even more impressively esoteric material about the creation of humankind and the origins of the world. So the idea that the people who compiled them in whatever form were operating under the spell of relatively primitive superstition is questionable to say the least.

Overall then there's good reason to suggest that the catastrophe reported in the various texts we've considered may have indeed have represented a karmic reboot – driven from higher planes of awareness.

CONCLUSION

The Near and Far Eastern texts of varying antiquity that we've considered in this chapter are not the easiest to decipher. But we've started with them because they're some of the best known, and are all to varying degrees germane to our central theme of a highly spiritual forgotten race who became so debased that a reboot via catastrophe was deemed spiritually necessary.

Of course if this were the only evidence available to support this contention then it would be fair to regard it as interesting but hardly conclusive. Yet in due course we'll find it echoed, often with far more clarity, in various other texts and traditions from around the world that have a rather different primary context.

3

THE ARTS OF CIVILISATION

In the last chapter we discussed various texts that describe angels, demigods or sages appearing to introduce humanity to mathematics, astronomy, divination and various other magical practices. We also saw that this theme of knowledge transfer often tended to be mistakenly interwoven with that of debasement. So now we'll turn to a few additional traditions that perhaps preserve the original meaning rather better.

KNOWLEDGE TRANSFER

More specifically in the last chapter we saw that one theme relating to the fallen angels in the Judaic texts was their teaching the arts of civilisation to humankind. In terms of potential forerunners we also briefly encountered the Akkadian tradition of Enki sending seven sages to effect the same end. This theme is not fully developed in any of the original Mesopotamian source texts so far discovered, but survives mainly through the writings of Berossus, a Babylonian historian-priest of the third century BCE. Although his original *Babyloniaca* hasn't survived, much of it has been preserved for us in the commentaries of subsequent historians such as Alexander Polyhistor, George Syncellus and Eusebius.

Polyhistor's account describes how the sages' leader Oannes – referred to in the original Mesopotamian sources as Adapa – 'emerged from the Erythraean sea', how he was 'part-man and part-fish', how his voice was 'articulate and human' and how 'a representation of him is preserved even to this day'.[1] This latter is born out by depictions of a man wearing fish scales as a headdress in multiple Mesopotamian and Babylonian reliefs. In addition the lesser-known historian Helladius reports that 'some accounts say that... he was actually a man, but only seemed a fish because he was clothed in the skin of a sea creature'.[2] All this tends to suggest that the sages were not monstrous amphibious creatures, nor for that matter extraterrestrials as some would have us believe, but real humans. It may even be that the fish motif is symbolic of wisdom, given that Enki himself is associated primarily with both water and wisdom.[3]

Meanwhile Berossus, via Polyhistor, continues as follows:

> This Being in the day-time used to converse with men; but took no food at that season; and he gave them an insight into letters and sciences, and every kind of art. He taught them to construct houses, to found temples, to compile laws, and explained to them the principles of geometrical knowledge. He made them distinguish the seeds of the earth, and shewed them how to collect fruits; in short, he instructed them in every thing which could tend to soften manners and humanise humankind. From that time, so universal were his instructions, nothing has been added material by way of improvement.

We can see that this has none of the negative tone of the accounts in the last chapter. We don't know what Berossus' source was for this particular information, but it must have been old enough to have avoided the late-Mesopotamian distortions we encountered previously in *Erra and Ishum*. Moreover Polyhistor goes on to report that 'after this there appeared other animals like Oannes, of which Berossus promises to give an account when he comes to the history of the kings'. Were there indeed a number of these sages, and did they perhaps assist their peers over a prolonged period?

Although none of the earlier Mesopotamian texts that we now have completely mirrors Berossus' account, certain of them do reveal important details that considerably predate the Babylonian tradition. The introduction to the short and incomplete Akkadian text *Adapa*, which dates to around 1500 BCE, reveals the following about him:[4]

> Ea made broad understanding perfect in him, to disclose the design of the land. To him he gave wisdom, but did not give eternal life. At that time, in those years, he was a sage, son of Eridu. Ea created him as a protecting spirit among humankind. A sage – nobody rejects his word – clever, extra-wise, he was one of the Anunnaki.

This description of Adapa as 'extra-wise' is in fact the same as the epithet given to the flood heroes Atrahasis, Ziusudra and Utnapishtim, while they all have the additional epithet 'far-distant'.[5] As for the other six sages, unsurprisingly we find that in *Erra and Ishum* they're all described in similar terms as 'the holy carp, who are perfect in lofty wisdom like Ea their lord'.[6] Although they are semi-deified they don't have 'eternal life', which is perhaps just a way of saying they're really just incarnate humans. Nevertheless it's surely not going too far to suggest that these descriptions are intended to convey a high degree of spiritual awareness? This in addition to a practical knowledge of the way to kickstart the civilisation process on Earth.

There exists an even older, Sumerian text entitled *Inanna and Enki: the Transfer of the Arts of Civilisation from Eridu to Erech*. The title itself is revealing, although we should appreciate that the text has an obvious political message in that it attempts to justify the ascendancy of Inanna's ancient city of Erech over that of Enki in Eridu. Nor does it contain any details of who bestowed these gifts on humankind in the first place. Yet it does include a detailed description of more than one hundred of these so-called 'arts' – an approximate translation of the Sumerian word *me*. In his 1963 work *The Sumerians* Mesopotamian scholar Samuel Noah Kramer points out that 'only some sixty-odd are at present intelligible, and some of these are only bare words which, because of lack of context, give but a hint of their real significance'.[7] But as well as more mundane arts such as those of the metalworker, smith, leatherworker, builder and basket weaver, the list includes words and phrases that have been translated as godship, kingship, truth, ascent from and descent into the netherworld, various unidentified priestly offices, law, art, music, scribeship, wisdom, attention, judgment and decision. If the less politicised elements of the traditions of Adapa and various flood heroes are correct, it suggests that these skills were indeed introduced to humanity at some time in our *pre-catastrophe* past.

What is more these accounts of knowledge transfer are by no means restricted to the Near East. For example Chinese tradition reports that the Yellow Emperor, Huang Ti:[8]

> Taught the arts of divination and mathematics, composed the calendar, invented musical instruments of bamboo, taught the use of money, boats and carriages, and the arts of work in clay, metal, and wood. He established the rituals of address to *shang ti,* built the first temple and the first palace, studied and taught the properties of healing herbs.

As an isolated case this could of course be interpreted entirely prosaically as a political text extolling the virtues of the culture's main ancestors. Yet there are accounts from other parts of the world that back up the idea of knowledge bringers *from afar*, a celebrated example being the tradition of Quetzalcoatl of the Mexican Toltecs.[9] However sometimes it appears that they're catastrophe *survivors* rather than original pre-catastrophe *civilisers*. Indeed we might go as far as to suggest that the association of Oannes-Adapa with a fish emerging from the sea gives him a hint of the same context, even if in their broader context the Oannes-Adapa traditions point towards the pre-catastrophe transfer of knowledge to the golden race.

This factor somewhat complicates our interpretation of knowledge transfer traditions, in as much as they may relate to vastly different periods in our history. So let's attempt to build on the scenario presented in the last chapter. Those with a clearly *pre-catastrophe* context provide support for my suggestion that, at various points in early human history, highly aware souls deliberately incarnated to help the civilisation process move forwards. Of course this wouldn't have been a one-off but more likely a gradual one that was repeated over a lengthy period.

On the other hand we've seen that there are hints that this knowledge transfer process also had to be carried on *after* the catastrophe, to help the rebuilding process, so from this perspective we can construct a further scenario. There is good reason to believe that the most culturally advanced elements of our pre-catastrophe race would have lived in coastal areas, especially if their whole system of trade relied on ocean navigation. Of course these would have been the very areas worst affected by any global catastrophe that involved tsunamis and sea-level rise, so most pockets of survivors would have been inland farmers or still nomadic hunter-gatherers who led a more basic existence. But it's also highly likely that a few people from the more culturally advanced settlements would have survived, for example because they were at sea in the deep ocean when disaster struck, or because they were in a less affected part of the globe – maybe even because they somehow foresaw what was coming.

These are all issues that we'll examine more fully in Part 2. But the key point here is that, although all survivors would probably have had a hard time for several generations, if those who were more culturally advanced then came into contact with those who were less so they might well have been seen as 'educating gods' of some sort. At the very least they'd have had a sufficiently significant impact on the 'receiving' culture that they'd have become highly prominent in its traditions.

This kind of speculation is based on the 'cargo cult' theory that many alternative researchers have promoted for decades, and it may well have a role to play in the interpretation of some of these knowledge transfer traditions. But the story is unlikely to end there, because there's every reason to suspect that more aware souls also continued to incarnate after the catastrophe to assist the rebuilding and re-education process – perhaps in particular to ensure that the spiritual understanding that had been lost was reintroduced. On that basis a variety of different interactions at different times may well underlie these traditions.

KNOWLEDGE PRESERVATION

By way of contrast we also find accounts of knowledge being *preserved* for the future by our ancient forebears, and sometimes these two types of tradition tend to overlap and become confused too. The earliest record of this idea seems to come from the opening lines of the Akkadian *Epic of Gilgamesh*, in which the hero is described as having 'found out all things... experienced everything... gained complete wisdom... found out what was secret and uncovered what was hidden' and, especially, as engraving all this on 'a memorial monument of stone'.[10] Similarly Polyhistor informs us of the Babylonian records that Berossus said existed in his time:[11]

> He mentions that there were written accounts preserved at Babylon with the greatest care, comprehending a term of fifteen myriads of years [ten thousand]. These writings contained a history of the heavens and the sea; of the birth of humankind; also of those who had sovereign rule; and of the actions achieved by them.

These records are often said to have been prepared just before the flood, in order to preserve the knowledge of what went before. For example, again via Polyhistor we find that in Berossus' version of the tradition the hero Xisuthros is asked by the deity to 'commit to writing a history of the beginning, procedure, and final conclusion of all things, down to the present term', and to 'bury these accounts securely in the city of the Sun at Sippara'.[12] The same idea is found in Josephus' biblical commentary when he describes how the descendants of Adam's favoured son Seth took precautions before the onset of the flood:[13]

And that their inventions might not be lost before they were sufficiently known, upon Adam's prediction that the world was to be destroyed at one time by the force of fire, and at another time by the violence and quantity of water, they made two pillars; the one of brick, the other of stone: they inscribed their discoveries on them both, that in case the pillar of brick should be destroyed by the flood, the pillar of stone might remain, and exhibit those discoveries to humankind; and also inform them that there was another pillar of brick erected by them. This remains in the land of Siriad to this day.

It is not entirely obvious why the church fathers decided to omit this aspect of the flood story from Genesis. As to where Josephus obtained this information, we know that before writing his account he spent time at Qumran in the company of another breakaway sect known as the Essenes.[14] They were the authors of the Dead Sea Scrolls, discovered in various caves there in 1947, and most scholars accept they had a rather more esoteric take on the Judaic and other material available to them than the founders of the Christian church. We also find that the Gnostic literature contains many texts that extol Seth as the father of the bloodline of the aforementioned 'immovable race', and one in particular entitled *The Three Steles of Seth* is clearly based on the same theme, although unfortunately the contents are not particularly revealing.[15]

Intriguingly this idea of knowledge preservation is not found in the Ethiopian version of *The Book of Enoch*, although in a sense the information recorded therein constitutes its own 'preserved' revelations. However the Slavonic version does make it clear that Enoch was instructed to record everything that the archangels showed and taught him during his visionary trip to the 'seven abodes of heaven':[16]

And now, my children, I know all things from the lips of the Lord; for my eyes have seen from the beginning to the end. I know all things and have written all things in the books.

The list of the 'things' that follows mainly includes details of astronomy, calendars and the seasons. Yet there's always been a strong suspicion that the original Enochian material contained far more esoteric knowledge that was hidden from the masses but preserved in Masonic tradition. Here, for example, is George Oliver discussing what are normally referred to as the 'Pillars of Enoch' in his 1843 *Antiquities of Freemasonry*:[17]

Enoch formed his plans for preserving the knowledge he had acquired, amidst the devastation necessarily attending the predicted calamity [the flood]... He built a temple in the bowels of the earth, the entrance to which was through nine several porches, each supported by a pair of pillars... He then made a plate of gold in the form of an equilateral triangle, each of whose sides was eighteen inches; which he enriched with precious stones, and encrusted it on a triangular agate of the same dimensions. On this plate he engraved the ineffable characters he had seen in his vision; and alone, in silence and solitude, he descended through the nine portals into the temple, and placed this invaluable treasure upon a cubical pedestal of white marble. When the temple was completed, Enoch made nine secret doors of stone, and placed them at the entrance of the portals, with an iron ring inserted in each for the facility of raising, in case any wise and good man of future ages should be led to explore the secret recesses of this sepulchral vault... Upon a high mountain... he erected two great pillars, one of marble and another of brass, to preserve the true principles of science for the benefit of a future world; the former of which he conceived would withstand fire and the latter water. On these he engraved the elements of the liberal sciences, including Masonry; and also a notification that he had concealed a valuable treasure in the bowels of the earth.

These accounts are echoed in other traditions. For example in the *Hermetica* Hermes is said to have inscribed 'knowledge of all' on certain tablets.[18] Meanwhile Eve Reymond, former professor of Egyptology at the University of Manchester, has this to say about the *Edfu Documents* that date to the last half of the first millennium BCE in her 1969 work *The Mythical Origin of the Egyptian Temple*:[19]

The introduction of the first Edfu cosmogonical record discloses the tradition that the contents of these records were the words of the Sages. We are told that this sacred book was believed to be a copy of writings which Thoth [the Egyptian Hermes] made according to the words of the Sages of Mehweret.

This appears to have parallels with the Mesopotamian knowledge transfer tradition of the seven sages. Then, sticking with Egypt, we also have the Arab accounts preserved by the ninth-century chronicler Abd al Hokm. These describe a pre-flood king named Saurid who supposedly built the three pyramids of Giza *before* the flood to secrete and preserve knowledge of the 'profound sciences... of astrology, arithmetic, geometry and physics', and also 'the commentaries of each priest... concerning what was done in his time, and what is, and what shall be, from the beginning of time, to the end of it'.[20] As we'll see in Part 2 there's overwhelming evidence that these monuments were indeed built only around 2500 BCE as orthodox scholars suggest. But what about the many other accounts from Egyptian, Greek and Roman sources that suggest some sort of secret knowledge of the remote past was preserved in Egypt in particular? For example, here is al Hokm's fifteenth-century successor Makrizi echoing the Masonic traditions but transposing them to Egypt:[21]

> The temple at Akhmim was among the finest and largest. The Egyptians had built it to store their wheat because they had been warned in advance of the coming of the Flood. But they disagreed about the nature of the destruction; according to some, it would be a fire that would burn everything on the surface of the earth; according to others, it would be a flood. Therefore, they constructed this temple before the Flood. In it they depicted portraits of the kings who ruled Egypt. The temple was built of marble blocks, each measuring five cubits wide and two cubits thick. It included seven rooms constructed from stones each eighteen cubits long and five wide... Each room was named after one of the seven planets, and all the walls were engraved with images of different shapes and sizes, along with signs explaining the sciences of the Copts: chemistry, cosmography, the art of talismans, medicine, astronomy, geometry, etc., all of which are represented by these images.

These accounts would eventually lead to the now celebrated suggestion that a 'Hall of Records' awaits discovery somewhere in Egypt, perhaps along with others elsewhere.[22] Such intriguing possibilities have provided massive incentives to a variety of researchers and explorers who have devoted their lives to attempting to locate such records, and perhaps even caches of artifacts developed using lost technology. However it seems likely that the bulk of these traditions have built up from the sort of rumour and exaggeration that has always been associated with the Giza plateau especially. To take the most celebrated example there's no genuine evidence whatsoever for hidden chambers underneath the Sphinx.[23] What is more, as we'll see in Part 2 everything points towards it being of at least similar age to the pyramids it stands next to. Indeed there's perhaps a strong argument that, rather than a *physical* repository containing evidence of our forgotten race and their knowledge, the Hall of

Records is far better seen as a spiritual concept similar to that of the 'akashic records' of the lives of every soul who has ever incarnated on Earth, which are said to exist in the collective consciousness of the afterlife planes.

Yet, despite all this, does the possibility remain that historical records of a highly cultured pre-catastrophe race *do* survive, which are far more detailed than those currently in the public domain? Rumours abound of caches of ancient documents being secreted away in hidden vaults in the Vatican, or in remote hideaways in Tibet. But as yet that's all they are... fascinating *rumours*.

CONCLUSION

It is surely reasonable to suggest that, taken all together, the various knowledge transfer traditions described in this chapter and the last do point towards an underlying reality: that the development of human culture, civilisation and spiritual understanding has received a significant boost from the catalyst of the incarnation of highly aware souls at various times throughout human history, which means both before and after any worldwide catastrophe. This is coupled with the more prosaic possibility of more civilised catastrophe survivors educating their more primitive counterparts.

As for the knowledge preservation traditions, *if* they have any validity at all, they do provide general support for the idea that a cultured, pre-catastrophe race existed. However the validity of these particular traditions is more than usually questionable.

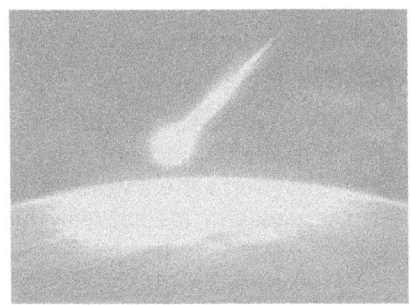

4

THE GOLDEN AGE

We have now started to build up a picture of a forgotten race who were originally highly aware of their true spiritual roots, but then began to concentrate unduly on the material. They were then pretty much wiped out in a catastrophe that may have been universally agreed at a soul level, to institute some form of karmic reboot. But we've also seen that the traditions we've studied so far tend to omit or only hint at any description of what life was really like before the process of degeneration commenced. So we'll now turn to those texts that fill in this gap, with their widespread references to a pre-catastrophe 'golden age' – and we'll leave a discussion of whether or not they can be explained in purely psycho-materialist terms until the conclusion.

PARADISE IN EDEN

Although the details of the biblical Eden are sparse and fairly prosaic in Genesis, only mentioning an abundance of food for humans and animals, since time immemorial it's been regarded as a paradise from which Adam and Eve were expelled after the first fall. Does this represent a thinly veiled reference to a golden age in the distant past? A passage from the Slavonic version of *The Book of Enoch* describes the conditions God provided for Adam in Eden as follows:[1]

> I made for him the heavens open that he should perceive the angels singing the song of triumph. And there was light without any darkness continually in paradise.

This 'continual light' should clearly not be taken literally, so is it an esoteric reference to the idea that Eden was filled with 'spiritual light'?

Meanwhile we saw in chapter 2 that Josephus reports on how 'evil' Cain altered the 'simple and innocent lives that men lived before', but he then goes on to describe 'good' Seth's descendants as follows:[2]

> All these proved to be of good dispositions. They inhabited the same country without dissensions, and in a happy condition, without any misfortunes falling upon them, till they died. They were the inventors of that peculiar sort of wisdom which is concerned with the heavenly bodies, and their order.

So perhaps, even in the often-distorted Judaeo-Christian traditions, we can perceive the message that our pre-catastrophe ancestors originally lived in a 'paradisial' spiritual state.

As we saw previously the Mesopotamian texts too aren't exactly effusive on this issue, but one at least continues the theme that Judaic traditions were informed by these far earlier predecessors. *Enki and Ninhursag* has been dubbed 'A Sumerian Paradise Myth' and, although the version we now have was composed primarily to entertain visiting merchants from Dilmun i.e. Bahrain, it was clearly composed from at least two, separate, original sources. Both of these appear to have been ruthlessly culled judging by the contextual jumps that remain, yet the opening stanzas contain a description of a paradisial land that scholars suggest may originally have been much longer and more detailed, and not associated with Dilmun at all. It is described as 'pure' and 'virginal', and a place where there was no disease.[3]

THE FIRST TIME

Most scholars don't emphasise the idea that a golden age formed part of Ancient Egyptian tradition, but one of the few who does is RT Rundle Clark, a former professor of Egyptology at the University of Birmingham. In his 1959 study *Myth and Symbol in Ancient Egypt* he provides this description of the 'first time':[4]

> The basic principles of life, nature and society were determined by the gods long ago, before the establishment of kingship. This epoch – '*Tep Zepi*' – 'the First Time' – stretched from the first stirring of the High God in the Primeval Waters to the settling of Horus upon the throne and the redemption of Osiris. All proper myths relate events or manifestations of this epoch.
> Anything whose existence or authority had to be justified or

explained must be referred to the 'First Time'. This was true for natural phenomena, rituals, royal insignia, the plans of temples, magical or medical formulae, the hieroglyphic system of writing, the calendar – the whole paraphernalia of the civilisation...

All that was good or efficacious was established on the principles laid down in the 'First Time' – which was, therefore, a golden age of absolute perfection – 'before rage or clamour or strife or uproar had come about'. No death, disease or disaster occurred in this blissful epoch, known variously as 'the time of Re', 'the time of Osiris', or the 'time of Horus'.

The Golden Age was disturbed. The entry of evil was generally thought to have happened when the eye of the High God grew angry seeing that it had been supplanted by another in its absence. The partial restoration of this Golden Age – *hetep* – is the chief theme of the ritual. Hence the emphasis on the constraint of evil forces and the defeat of the powers of chaos. After the triumph of the Osiris cult the chief disturber of cosmic harmony was Seth [not to be confused with the Judaic deity of the same name].

A number of alternative researchers rely quite heavily on Rundle Clark's work.[5] It stands somewhat alone in scholarly circles because, although the concept of the first time displays clear parallels with the original 'dream time' of indigenous peoples in Australasia and elsewhere, the main reference books on Egyptian mythology don't seem to contain much in the way of references to it – or to a golden age.

One other possibly relevant source is the *Edfu Documents* primarily discussed by Egyptologist Eve Reymond, which we introduced in the last chapter and which have also been referenced extensively by various alternative researchers. As with the Sumerian Paradise Myth above, Reymond suggests that they appear to represent highly edited extracts from original compositions, perhaps of extreme antiquity, which weren't specifically associated with Edfu – but unfortunately haven't survived.[6] Yet, even though the first of these later texts is entitled *Sanctified God Who Came into Being at the First Occasion*, we should recognise that Reymond's commentary thereon has very little to say about this first occasion, and nowhere do either she or the texts themselves elaborate on this as a golden age. It is merely described as a time when the earliest gods inhabited the Earth. The only other relevant source is the celebrated *Story of Re* reproduced in chapter 2, which hints at a golden age with its brief allusion to 'the good things in the time of Re'.

THE DAYS OF DASA-RATHA

We saw in chapter 2 how Brahmanism emerged in India around the start of the first millennium BCE. Then around 400 years later the teachings of one of the archetypal 'world saviours', Gautama Buddha, led to the emergence of Buddhism in Northern India. The two main strands that developed were the broad-based Mahayana school and the more orthodox Hinayana school, and their teachings were recorded for the first time in writing late in that same millennium – the former in a number of sutras, the most important of which is the *Avatamsaka Sutra*, and the latter in the *Pali Canon*. But while Buddhism spread to the Orient in the early centuries of the first millennium, in Northern India Hinduism developed out of a resurgent Brahmanism.

The two main Sanskrit epics of Indian literature are the Hindu *Mahabharata* and *Ramayana*. The former is described by Joseph Campbell as 'the chief mythological document of the Indian golden age... much of the material of which is indefinitely old, perhaps ante 400 BC, but of which the final style and tone are rather of around AD 400 and thereafter'.[7] Both epics are lengthy and full of references to a golden age, although it tends to be placed in the context of *multiple* ages as we'll see in the next chapter. But for now, by way of example, here's a passage from the *Ramayana* as rendered into English by Romesh Dutt at the beginning of the twentieth century. Taken from the first book entitled 'The Bridal of Sita', it's lengthy – but to paraphrase or edit would be to miss out on the beautiful poetry of his translation:[8]

> Rich in royal worth and valour, rich in holy Vedic lore,
> Dasa-ratha ruled his empire in the happy days of yore,
> Loved of men in fair Ayodhya, sprung of ancient Solar Race,
> Royal rishi in his duty, saintly rishi in his grace,
> Great as Indra in his prowess, bounteous as Kuvera kind,
> Dauntless deeds subdued his foemen, lofty faith subdued his mind!
> Like the ancient monarch Manu, father of the human race,
> Dasa-ratha ruled his people with a father's loving grace,
> Truth and Justice swayed each action and each baser motive quelled,
> People's Love and Monarch's Duty every thought and deed impelled,
> And his town like Indra's city – tower and dome and turret brave –
> Rose in proud and peerless beauty on Sarayu's limpid wave!
> Peaceful lived the righteous people, rich in wealth in merit high,
> Envy dwelt not in their bosoms and their accents shaped no lie,

Fathers with their happy households owned their cattle, corn, and gold,
Galling penury and famine in Ayodhya had no hold,
Neighbours lived in mutual kindness helpful with their ample wealth,
None begged the wasted refuse, none lived by fraud and stealth!
And they wore the gem and earring, wreath and fragrant sandal paste,
Their arms were decked with bracelets, their necks with nishkas graced,
Cheat and braggart and deceiver lived not in the ancient town,
Proud despiser of the lowly wore not insults in their frown,
Poorer fed not on the richer, hireling friend upon the great,
None with low and lying accents did upon the proud man wait!
Men to plighted vows were faithful, faithful was each loving wife,
Impure thought and wandering fancy stained not holy wedded life,
Robed in gold and graceful garments, fair in form and fair in face,
Winsome were Ayodhya's daughters, rich in wit and woman's grace!
Twice-born men were free from passion, lust of gold and impure greed,
Faithful to their Rites and Scriptures, truthful in their word and deed,
Altar blazed in every mansion, from each home was bounty given,
Stooped none to fulsome falsehood, questioned not the will of Heaven.
Kshatras bowed to holy Brahmans, Vaisyas to the Kshatras bowed,
Toiling Sudras lived by labour, of their honest duty proud,
To the Gods and to the Fathers, to each guest in virtue trained,
Rites were done with true devotion as by holy writ ordained.
Pure each caste in due observance, stainless was each ancient rite,
And the nation thrived and prospered by its old and matchless might,
And each man in truth abiding lived a long and peaceful life,
With his sons and with his grandsons and his loved and honoured wife.
Thus was ruled the ancient city by her monarch true and bold,
As the Earth was ruled by Manu in the misty days of old.

This passage doesn't deal with the original golden age itself, which is presumably the time when 'the Earth was ruled by Manu in the misty days of old', but it's clearly attempting to describe a period of rule in which this was recreated. Admittedly it's reasonably prosaic and moralistic in tone – apart from its reference to 'twice-born' men, which means those who have been initiated into spiritual awareness. But we'll find plenty more esoteric wisdom to back this up in the broader and earlier Indian material that will be covered in future chapters.

THE AGE OF PERFECT VIRTUE

We haven't yet considered the important Chinese texts and traditions. The first formalised religion to emerge in China was Confucianism around the middle of the first millennium BCE. Its main texts include the *Shu King* or 'Book of History', which commences with the 'Canon of Yeo' who ruled around 2300 BCE; the *Shih King*; the *Hsiao King*; the *Yi King*, the basis for the I Ching system of divination; and the *Li Ki*. Its emergence was accompanied by a purge of earlier literature and traditions that culminated in the 'burning of the books' by the emperor Shih Huang Ti in 213 BCE, at about the same time the Great Wall was constructed. But after this the rulers of the Han dynasty set about reinventing their early traditions, so scholars have found it extremely difficult to piece back together the original traditions of the earliest historical dynasties of Shang and Chou. Meanwhile Taoism emerged shortly after Confucianism, its main texts being the *Tao Teh King* and the *Writings of Kwang Tze*. As mentioned above, Buddhism didn't come to China until some time in the first half of the first millennium.

Translations of and commentaries on all of these main texts are available in a monumental forty-volume compilation entitled *The Sacred Books of the East,* compiled in the late nineteenth century by Max Müller – specifically in the subset entitled *The Sacred Books of China* prepared by the leading contemporary Orientalist James Legge.[9] His translation of the Taoist *Writings of Kwang Tze* contains a number of excellent descriptions of the nature of man in the 'Age of Perfect Virtue', for example:[10]

> In the age of perfect virtue, men lived in common with birds and beasts, and were on terms of equality with all creatures, as forming one family; how could they know among themselves the distinctions of superior men and small men? Equally without knowledge, they did not leave the path of their natural virtue; equally free from desires, they were in the state of pure simplicity. In that state of pure simplicity, the nature of the people was what it ought to be.

> In the age of perfect virtue they attached no value to wisdom, nor employed men of ability. Superiors were but as the higher branches of a tree; and the people were like the deer of the wild. They were upright and correct, without knowing that to be so was Righteousness; they loved one another, without knowing that to do so was Benevolence; they were honest and loyal-hearted, without knowing that it was Loyalty; they fulfilled their engagements, without knowing that to do so was Good Faith; in their simple movements they employed the services of one another, without thinking that they were conferring or receiving

a gift. Therefore their actions left no trace, and there was no record of their affairs.

To add to this picture we have extracts from another Taoist text, this time translated by Evan Morgan of the University of Wales in his *Essays from Huai Nan Tzu*. Here is a passage from one entitled 'Beginning and Reality':[11]

> The ancients lodged within the realm of the Tao; desire was controlled and passion mastered; and, in consequence, the spirit did not wander into the extraneous. They derived repose from the calm of creation: they were not disturbed by the baneful effects of comets and the tail of the Great Bear. Though noxious, they refused to be disturbed by their appearances.
>
> During this period, the people were in a state of Arcadian simplicity; they ate and rambled about: they smacked their stomachs and rejoiced. All together enjoyed the blessings of heaven and ate of the fruits of the earth. They did not wrangle in mutual recriminations, nor dispute over rights and wrongs. Peace and plenty existed. This may be called the Ideal Rule...
>
> The perfect man of ancient time stood in the very root and centre of being, the foundations of Heaven and Earth themselves, and wandered at will, unhasting and free, in this central seat of being. He cherished and diffused virtue, he enkindled the spirit of harmony of existence and thus enabled creation to come to full maturity.

The following extract from another essay, 'Natural Law', reinforces the point:[12]

> The rule of the T'ai Ch'ing was in accord with Heaven, and beneficial to creation. Nature was constant, the spirit simple and centred. The mind had no appetites: it was quiescent: it was active, not stagnant. Mental activities were consistent with the Tao, and outward activities were in agreement with right. The activities of the mind worked artistically; action was correct with benefit to things. Words were prized and in accord with reason. Actions were simple and direct, in accordance with nature. The mind was contented and without cunning. Actions were simple and without ostentation.

These are all highly eloquent descriptions of a golden race whose mode of being can clearly *only* be interpreted in spiritual terms. But the latter essay continues with a description of the decadence that resulted when the way of the Tao was eventually forsaken:

When we arrive at the decadent age, we find that men dug into the mountains for precious stones. They wrought metal and jade into cunning vessels and broke open oysters in search of pearls: they melted brass and iron; the whole of nature withered under the exploitation. They ripped open the pregnant and slew the young, untimely, in order to get skins and furs. The Chilin, as a result, did not visit the land. They broke down nests and despoiled birds that had not lain, so that the phoenix no longer hovered around. They drilled wood for fire: they piled up timber to make verandas and balustrades: they burnt forests to drive out game and drained the waters for fish. In spite of this, the furniture at the service of the people was not enough for their use, whilst the luxuries of the rulers were abundant. Thus, the world of life partially failed and things miscarried so that the larger half of creation failed of fruition.

Does this message of the fall of our forgotten race strike a cord as it reaches out to us across the millennia?

THE RACE OF GOLD

Whenever the idea of a golden age is discussed the primary reference is to classical Greek tradition, although as with India this tends to place it within the context of *multiple* ages that we'll examine in the next chapter. But this is what one of their earliest historians, Hesiod, had to say about it in the middle of the eighth century BCE in his *Works and Days*:[13]

> The race of men that the immortals who dwell on Olympus made first of all was of gold. They were in the time of Kronos, when he was king in heaven; and they lived like gods, with carefree heart, remote from toil and misery. Wretched old age did not affect them either, but with hands and feet ever unchanged they enjoyed themselves in feasting, beyond all ills, and they died as if overcome by sleep. All good things were theirs, and the grain-giving soil bore its fruits of its own accord in unstinted plenty, while they at their leisure harvested their fields in contentment amid abundance. Since the Earth covered up that race, they have been divine spirits by great Zeus' design, good spirits on the face of the Earth, watchers over mortal men, bestowers of wealth: such is the kingly honour that they received.

This theme persisted in Greek literature for nearly a thousand years. Here, for example, is Ovid repeating it in *Metamorphosis* at the start of the first century:[14]

Golden was that first age which unconstrained,
With heart and soul, obedient to no law,
Gave honour to good faith and righteousness.
No punishment they knew, no fear; they read
No penalties engraved on plates of bronze;
No suppliant throng with dread beheld their judge;
No judges had they then, but lived secure.
No pine had yet, on its high mountain felled,
Descended to the sea to find strange lands afar;
Men knew no shores except their own.
No battlements their cities yet embraced,
No trumpets straight, no horns of sinuous brass,
No sword, no helmet then – no need of arms;
The world untroubled lived in leisured ease.

These Greek accounts are also similar to some Indian compositions in their somewhat prosaic tone, and the original spiritual message seems to have been left behind. Nevertheless Hesiod's description of how the golden race went on to become 'divine spirits' perhaps hints at it.

THE DIVINE ATLANTEANS

Although the bulk of the classical Greek writers failed to retain the original spiritual message of the golden age, there's one notable exception – the celebrated philosopher Plato. Alternative researchers have spent a great deal of time analyzing his *Timaeus* and *Critias* dialogues, written in the fourth century BCE, because they contain a detailed description of the location and layout of Atlantis – a subject to which we'll return in Part 2. Much less well known, yet arguably far more important at least for our current purposes, are the passages at the very end of *Critias*. It actually stops in mid-sentence, apparently because he was getting old and suddenly decided to switch to his last book, the *Laws*, but it still contains a detailed description of the nature of the Atlantean *people* – and what a revelation it is:[15]

> For many generations, so long as the divine element in their nature survived, they obeyed the laws and loved the divine to which they were akin. They retained a certain greatness of mind, and treated the vagaries of fortune and one another with wisdom and forbearance, as they reckoned that qualities of character were far more important than their present prosperity. So they bore the burden of their wealth and

possessions lightly, and did not let their high standard of living intoxicate them or make them lose their self-control, but saw soberly and clearly that all these things flourish only on a soil of common goodwill and individual character, and if pursued too eagerly and overvalued destroy themselves and morality with them. So long as these principles and their divine nature remained unimpaired the prosperity which we have described continued to grow.

But when the divine element in them became weakened by frequent admixture with mortal stock, and their human traits became predominant, they ceased to be able to carry their prosperity with moderation. To the perceptive eye the depth of their degeneration was clear enough, but to those whose judgment of true happiness is defective they seemed, in their pursuit of unbridled ambition and power, to be at the height of their fame and fortune. And the god of gods, Zeus, who reigns by law, and whose eye can see such things, when he perceived the wretched state of this admirable stock decided to punish them and reduce them to order by discipline.

He accordingly summoned all the gods to his own most glorious abode, which stands at the centre of the universe and looks out over the whole realm of change, and when they had assembled addressed them.

Whatever we may think of the Atlantis myth itself, how can we ask for a clearer elucidation of our main theme of a highly spiritual, pre-catastrophe race who became debased? It has often been suggested that Plato spent a number of years in the company of Egyptian priests who initiated him into their sacred mysteries, and that his writings were a coded 'story' version of what he learned – coded because, like other initiates, he was not allowed to reveal the full extent of his knowledge to the common people. Whether or not this is the case, this final passage appears to provide an extremely clear and lucid account of the nature and fate of our forgotten race. In fact there's a strong argument that any coding and fabrication is encountered far more in the prosaic details of Plato's account of Atlantis – that is, its location and layout – than in its spiritual content.

The only possible criticism would be of the idea that the original Atlanteans' divine nature was diluted by 'admixture with mortal stock', suggesting they were somehow divine beings rather than mortal humans imbued with a high degree of spiritual awareness. But as we've seen this was something of a confusing and grey area for many early writers who seem to have forgotten the true spiritual dynamics underlying what they were describing.

CONCLUSION

In chapter 2 I briefly considered and argued against a purely psycho-materialist interpretation of the flood tradition. But we must now do the same for the broader theme of a golden age that came to an end. Of course it's easy to suggest that this stems from the innate human tendency to view the past through rose-tinted spectacles, and to hark back to simpler times before progress ruined everything. To some extent the idea of a golden age is also consistent with the cyclical worldview that will come into play more in the next chapter, whereby all things are born or created and then degenerate until they're destroyed or die. Perhaps we could even see in these traditions a relatively simplistic attempt to account for how evil entered the world – especially when so many people even today are troubled by the apparent conundrum of how an all-powerful God could allow terrible things to happen.

There is also the possibility that the psychology of politics and control fuelled these traditions, just as it did the separation of God and man as we saw in chapter 2. That is to say, if the common people acted as their priests or shamans told them to, and in accordance with whatever 'divine laws' they deemed appropriate for that culture at that time, then they would succeed in recreating the golden age. If not, and they continued with their debased ways, they too would ultimately be destroyed. Indeed this is merely a more collective alternative to the personal threat of a hellish realm. What is more, this time psycho-materialists don't need to dismiss the composers of these texts as simplistic; instead they can assert that their attempts to use a religious or spiritual message to exert control over the masses were ingenious and imaginative.

There is much to be said for these alternatives, and they surely do have *a* part to play. Nevertheless there's one overriding argument against them and that is, again, the depth of spiritual and esoteric wisdom displayed in at least some of these texts and traditions that have been less ravaged by editorial distortions – particularly in relation to the themes of the creation of humankind and the origins of the world that we'll discuss in chapters 7 and 8. Psycho-materialist interpretations can really only work on the basis that no part of the whole mythic ensemble from across the globe has any valid, spiritual basis underlying it. Whereas, of course, prima facie I take the opposite approach and place these worldwide traditions in what I believe to be their correct context of exactly the sort of typical, modern, spiritual worldview introduced in earlier chapters.

To conclude, then, we've now collated a significant body of evidence that there was a time when humankind possessed a high degree of awareness and adopted a simple and predominantly spiritual approach to life. Indeed we've now come nearly full circle around the globe in our review of these traditions – with the exception that we've yet to discuss the indigenous American variants. But we'll find in the next chapter that they too strongly exhibit this theme.

5

WORLD AGES
& UNIVERSAL
CYCLES

The theme of multiple world eons exists in a number of cultures and can be split into two main categories, although these sometimes overlap. On the one hand we have the world *ages* traditions that are most obviously found in Ancient Greece and the Americas, which tend to be relatively unstructured. On the other we have the world *cycle* traditions found primarily in the East that are based on regulated, long-term cycles.

We will examine each in turn before considering how they can best be interpreted, and whether any aspects thereof provide any sort of support for the themes already developed.

OF SILVER, BRONZE AND IRON

We saw in the last chapter that Greek traditions are best known for their descriptions of multiple world ages – so that, for example, Hesiod's account of the golden age sees it followed by four further 'races' of humankind. As usual we'll look at the extract in full to try to obtain a proper perspective:[1]

> A second race after that, much inferior, the dwellers on Olympus made of silver. It resembled the golden one neither in body nor in disposition. For a hundred years a boy would stay in the care of his mother, playing childishly at home; but after reaching adolescence and the appointed span of youthful manhood, they lived but a little time, and in suffering, because of their witlessness. For they could not restrain themselves from crimes against each other, and they would not serve the immortals or sacrifice on the sacred altars of the blessed ones, as is laid

down for men in their various homelands. They were put away by Zeus son of Kronos, angry because they did not offer honour to the blessed gods who occupy Olympus. Since the Earth covered up this race in its turn, they have been called the mortal blessed below, second in rank, but still they too have honour.

Then Zeus the father made yet a third race of men, of bronze, not like the silver in anything. Out of ash-trees he made them, a terrible and fierce race, occupied with the woeful works of Ares and with acts of violence, no eaters of corn, their stern hearts being of adamant; unshapen hulks, with great strength and indescribable arms growing from their shoulders above their stalwart bodies. They had bronze armour, bronze houses, and with bronze they laboured, as dark iron was not available. They were laid low by their own hands, and they went to chill Hades' house of decay leaving no names: mighty though they were, dark death got them, and they left the bright sunlight.

After the Earth covered up this race too, Zeus son of Kronos made yet a fourth one upon the rich-pastured Earth, a more righteous and noble one, the godly race of the heroes who are called demigods, our predecessors on the boundless Earth. And as for them, ugly war and fearful fighting destroyed them, some below seven-gated Thebes, the Cadmean country, as they battled for Oedipus' flocks, and others it led in ships over the great abyss of the sea to Troy on account of lovely-haired Helen. There some of them were engulfed by the consummation of death, but to some Zeus the father, son of Kronos, granted a life and home apart from men, and settled them at the ends of the Earth. These dwell with carefree heart in the Isles of the Blessed Ones, beside deep-swirling Oceanus: fortunate Heroes, for whom the grain-giving soil bears its honey-sweet fruits thrice a year.

Would that I were not then among the fifth race of men, but either dead earlier or born later! For now it is a race of iron; and they will never cease from toil and misery by day or night, in constant distress, and the gods will give them harsh troubles. Nevertheless, even they shall have good mixed with ill. Yet Zeus will destroy this race of men also, when at birth they turn out grey at the temples. Nor will father be like children nor children to father, nor guest to host or comrade to comrade, nor will a brother be friendly as in former times. Soon they will cease to respect their ageing parents, and will rail at them with harsh words, the ruffians, in ignorance of the gods' punishment; nor are they likely to repay their ageing parents for their nurture. Fist-law men; one will sack another's town, and there will be no thanks for the man who abides by his oath or for the righteous or worthy man, but instead they will honour the miscreant and the criminal. Law and decency will be in fists. The villain will do his better down by telling crooked tales, and will swear his oath upon it. Men in their misery will everywhere be dogged by the evil commotions of that Envy who exults in misfortune with a face full of hate. Then verily off to Olympus from the wide-pathed Earth, veiling their fair faces with white robes, Decency and Moral Disapproval will go to join the family of the immortals, abandoning humankind; those grim woes will remain for mortal men, and there will be no help against evil.

Like most of the other world age traditions we'll encounter this heady concoction isn't easy to interpret. Although it's a relatively early text it appears to be heavily infected by distortions that we know have little basis in reality. The bronze race appears to reflect the fixation with a race of giants that, as we saw earlier, came to infect the Judaic traditions of the offspring of the fallen angels, the Nephilim. Then, coming after the apparently regressive silver and bronze races, we have a somewhat more progressive shift to the 'demigods' – who were 'more righteous and noble' yet still managed to perish through 'ugly war and fearful fighting'. Finally we have the iron race, apparently our own, which appears destined to be more regressive than any of its predecessors. So to some extent the silver, bronze and iron races exhibit the spiritual debasement we've already encountered on numerous occasions – but, apart from that, Hesiod's account provides little credible support for the idea that multiple races of humans have existed on Earth, each in turn destroyed. In fact the clear message that these races were 'created' makes this account in some respects comparable with the multiple-creation-of-humankind traditions we'll consider in chapter 7 – albeit that in these, by contrast, the last-created race tends to be the most perfect.

Ovid's much later account contains a number of major differences.[2] The silver and bronze races are dealt with swiftly and don't differ substantially from Hesiod. The demigods are then omitted, which leaves a clear path for the even more regressive iron race that's no longer our own, as in Hesiod, but whose members are this time actually destroyed for their debased behaviour. As a result there's another race thereafter, unnamed but presumably our own, which unfortunately is just as bad. Of course it could be argued that this is consistent with our main themes, in that we have a golden age followed by a progressive debasement that ends in the destruction of the iron race, with our own modern race then arguably repeating the same mistakes. But it's just as easy to maintain there's so much confusion in these classical Greek traditions of multiple world ages that for our current purposes they deserve little credence.[3]

SOLON'S SOJOURN

Just as in the last chapter Plato takes a somewhat different tack from the other Greek historians when he discusses the theme of world ages. The *Timaeus* and *Critias* dialogues remain his most relevant works here, but first we need to understand their structure because it's somewhat confusing and often poorly explained. Although, unusually for Plato, each is primarily a monologue by the two title characters, *Timaeus* commences in his more usual style with a dialogue involving these two, Socrates and Hermocrates. It opens with Critias describing a world age tradition told to him by his grandfather, also called Critias, who in turn received it from Solon. This is the celebrated Platonic figure who, with echoes of the Mesopotamian sages, is described as 'the wisest of the seven wise men', and here we find him in the company of some Egyptian priests at Sais on the Nile delta:[4]

> And a very old priest said to him, 'Oh Solon, Solon, you Greeks are all children, and there's no such thing as an old Greek.'
> 'What do you mean by that?' enquired Solon.
> 'You are all young in mind', came the reply. 'You have no belief rooted in old tradition and no knowledge hoary with age. And the reason is this. There have been and will be many different calamities to destroy humankind, the greatest of them by fire and water, lesser ones by countless other means. Your own story of how Phaethon, child of the sun, harnessed his father's chariot, but was unable to guide it along his father's course and so burnt up things on the Earth and was himself destroyed by a thunderbolt, is a mythical version of the truth that there is at long intervals a variation in the course of the heavenly bodies and a consequent widespread destruction by fire of things on the Earth.'

Plato is clearly suggesting that multiple catastrophes have plagued the Earth, and that these occur in cycles related to variations 'in the course of the heavenly bodies'. He could therefore be referring to the phenomenon of precession, something we'll return to later in the chapter. In any case this passage is followed by another in which the Egyptian priest describes how they managed to preserve far more ancient records than the Greeks:

'On such occasions [fire-based catastrophes] those who live in the mountains or in high and dry places suffer more than those living by rivers or by the sea; as for us, the Nile, our own regular saviour, is freed to preserve us in this emergency. When on the other hand the gods purge the Earth with a deluge, the herdsmen and shepherds in the mountains escape, but those living in the cities in your part of the world are swept into the sea by the rivers; here water never falls on the land from above either then or at any other time, but rises up naturally from below. This is the reason why our traditions here are the oldest preserved; though it is true that in all places where excessive cold or heat does not prevent it human beings are always to be found in larger or smaller numbers.

But in our temples we have preserved from earliest times a written record of any great or splendid achievement or notable event which has come to our ears whether it occurred in your part of the world or here or anywhere else; whereas with you and others, writing and the other necessities of civilisation have only just been developed when the periodic scourge of the deluge descends, and spares none but the unlettered and uncultured, so that you have to begin again like children in complete ignorance of what happened in our part of the world or in yours in early times.

So these genealogies of your own people which you were just recounting are little more than children's stories. You remember only one deluge, though there have been many, and you do not know that the finest and best race of men that ever existed lived in your country; you and your fellow citizens are descended from the few survivors that remained, but you know nothing about it because so many succeeding generations left no record in writing. For before the greatest of all destructions by water, Solon, the city that is now Athens was pre-eminent in war and conspicuously the best governed in every way, its achievements and constitution being the finest of any in the world of which we have heard tell.'

Apart from Plato's clear political message of the pre-eminence of the earliest Athenian civilisation at the end of this passage, it also shows some interesting parallels with the scenario I painted in chapter 3 of who might survive, and what might happen, after a major flood catastrophe. These ideas are echoed further in a later reprise in *Critias*:[5]

Their names have been preserved but what they did has been forgotten because of the destruction of their successors and the long lapse of time. For as we said before, the survivors of the destruction were an unlettered mountain race who had just heard the names of the rulers of the land but knew little of their achievements. They were glad enough to give their names to their own children, but they knew nothing of the virtues and institutions of their predecessors, except for a few hazy reports; for many generations they and their children were short of bare necessities, and their minds and thoughts were occupied with providing for them, to the neglect of their earlier history and tradition. For an interest in the past and historical research came only when communities had leisure and when men were already provided with the necessities of life. This is how the names but not the achievements of these early generations came to be preserved.

To sum up, Plato's general theme of multiple catastrophes seems to be contextually quite different from his description of the divine Atlanteans who were destroyed in a single major catastrophe. Indeed to the extent that their context appear to be more cyclic and possibly related to the precessional cycle, it's difficult to interpret them as having any real historical value.

DEPARTURE FROM TAO

We saw in the last chapter that the Chinese Taoists had a flourishing tradition of a golden age that was terminated by debasement. We find hints that this too is mixed in with a tradition of world *ages*, for example in Donald Mackenzie's 1923 work *Myths of China and Japan*:[6] 'Here we touch on the doctrine of the World's Ages... The Chinese Taoists believed that the first age was a perfect one, and that humankind gradually deteriorated.' This is substantiated by a brief passage from the *Tao Teh King*:[7] 'In the highest antiquity, the people did not know that there were rulers. In the next age they loved and praised them. In the next they feared them. In the next they despised them.'

Accounts such as these that don't explicitly involve multiple and especially cyclic catastrophes could be argued to support the proposition that there was a gradual increase in debasement over a prolonged period. But it's difficult to completely remove them from the more general global context of catastrophic endings to each age.

THE FOUR WORLDS

The most abundant sources of world age traditions are indigenous

American cultures, every one of which appears to have some sort of variant thereof. The finest example of the North American genre comes from the Hopi of Northern Arizona. Although never written down in antiquity their traditions were transmitted orally from generation to generation for centuries, and kept a closely guarded secret from the outside world. That is until 1963 when the elders allowed them to be recorded for the first time by Frank Waters, who since childhood had cultivated close ties with various indigenous cultures. Working from the information provided by thirty elders, especially Oswald White Bear Fredericks, his *Book of the Hopi* has gained widespread acclaim. In general its contents demonstrate the deep erudition and spirituality of these people, and anyone who reads it must surely question the long-held view that indigenous tribes around the world are backward or primitive, and that modern technological progress makes us superior.

The Hopi commence by describing the creation of the Earth by the god Sotuknang, acting under instructions from the all-powerful creator Taiowa, and then of the first humans by the creator goddess Spider Woman – which themes we'll return to in chapters 7 and 8. They then proceed to how the human race multiplied during the first 'world', Topkela, which in our terms is clearly another report of a golden age:[8]

> The First People knew no sickness. Not until evil entered the world did persons get sick in the body or head... they understood themselves... were pure and happy... they felt as one and understood one another without talking.

This is yet another revelation of the 'awareness' of our earliest ancestors, this time including the concept of telepathy. But this golden age didn't last:

> Gradually there were those who forgot the commands of Sotuknang and the Spider Woman to respect their Creator. More and more they used the vibratory centres of their bodies solely for earthly purposes, forgetting that their primary purpose was to carry out the plan of Creation... It was then that animals drew away from people... In the same way, people began to divide and draw away from one another – those of different races and languages, then those who remembered the plan of Creation and those who did not.

We can see that this account is even more explicit in its confirmation that the debasement was based on a loss of *spiritual* roots that departed from the 'plan of creation'. In any case, as the situation worsened Sotuknang decided to destroy the first race by fire and volcano, but not before he'd selected an untainted group to survive and father a new race. These were secreted under the earth with the 'ant people'. Then Sotuknang created the second world, Tokpa, 'changing its form completely, putting land where the water was and water where the land had been'. When the second race first emerged they 'multiplied rapidly, spreading... even to the other side of the world'. But 'this did not matter, for they were so close together in spirit they could see and talk to each other from the centre on top of their head'. Ultimately, however, they too fell into wicked ways:

> More and more they traded for things they didn't need, and the more goods they got, the more they wanted... They forgot to sing joyful praises to the Creator and soon began to sing praises for the goods they bartered and stored. Before long it happened as it had to happen. The people began to quarrel and fight, and then wars between villages began.

We can see that this second debasement clearly emphasises the dominance of materialism, and again Sotuknang was forced to destroy the world except for a chosen few survivors hidden under the ground. This time the Hopi's description of the destruction seems to suggest a huge shift of the Earth's axis followed by a prolonged absence of the sun:

> The world, with no one to control it, teetered off balance, spun around crazily, then rolled over twice. Mountains plunged into seas with a great splash, seas and lakes sloshed over the land; and as the world spun through cold and lifeless space it froze into solid ice.

For many years the Earth lay frozen and dormant, and the survivors remained underground. Finally Sotuknang created the third world, Kuskurza, and after they emerged the third race 'multiplied in such numbers and advanced so rapidly that they created big cities, countries, a whole civilisation'. But we can now guess what happened next:

> More and more of them became wholly occupied with their own earthly plans. Some of them, of course, retained the wisdom granted them upon their Emergence. With this wisdom they understood that the farther they proceeded on the Road of Life and the more they developed, the harder it was. That was why their world was destroyed every so often to give them a fresh start... Some of them made a

patuwvota (shield made of hide) and with their creative power made it fly through the air. On this many of the people flew to a big city, attacked it, and returned so fast no one knew where they came from. Soon the people of many cities and countries were making *patuwvotas* and flying on them to attack one another. So corruption and war came to the Third World as it had to the others.

Once again Sotuknang called for destruction, this time by flood, although a select group was again to be saved, this time by being sealed inside hollow reeds:

He loosed the waters upon the Earth. Waves higher than mountains rolled in upon the land. Continents broke asunder and sank beneath the seas. And still the rains fell, the waves rolled in.

When the survivors emerged into the fourth world, Tuwaqachi, all they could see was water. Having crossed a number of seas and islands, heading eastward, they reached land proper. At this point he instructed them to look west and south, at the way they'd come, and then he made all the islands disappear:

'I have washed away even the footprints of your Emergence: the stepping-stones which I left for you. Down on the bottom of the seas lie all the proud cities, the flying *patuwvotas,* and the worldly treasures corrupted with evil, and those people who found no time to sing praises to the Creator from the tops of their hills. But the day will come, if you preserve the memory and the meaning of your Emergence, when these stepping-stones will emerge again to prove the truth you speak... What you choose will determine if this time you can carry out the plan of Creation on it or whether it must in time be destroyed too. Now you will separate and go different ways to claim all the Earth for the Creator. Each group of you will follow your own star until it stops. There you will settle. Now I must go. But you will have help from the proper deities, from your good spirits. Just keep your own doors open and always remember what I have told you.'

According to the Hopi this is the world in which we now live. There is much in this narrative that's clearly symbolic and can't be taken literally, for example the subterranean ant people. The apparently advanced technology of the third race too can probably be taken with a pinch of salt, as we'll see in Part 2. But an interesting aspect of the Hopi world age tradition is that each time a new race emerges it is given a fresh start, and initially has its spirituality or awareness restored. Does any of this provide us with any genuine support for our main themes of a golden age followed by debasement and destruction? We are given no timescales for any of this, so for now let's reserve judgment.

THE FIVE SUNS

Let us now turn to Central America, and specifically to the Aztecs of Mexico. Despite the atrocities committed by the Spanish conquistadors in the early sixteenth century, and their attempts to stamp out indigenous traditions, a number of texts written in alphabetic script that date to this period have survived. The primary source for world age traditions is the three-part *Codex Chimalpopoca*, as translated by John Bierhorst in his 1992 work *History and Mythology of the Aztecs*. One part, the *Leyenda de los Soles* or 'Legend of the Suns', is summarised in Figure 2.

Age/Sun	Details
Jaguar	Lasted 676 (13 x 52) years. This age ended when all the people were devoured by jaguars.
Wind	Lasted 364 (7 x 52) years. This age ended when everything was swept away by the wind.
Rain	Lasted 312 (6 x 52) years. This age ended when everything was destroyed by a rain of fire.
Water	Lasted 676 (13 x 52) years. This age ended when everything was destroyed by flood: 'the skies came falling down... all the mountains disappeared'.
Movement	Because of its name, it's assumed that an earthquake will bring this, our current age, to an end.

Figure 2: The Aztec Legend of the Suns [9]

The periods shown therein are actually extremely short and fall well within our known historical epoch. The first age is reported to have begun 2513 years before its composition in 1558 – that is, in 955 BCE – so, given that the first four ages total 2028 years, we'd have been 485 years into the current age even by the time it was written. If the length of the others is anything to go by, the volcanic destruction promised for our current race should have occurred at the latest by the middle of the eighteenth century. Having said that perhaps these numbers should be taken symbolically rather than literally. For example 364, the length in years of the wind age, is roughly the number of days in a year, while the length of every age is a multiple of 52, the number of weeks in the year but also the length in years of a Mayan century, as we'll shortly see. What is more the length of the second and third ages combined is the same as that of the first and fourth.

Another section of the same codex, the *Anales de Cuauhtitlan*, is even less revealing in that it contains no durations and, although the details are broadly the same, the ages are in the different order of water, jaguar, rain, wind and movement.[10] Meanwhile in a separate source called the *Historia de Colhuacan y de Mexico*, discussed by Eric Thompson in his *Maya Hieroglyphic Writing*, the four preceding ages once again total 2028 years.[11]

However a further Mexican source known as the *Codex Rios* – also referred to as *Codex 3738* or *Codex Vaticanus A* – records a completely different set of numbers, with each age lasting 4008, 4010, 4801 and 5042 years respectively, giving a total of 17,861 years.[12] This text also contains the following interesting passage about the survivors of the flood that ended what it too deems to be the *first* age:[13]

> Others say that not only the two inside the tree survived the flood, but that other people found refuge in certain caves, and after the flood... they spread all over the world, and the following populations worshipped them as Gods, each in his nation.

This is of course exactly the sort of 'cargo cult' survivor scenario we discussed in chapter 3. Sadly, however, the remainder of this codex contains a number of superimposed Christian distortions, including an early race of giants, a 'tower of Babel' and a 'virgin birth'.

Moving down to South America, the world age traditions of the Peruvian Incas were recorded by several of their own scholars in the sixteenth century. They are summarised by Hartley Burr Alexander in his Latin American volume of *The Mythology of All Races* – a monumental, thirteen-volume work dating to the early part of the twentieth century, which is an invaluable source of traditions from all over the world:[14]

> Molina, Cieza de Leon, Sarmiento, Huaman Poma tell of the making of sun and moon, and of the generations of men, associating this creation with the lake of Titicaca, its islands, and its neighbourhood. Viracocha is

almost universally represented as the creator, and the story follows the main plot of the genesis narratives known to the civilised nations of both Americas – a succession of world eons, each ending in cataclysm. As told by Huaman Poma, five such ages had preceded that in which he lived. The first was an age of Viracochas, an age of gods, of holiness, of life without death... the second was an age of skin-clad giants, the Huari Runa, or 'Indigenes', worshippers of Viracocha; third came the age of Puron Runa, or 'Common Men', living without culture; fourth, that of the Auca Runa, 'Warriors', and fifth that of the Inca rule, ended by the coming of the Spaniards. As related by Sarmiento the first age was that of a sunless world inhabited by a race of giants, who, owing to the sin of disobedience, were cataclysmically destroyed.

Although we can see that these various Central and South American traditions do contain a degree of support for our main themes, in general they're inconsistent – even amongst each other – relatively brief, highly symbolic and have been significantly distorted by late Christian influences.

COUNTING LONG

So far we've only made passing reference to the celebrated Mayan culture that flourished in Central America from Mexico right across to the Yucatán. They too have a world ages tradition of sorts contained in their most famous surviving text, the *Popol Vuh*, but it slants much more towards the multiple-creation-of-humankind theme so we won't discuss it until chapter 7.

In the meantime this culture represents a point of crossover between the world age and world cycle traditions, because the Maya also developed an extremely sophisticated calendar that incorporated the notion of long-term cycles. Unlike many of their counterparts in other parts of the Americas, the Maya had an extensive literature and a sophisticated form of pictographic writing that used distinctive glyphs. Fortunately three main hieroglyphic texts survived the Spanish conquest, during which almost all copies of such texts were avidly sought out and destroyed, and they're named after the cities in whose institutions they reside:[15]

- The *Dresden Codex* mainly contains almanacs of complex and accurate astronomical and calendrical data, for example on lunar cycles and the heliacal rising of Venus.

- The *Madrid Codex*, also known as the *Codex Tro-Cortesianus*, is made up of several parts including the *Troano Codex*, and merely contains divinations.
- The *Paris Codex* shares similarities with the others but isn't fully translatable because incomplete.

The *Dresden Codex* is thought to date to the twelfth century because its latest dates for astronomical calculations are for this period, while the other two appear to be somewhat later compositions. The only other Mayan texts of note are the *Books of Chilam Balam*, various versions of which have been found because each settlement had its own copy. Although they're in alphabetic script they're similar to the codices, but are again distorted by being interwoven with later Christian infusions.

From these written texts and from various inscriptions on steles and temples, scholars have been able to establish the details of the Mayan calendrical system. Their short-count calendar had two types of year – a sacred one of 260 days called a tzolkin, and a normal one of 365 days. Any given day was identified by both systems, so that the calendar lasted 52 years or 73 tzolkins before it repeated itself, and this was the Mayan equivalent of a century. It was then supplemented by a long-count calendar in which 20 days or kins made up a 20-day month or uinal; 18 uinals made up a 360-day year or tun; 20 tuns made up a katun of approximately 20 years; 20 katuns made up a baktun of 394.3 years; and longer cycles of 13 and 20 baktuns are also referenced, representing 5125 and 7886 years respectively.[16] This long-count calendar is generally reckoned to have a starting date of 11 August 3114 BCE under our Gregorian system – and it neatly leads us on to the more complex world cycle traditions of the East.

DAYS AND NIGHTS OF BRAHMA

The Indian concept of world cycles doesn't really come to the fore in the Vedic literature, although it would surely be a mistake to suggest that it was newly created in the Hindu epics in which it's most clearly expounded. This time we'll concentrate on the *Mahabharata*, which contains 18 main books or 'parvas' including the celebrated 'Bhagavad-Gita'. The full epic was meticulously translated by Chandra Ray over a period of ten years at the end of the nineteenth century and in Book 3, the 'Vana Parva', we find the following:[17]

After the dissolution of the universe, all this wonderful creation again comes into life. Four thousand years have been said to constitute the Krita Yuga. Its dawn also, as well as its eve, hath been said to comprise four hundred years. The Treta Yuga is said to comprise three thousand years, and its dawn, as well as its eve, is said to comprise three hundred years. The Yuga that comes next is called Dwapara, and it hath been computed to consist of two thousand years. Its dawn, as well as its eve, is said to comprise two hundred years. The next Yuga, called Kali, is said to comprise one thousand years, and its dawn, as well as eve, is said to comprise one hundred years... And after the Kali Yuga is over, the Krita Yuga comes again. A cycle of the Yugas then comprises a period of twelve thousand years. A full thousand of such cycles would constitute a day of Brahma. O tiger among men, when all this universe is withdrawn and ensconced within its home the Creator himself, that disappearance of all things is called by the learned to be Universal Destruction.

With echoes of our main themes except in a clearly cyclical context, the text goes on to describe in great detail how each age becomes successively less enlightened and more debased; how depravity overtakes humankind toward the end of the 'dark' Kali Yuga; how it's destroyed by drought, then fire, then flood; and how the new 'golden' Krita Yuga then dawns again.[18]

Later on, in Book 12, the 'Santi Parva', we find the same details but with more added.[19] First we're told that 'a year is equal to a day and night of the gods', which Hindu scholars regard as a 'divine year' of 360 'human years', for reasons we'll come to shortly. We are then told that:

With the commencement of Brahman's day the universe begins to start into life. During the period of universal dissolution the Creator sleeps, having recourse to yoga-meditation. When the period of slumber expires, He awakes. That then which is Brahman's day extends for a thousand such Yugas. His night also extends for a thousand similar Yugas.

In the succeeding passages we're given detailed descriptions of the processes of creation and destruction at the beginning and end of each Day of Brahma. So under this schema humanity on Earth is wiped out to start again at the end of each four-Yuga cycle lasting 4.3 *million* human years, while the universe as a whole is completely 'reabsorbed' back into its primal state at the end of each Day of Brahma lasting 4.3 *billion* human years, after which it lies dormant for an equivalent period. All this is summarised in Figure 3.

Age or Yuga	Dawn	Age	Twilight	Total	Total
				Divine Years	Normal Years
Krita	400	4000	400	4800	1,728,000
Treta	300	3000	300	3600	1,296,000
Dwapara	200	2000	200	2400	864,000
Kali	100	1000	100	1200	432,000
Maha				12,000	4,320,000
Manvantara (approx)				0.86 million	0.3 billion
Kalpa or Day/Night of Brahma (1000 Maha Yugas/14 Manvantaras)				12 million	4.32 billion
Year of Brahma (720 Kalpas)				8.64 billion	3.11 trillion
Life of Brahma (72,000 Kalpas)				864 billion	311 trillion

Figure 3: The Hindu World Cycles

If we now turn to the later *Puranas* that were compiled mainly in the middle of the first millennium, again there are 18 major works in this group, although most record similar information. Perhaps the best known is the *Vishnu Purana*, and here we find the same cycles but augmented in various ways.[20] First, with echoes of other cultures' traditions of races of giants and of longer lifespans, it reports that in each Yuga humankind's longevity and stature – as well as virtue – decrease. Then in terms of time cycles it explicitly confirms that each divine year is the equivalent of 360 human years. What is more it introduces new terminology, in that a complete cycle of the four Yugas is referred to as a Maha Yuga, and the length of a Day or Night of Brahma as a Kalpa, while each Day of Brahma is now divided into 14 Manvantaras, each of which lasts approximately 71 Maha Yugas or 308 million years. But the most profound change is the introduction of a *Year* of Brahma, made up of 360 Days and Nights of Brahma, or 720 Kalpas, or 3 trillion human years; and of a *Life* of Brahma, which is made up of 100 Years of Brahma, or 72,000 Kalpas, or 311 *trillion* human years. According to the Puranic model, it's only at the end of *this* almost inconceivably long period that complete reabsorption of the universe takes place. These extra details have been added into Figure 3.

So what are we to make of all this? Arguably to give these cycles any sort of meaningful context we need to split them into two and consider each element separately. First we have the Yugas or what we might term *world* cycles that appear to relate to Earth only. The first thing we can say is that even their timescales are ridiculously lengthy in the context of what we know about human history, even if there was only one cycle. For this reason various modern commentators have attempted to shorten them, with varying degrees of scholarship and success, and even to identify where in the cycles we currently stand. The most important issue here is whether or not the years mentioned in the earlier texts, such as the Vana Parva, are normal or divine – because if the former then the time periods become reasonable again. Even allowing for this, though, we're still left with the fact that they seem to describe how the Earth is completely subsumed by the 'waters' at the end of each Yuga cycle, leading to the apparently *complete* annihilation of humankind even if not of Earth itself, and its subsequent re-emergence in a new Krita age with no period of evolutionary development – again, and again, and again. This 'Hindu Creationist' approach must surely be seen as going against all the evidence of multiple disciplines, from archaeology through to geology and beyond – although we'll briefly return to it in chapter 9. Nevertheless we can surely argue that, if the cyclical element of these Yuga traditions is removed, in general they do provide some degree of support for our main theme of a golden age followed by progressive debasement.

We then have the ostensibly separate concept of far longer *universal* cycles that deal with the dissolution and re-emergence of the entire universe at the end of a Day, Year or even Life of Brahma. Yet in the Vana Parva we not only encounter the theme of how the waters subsume the Earth at the end of each Yuga cycle, but also of the lotus-boy who is the only thing left and whose stomach contains all the potential for re-emergence and recreation – remembering that this flower closes its petals at night and draws back into the water, only to re-emerge and unfold in the dawn.[21] All this seems to bear more than a passing resemblance to the ideas about the emergence of the universe as a whole that are found not only in Vedic but other origin traditions too, as we'll see in chapter 8. Indeed in Ray's translation these passages seem to swap seamlessly between the words *Earth* and *universe* with little rhyme or reason. So there seems to be a good deal of overlap between the two sets of cycles, at least in the Vana Parva.

Indeed a strong argument can be presented that in fact the Yuga *ages* have much more in common with the other *non-cyclical* world age traditions we've discussed, while the concept of *universal cycles* should be seen as entirely separate. As to what these latter might really represent, and whether they might have at least a theoretical connection to certain postulations of modern physics and cosmology, we'll return to these topics in the conclusion.

THE WHEEL OF TIME

We haven't yet considered the Jain religion, which emerged in India at about the same time as Buddhism in the latter half of the first millennium BCE, and was of similar influence. Its tradition of world cycles is similar to that of the Hindus that we've just considered, but with an interesting twist. It is described briefly by Arthur Berriedale Keith in his Indian volume of *The Mythology of All Races*:[22]

> To the Jain time is endless and is pictured as a wheel with spokes... normally with twelve, divided into two sets of six, one of which belongs to the avasarpini, or 'descending', and the other to the utsarpin, or 'ascending'. In the first of these eras good things gradually give place to bad, while in the latter the relation is reversed. Of these eras the fifth 'spoke', or era, of the avasarpini is that in which we live.

This is possibly a similar idea to that of the fourteen Manvantaras within a Day of Brahma, except with only twelve. Moreover we again find that the periods involved are incredibly lengthy, while the theme of progressively reducing lifespans and human stature recurs.[23] Yet the Jain tradition can clearly be differentiated in that it suggests that only the first half of the cycle is one of progressive debasement, while the second half is one of upward spiritual progression. This is an issue to which we'll return shortly.

A possibly similar theme is found in the Zoroastrian religion, which dominated the mighty Persian Empire at its height in the first millennium BCE and had a significant influence on the development of Judaism.[24] In their most sacred text, the *Zend Avesta*, we find that their cycle is unique in that it contains only two non-repeated rounds of 12,000 years each – the potential similarity being that the first is dominated by the benign deity Ahura Mazda and the second by his evil counterpart Angra Mainyu.[25]

We might also note that a less specific cyclic theme exists in Ancient Egyptian tradition. Egyptologists John Baines and Geraldine Pinch make the following observation in their essay in *World Mythology*:[26]

> The cosmos would not last forever, the Egyptians believed. The time would come when the creator would grow so weary that he and all his works would dissolve back into chaos. Then the cycle of creation would recommence.

CYCLES AND PRECESSION

Because the polar axis around which the Earth rotates has a wobble akin to that of a spinning top, the stars appear to move in the sky over prolonged periods. This phenomenon is referred to as precession. Currently it's estimated that it takes approximately 2150 years for the Earth to move through each of the 12 constellations of the zodiac, with a complete cycle estimated to be 25,765 years.[27] This is why people refer to us moving out of the Age of Pisces into the Age of Aquarius, although the point at which one age ends and another begins relies on rough observation alone and can't be accurately pinpointed.

How is this relevant to cycles? First of all, if we recall the extract from Plato's *Timaeus* quoted early in this chapter, we questioned whether in saying that 'at long intervals there is a variation in the course of the heavenly bodies' he could be referring to this phenomenon. The problem with this is, of course, the phrase that comes next: 'and a consequent widespread destruction by fire of things on the Earth'. There is no obvious scientific mechanism by which precession produces regular catastrophes.

Second, various alternative researchers have attempted to tie together the numbers in the precessional cycle with those of various Amerindian traditions. For example, Gregory Severin works off the 2028 years quoted for Aztec ages as discussed above – but among other problems he makes the mistake of assuming that each age lasts this long, whereas in fact it's the stated duration of *all four* previous ages.[28] If we turn now to the Maya, in his 1998 work *Maya Cosmogenesis 2012* John Major Jenkins argues that their long-count calendar can also be tied into the precessional cycle because five 13-baktun cycles of 5125 years produce a total of 25,625.[29] This analysis formed part of the lead up to the year 2012, when various forecasts of the end of the world or the beginning of a whole new phase in human history were forecasted. These were not least based on this date marking the endpoint in the 13-baktun Mayan long-count calendar. But we've already seen that there's no significant Mayan tradition of world ages to go with their calendar, the whole context of the *Popol Vuh* being more one of multiple-creation-of-humankind experiments. Nor did the Mayans necessarily tie their calendar into cyclic catastrophes. So, as is so often the case, 2012 came and went without major incident. Returning to precession, even if the concept of world ages could be applied to the Mayan calendar, Jenkins uses the factor 5 to arrive at 25,625 years above, but we'll see in chapter 7 that there are only 4 ages, including our own, recorded in the *Popol Vuh*. Meanwhile if his intention is to fall back on the idea that many other Amerindian traditions do report 5 ages, he's forgetting that in these the lengths aren't the same as in the Mayan calendar and vary wildly – not only from one culture to another but even sometimes within themselves. Overall, then, this isn't a persuasive argument.

More interesting are attempts to tie precessional numbers into the Hindu Yuga cycles. The first thing that has to be established in order for this to have any hope of working is that the concept of divine years has to be seen as a late distortion. One line of support for this argument comes from another version of this tradition contained in *The Laws of Manu*, a text that seems to stir up controversy because of its debatable authority.[30] Nevertheless it dates to around the same time as the *Mahabharata* and the concept of divine years isn't specifically mentioned.[31] We saw that the same was true of the Vana Parva, one of the earlier books in the same epic, and that the concept of divine years was only introduced *implicitly* in the numerically later Santi Parva, and *explicitly* in the completely separate and chronologically later *Vishnu Purana*.

At this point we need to bring in Sri Yukteswar, the guru whose pupil Paramhansa Yogananda became even more celebrated in the West. In *The Holy Science*, published in 1894, he was arguably the first Hindu scholar to propose that the concept of divine years was a late fabrication.[32] But he further suggests that the four Yuga cycles should be seen in the context of a descending cycle followed by an ascending cycle, making for a total of 24,000 years. This seems to have much more of a Jain flavour, and it also brings the length of the total cycle closer to that of precession. Yet the numbers are still significantly different and, in any case, Yukteswar himself wasn't trying to make such a correlation.

Joseph Campbell did however attempt to correlate them and, on the basis that the length of the full precessional cycle changes over time, he worked off a period of 25,920 years as opposed to the current 25,765 quoted above.[33] A twelfth of this larger figure – that is, the time taken to pass through one sign of the zodiac – is 2160, which when multiplied by 800, 600, 400 and 200 gives the length of each traditional Yuga in normal years as per Figure 3. Campbell therefore argues that these numbers are merely symbolic and demonstrate a knowledge of precession.

CONCLUSION

These different types of traditions can broadly be split into three categories of a) repeating *universal* cycles, b) repeating *world* cycles and c) non-repeating world *ages*. We need to look carefully at each in turn because there are a number of different ways of interpreting them.

However before we do this it will be useful to consider the nature of cycles at the various levels of existence. The nature of all life at the microcosmic level is cyclical – for example individual cells divide and multiply then die off and are replaced, while on a broader scale one doesn't have to believe in reincarnation to see that both vegetable and animal lifeforms go through a similar sort of cycle. But these don't conform to any fixed time pattern and each one is, in relative terms, of extremely short duration.

If we then jump to the macrocosmic scale of the universe as a whole, modern physicists and cosmologists are by no means united on whether the universe operates cyclically. Yet even the celebrated concept of the 'Big Bang' begs the question as to what did or didn't exist prior to that point. More challenging still is the fact that many experts believe there are an infinite number of universes, all coexisting alongside each other. Some argue that these are only minutely differentiated, playing out all possible variations of all, for example, human decisions – the so-called 'many worlds' hypothesis first proposed by physicist Hugh Everett in 1957, as one way of interpreting quantum experiments. Meanwhile others concentrate on the three dozen or so 'fundamental constants', such as the speed of light, that govern our own universe – and on how incredibly 'fine-tuned' they are to the development of 'physical' life as we know it. On this basis they argue that there may be multiple other universes with different combinations of these constants that have never produced life at all – often referred to as 'multiverse' theory. Perhaps even more interesting for our current purposes are the ideas of Ervin Laszlo, a Hungarian philosopher of science. In 2004 he postulated the concept of a 'metaverse' in which an intelligent consciousness – he refers to it as the 'Akashic Field' – has been progressively fine-tuning these constants in a series of evolving universes.[34]

On that basis it's logical to argue that the primarily Hindu *universal cycle* traditions may be describing a process similar to Laszlo's metaverse, whereby each universe emerges into manifestation producing galaxies, stars and planets and any lifeforms that might evolve thereon. Then, after an immense time span, the whole ensemble dissolves and is reabsorbed back into its primal state, before starting up again with new, refined parameters. This suggestion will gain even more support when we look at the origin traditions from around the world in chapter 8.

By contrast the *world cycle* traditions found in Jain and also some Hindu literature seem to involve the mesocosm of stars and planets – that is, the middle ground between the two extremes of the microcosm of the individual lifeform and the macrocosm of the universe as a whole. Of course it goes against all modern reason to suggest that planets themselves might go through some sort of cycle of repeated creation and destruction, as part of a subcycle within the universal cycle. So how might this distortion have come about? First, it's entirely possible that it resulted from a desire to reflect the microcosm in the macrocosm and at all levels in between, so that the entirely sensible cyclical principles of the two extremes were mistakenly applied to the mesocosm as well. Second, at some point these traditions may have simply been edited so that the potentially authentic themes of human debasement and destruction on the one hand, and of universal cycles on the other, were incorrectly merged. A third option would be to adopt a more Qabalistic or theosophical approach, and to regard the various solar systems, planets and lifeforms thereon as cycling their way through different vibratory 'planes', most of which are much less 'physical' than ours.[35] This would be exactly the Jain approach described earlier if each era were to be interpreted as not necessarily involving the physical plane.

What, then, are we to make of our third category, the less rigidly cyclical *world age* traditions from Europe and the Americas with which we opened this chapter? Not only do they contain a number of clear distortions, sometimes with a late Christian influence, but we might also conjecture that they too have arisen because somewhere along the line the original themes of, first, universal cycles and, second, debasement and destruction, became mixed up and interwoven – although this time the distortion is ameliorated by them reporting only one overall cycle. On the other hand we've already mentioned that it's now generally accepted that the Earth has been rocked by repeated major catastrophes in its history. In particular as we'll see in Part 2 the peaks and troughs of the last ice age would have produced significant instability and upheaval on a local, continental and sometimes even global scale. So it's just possible that some of these traditions reflect that reality.

In conclusion, we shouldn't hide from the fact that the various universal cycle, world cycle and world age traditions undoubtedly present us with a minefield of confusion. However I hope that within this chapter I've been able to give them some sort of context that doesn't simply dismiss them all as irrelevant distortions on the one hand, or as purely symbolic on the other. Above all it does seem reasonable to argue that, in amidst all the confusion, some of them just might provide a degree of support for our main themes of a golden age followed by debasement and destruction.

6

TAKING ON THE
EXPERTS

In each of the last four chapters we've discussed the more obvious psycho-materialist interpretations that could be used to dismiss the idea that the themes we've been considering might have some historical authenticity. But if we now turn specifically to the opinions of the experts in comparative mythology, it's something of a surprise to find they don't have a great deal to say about these important themes, despite the considerable quantity of worldwide detail we can now see exists. Arguably the two foremost experts in the field are, as we saw in chapter 1, Joseph Campbell and Mircea Eliade, and we'll deal with each in turn.

CAMPBELL AND CYCLES

If we start with Joseph Campbell, he reviews the biblical themes of the fall of Adam and Eve and of the flood in some detail, but the fall of the angels that sits in between – a narrative that's arguably of the utmost importance – receives barely a mention. In fact he hardly comments on our main themes at all, despite the huge depth and breadth of his studies. To the extent that he does, though, he has a tendency to dismiss them as 'part and parcel of the heritage of civilisation itself' – which leaves us somewhat in the dark about his true feelings.[1] The only other thing we can say is that his attitude towards them is on the one hand angled towards a cyclical interpretation, the principles behind which were introduced in chapters 1 and 5; and on the other a mathematical one – no surprise given his attempts, as described in the last chapter, to link the numbers in the Hindu cycles to those of precession.

Nowhere is this more obvious than when he discusses the flood theme in Sumerian tradition in *The Masks of God*:[2]

The whole idea of the Flood rather as the work of a god of wrath than as the natural punctuation of an eon of say 432,000 years seems, indeed, to be an effect of later, secondary, comparatively simple cerebration.

Thus the evidence from a number of quarters suggests very strongly that in the earliest known Sumerian mythological texts the basic, mathematically inspired priestly vision has already been overlaid by an intrusive anthropomorphic view of the powers that motivate the world, far more primitive than that from which the earliest high civilisation had emerged; so that the myths that have survived to us represent a certain drop or devolution of tradition, which was either intentional, in the way of all devotional popularisation, or else unintentional following a loss of realisation. And the latter is the more likely, since, as Professor Poebel has let us know, the Sumerian idiom of these texts 'is no longer that of the classical period'. They are already of a late, epigonous age.

I would suggest, therefore, that the mathematics still evident in certain of the earliest known, yet late, Sumerian documents suffice to show that during the formative period of this potent tradition (which has by now reshaped humankind) an overpowering experience of order, not as something created by an anthropomorphic first being but as itself the all-creative, beginningless, and interminable structuring rhythm of the universe, supplied the wind that blew its civilisation into form. Furthermore, by a miracle that I have found no one to interpret, the arithmetic that was developed in Sumer as early as around 3200 BCE, whether by coincidence or by intuitive induction, so matched the celestial order as to amount in itself to a revelation. The whole archaic Oriental world, in contrast to the earlier primitive and later Occidental, was absolutely hypnotised by this miracle. The force of number was of far greater moment than mere fact; for it seemed actually to be the generator of fact. It was of greater moment than humanity; for it was the organising principle by which humanity realised and recognised its own latent harmony and sense. It was of considerably greater moment than the gods; for in the majesty of its cycles, greater cycles and ever greater, more majestic, infinitely widening cycles, it was the law by which gods came into being and disappeared. And it was greater even than being; for in its matrix lay the law of being.

To comment on this briefly, it's certainly true that the early Sumerians developed a sophisticated sexagesimal – or base-60 – numerical system that we still use to this day to measure time and angles, for example. However for what it's worth I'm unclear as to his evidence that they were heavily influenced by the concept of universal cycles. Indeed their literature seems to me to have had highly active, sometimes vengeful gods at its heart from the outset – and certainly, as we already saw in chapter 2, in the earliest recorded versions of the flood tradition. I will postpone further comment until the conclusion.

ELIADE AND RENEWAL

Eliade is a much more specialised commentator, so the fact that he fails to consider our main themes in any great depth is less surprising. In *Myth and Reality* he follows a similar tack to Campbell but with a few differences. His most pertinent comments come when, after discussing the rituals of annual or seasonal renewal at some length, he attempts to apply this to the idea of world ages and to certain flood traditions:[3]

> In other words, the End of the World in the past and that which is to take place in the future both represent the mythico-ritual system of the New Year festival projected on the macrocosmic scale and given an unusual degree of intensity... But now we no longer have what might be called the 'natural end' of the World... there is a real catastrophe, brought on by Divine Beings. The symmetry between the Flood and the annual renewal of the World was realised in some very few cases (Mesopotamia, Judaism, Mandan). But in general the Flood myths are independent from the mythico-ritual New Year scenarios. This is easy to understand, for the periodic festivals of regeneration symbolically re-enact the cosmogony, the creative work of the Gods, not the destruction of the old world; the latter disappeared 'naturally' for the simple reason that the distance that separated it from the 'beginnings' had reached its extreme limit.

As a corollary in his separate work *The Sacred and the Profane* he suggests that flood myths, especially of the submerged and lost continent type, can be compared to the concept of initiatory death and rebirth through baptism.[4] But that is pretty much it.

CONCLUSION

Quite apart from the fact that his work on hero myths was the inspiration for George Lucas' *Star Wars* films, Campbell's contribution to the study of comparative mythology is second to none. Yet in terms of our current themes his work surely leaves something to be desired. In particular his interpretation of catastrophe traditions can be summed up as 'early cyclical models good, later anthropomorphic models bad'. This is still a largely psychological approach and surely somewhat simplistic, in that it effectively suggests that the bulk of the traditions left to us contain nothing of any value in terms of possible pointers to a real hidden history. To be more specific he clearly argues that the idea of a single worldwide flood must be seen as an anthropomorphised distortion of the previously dominant cyclic view. He doesn't entertain the possibility that the two themes should perhaps be seen as entirely separate.

But here's the thing. What if, as I strongly suspect, the original Vedic and perhaps even earlier concept of universal cycles related only to the admittedly lengthy but periodic emergence and re-absorption of the universe as a whole – *with no suggestion of debasement and destruction being a part of this process*. As we'll see in chapter 8, this is an entirely plausible and highly esoteric worldview. In the meantime we have the quite separate tradition of a major catastrophe that wiped out our forgotten race, which just might be an echo of a genuine historical event on Earth. The problem is that some bright spark decided it would be a good idea to link them together.

Eliade too has much to offer and his observations about global catastrophe traditions quoted above appear highly erudite. Yet if we look behind the façade surely the obscure, symbolic, psychological explanations he pursues with such determination are rather less than convincing? Above all, as with most modern experts in this field, this apparent dismissal by Eliade and Campbell – of any possibility that the body of supposedly mythic texts and traditions from around the world that contain our key themes might have some genuine historical content – seems to be at least partly based on a lack of allowance for the sort of sophisticated but general spiritual worldview that I'd argue underpins much of it. Whether or not the alternative interpretations I'm putting forward in this work stand up, either partially or fully, surely – and however much their broader erudition is not in doubt – the shortcomings of the experts' approach to *these* traditions are there for all to see?

There are, moreover, two further themes that potentially strengthen our spiritual interpretations more than any other. We find these new pieces of the puzzle in yet more veiled secrets our ancestors have bequeathed to us – in their descriptions of the humankind and of the origins of the world. It is to these we'll now turn.

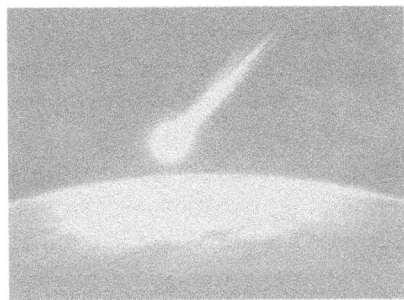

7

THE CREATION
OF HUMANKIND

Although many of the widespread accounts of the creation of humankind appear to be purely symbolic in describing how the first humans were fashioned from dust, clay or earth, some are more complex and just may provide a meaningful insight to add to our growing understanding of the deep spiritual insights our earliest global traditions contain. As usual we'll leave a discussion of orthodox opinion thereof for the conclusion.

To provide some context for this theme we again need to delve a little into the principles of a typical, modern, spiritual worldview. One of these is that energy, or indeed consciousness, underlies everything – in all planes, of all universes – and, by the way, not that long ago, in the first half of the twentieth century, some of the most brilliant scientists such as Max Planck, Niels Bohr, Albert Einstein and Werner Heisenberg more or less subscribed to this idea. This means that all animal and vegetable lifeforms, perhaps even mineral ones too, have some sort of underlying consciousness conferring varying degrees of awareness – for example, while it's self evident that many animal species possess quite sophisticated consciousness, modern biological research is showing this to be true of certain plant species too. Nevertheless it would appear that as humans ours is the most advanced, however hard that might be to believe given our crass stupidity sometimes. Indeed – despite the fact that many pets who spend a great deal of time with humans seem to possess strong individual characters – most modern evidence seems to suggest that each species of animal tends to have a more collective or group consciousness, compared to that of humans which is fully individuated.[1]

Of course for consciousness we might substitute the word *soul*. So this in turn *must* logically lead us to a question that is hugely interesting, yet hardly ever posed: *when* was it that this kind of fully individuated soul consciousness first started to incarnate on Earth – and in what *form*?

As we'll see in Part 2, not only was the evolution of modern *Homo sapiens* a gradual process, but there was a considerable buildup via earlier *Homo* strains. So we'll examine the evidence to attempt to establish roughly when our forebears made the dramatic cultural leap forward that the successful incarnation of a more evolved, individuated consciousness would surely produce. But for now there's another question we can ask: would this necessarily have been a simple, one-off process? We know that physical evolutionary processes involve an element of trial and error, but might this not apply to nonphysical aspects too? Now, in chapter 2 I proposed that our higher selves or supersouls, which reside in higher planes of consciousness, can take collective decisions to influence the course of events on Earth. Surely this would always have included a plan to project more individuated and aware souls, or aspects of themselves, into incarnation on this planet – not least because this would be one of the most fruitful ways to add to their databanks of experience. What is more, would they perhaps have been tempted to experiment with some of the earlier hominid forms they could see developing here? Might there even have been some disagreement as to whether or not this was too early? Might there even have been some *unsuccessful* early experiments? As far-fetched as this might sound, perhaps it is in fact what some of the traditions are hinting at.

IN HIS OWN IMAGE

If we start in the Near East, remember from chapter 2 that one aspect of the various confused narratives about the Nephilim may relate to the time when highly aware, individuated souls first incarnated on Earth to introduce the 'arts of civilisation' – in other words to act as the catalyst for a major cultural progression. Bearing that in mind, there are verses in the seventh chapter of the Ethiopian *Book of Enoch* that I deliberately omitted in chapter 2, but they now become relevant; because not only do the fallen angels decide to take 'wives from among the progeny of men', but there's also some consternation among them about this approach – with their leader concerned that he alone will 'suffer for so grievous a crime', while his fellows reassure him by 'swearing not to change their intention', and to 'execute their projected undertaking'.[2] What is more the Slavonic version seems to suggest there were two or even three groups of fallen angels, and that they fell at different times and suffered different fates.[3] Underneath it all, could these be distortions of an original description of disagreements amongst these 'angels' about when to first incarnate?

Meanwhile the Gnostic *On the Origin of the World* contains several intriguing accounts involving the creation of multiple versions of Adam – a Hebrew word that, depending on context, can often be translated as referring to 'mankind' generally:[4]

> And when they had finished Adam, he abandoned him as an inanimate vessel, since he had taken form like an abortion, in that no spirit was in him... He left his modelled form forty days without soul, and he withdrew and abandoned it.

> Sophia sent her daughter Zoe, being called Eve, as an instructor in order that she might make Adam, who had no soul, arise so that those whom he should engender might become containers of light.

> Now the first Adam, Adam of Light, is spirit-endowed and appeared on the first day. The second Adam is soul-endowed, and appeared on the sixth day, which is called Aphrodite. The third Adam is a creature of the earth, that is, the man of the law, and he appeared on the eighth day... which is called Sunday.

Again it's almost impossible to discern exactly what these probably distorted passages are supposed to convey. Having said that there's a clear sense of experimentation in that the first attempt to create humankind is clearly not a success, while the importance of Adam's offspring being 'containers of light' *could* be interpreted as meaning physical beings capable of successfully playing host to a highly aware, individuated soul energy. Similarly the following extract from the *Hermetica* could well be describing the point when such souls first incarnated in human form:[5]

> Mind, the father of all... gave birth to a man like himself... Having all authority over the cosmos of mortals and unreasoning animals, the man broke through the vault and stooped to look through the cosmic framework, thus displaying to lower nature the fair form of god... When the man saw in the water the form like himself as it was in nature, he loved it and wished to inhabit it; wish and action came in the same moment, and he inhabited the unreasoning form.

Moving back in time, some of the most detailed accounts of the creation of humankind are to be found in the Mesopotamian texts. The most explicit is the Sumerian *Birth of Man*, the version we have dating to some time in the second millennium BCE.[6] As we've seen so often this appears to be a composite of two original texts that have been merged none too seamlessly. The first part opens with the gods deciding to create humankind to relieve them of their excessive workload in digging and maintaining their extensive network of irrigation and drainage canals – which is nothing more than a somewhat prosaic piece of editing to reflect their localised experience of the massive effort involved in the annual 'corvée'. As a result:

> To his mother Namma he [Enki] called out:
> 'When you have drenched even the core of the Apsu's fathering clay...
> O mother mine, when you have determined its mode of being, may Ninmah put together the birth-chair
> And when, without any male, you have built it up in it, may you give birth to humankind!'
> Without the sperm of a male she gave birth to offspring, to the embryo of humankind.

The orthodox view is that this passage extols the symbolic role of the archetypal Earth Mother in producing humankind from her own self – that is, the earth or clay. The second part goes on to describe how Enki and Ninmah get drunk together, apparently to celebrate their creation. She boasts that she controls the 'build of men', be it good or bad, and he responds with the challenge that he can mitigate any 'badness' she produces. So she makes a variety of beings, described rather colourfully as follows: the 'man-unable-to-close-the-shaking-hand-upon-an-arrow-shaft-to-send-it-going'; the 'one-handing-back-the-lamp-to-the-men-who-can-see'; the 'hobbled-by-twisting-ankles'; the 'moron, the-engenderer-of-which-was-a-Subarean'; the 'man-leaking-urine'; the 'woman-who-is-not-giving-birth'; and the 'man-in-the-body-of-which-no-male-and-no-female-organ-was-placed'. He is then able to find a position in society for all these creations and, after creating his own being that is literally an abortion because it isn't gestated properly in the female womb, the text ends with them agreeing that both men and women have vital roles to play in the reproductive process.

We can see from the full context that it's hopelessly inappropriate for Zecharia Sitchin to use this text as a key plank in his theories by suggesting that it describes genetic experimentation – when in fact it's clearly a polemic on, first, the roles of men and women in reproduction and, second, of the disabled in society. Nor for that matter does it provide any support for our own current theme of *soul* experimentation. But it does allow a fuller understanding of the context and background of the Mesopotamian creation accounts.

In the hope of more interesting revelations let's turn to the Akkadian texts that deal with the creation of humankind, the most important of which is *Atrahasis*. As we saw in chapter 2 this too opens with the gods complaining about their workload, but then it carries on as follows:[7]

Enki made his voice heard
And spoke to the great gods,
'On the first, seventh, and fifteenth of the month
I shall make a purification by washing.
Then one god should be slaughtered.
And the gods can be purified by immersion.
Nintu shall mix clay
With his flesh and his blood.
Then a god and a man
Will be mixed together in clay.
Let us hear the drumbeat forever after,
Let a ghost come into existence from the god's flesh,
Let her proclaim it as his living sign,
And let the ghost exist so as not to forget (the slain god).'
They answered 'Yes!' in the assembly,
The great Anunnaki who assign the fates.
On the first, seventh, and fifteenth of the month
He made a purification by washing.
Geshtu-e, a god who had intelligence,
They slaughtered in their assembly.

Here we encounter the novel idea that humankind was not just created *by* the gods, but from *mixture with* at least one of them. In particular the parts of the god that humans receive are his 'ghost' and 'intelligence'. Is this a veiled reference to us playing host to an individuated soul for the first time? Support for this interpretation comes from the celebrated *Epic of Creation* or *Enuma Elish,* which dates to the first half of the first millennium BCE, in which a brief reference to the creation of humankind asserts that the 'blood' of one of the gods was involved:[8]

> They bound him [the chosen god, Qingu] and held him in front of Ea, imposed the penalty on him and cut off his blood. He created humankind from his blood.

Can this too be taken as a metaphor for humankind being endowed with a more 'godlike' soul energy for the first time? Certainly Berossus seems to support such an interpretation in his later commentary on this text, suggesting that it's 'on this account that men are rational and partake of divine knowledge'.[9] Of course in the first chapter of Genesis all this is distilled into the suggestion that humankind was created in 'the image of God', but perhaps we now have a different perspective on this brief and veiled reference.[10]

Another fascinating aspect of Mesopotamian accounts comes from the continuation of the above passage in *Atrahasis*:

> Mami made her voice heard
> And spoke to the great gods,
> 'I have carried out perfectly
> The work that you ordered of me.
> You have slaughtered a god together with his intelligence.
> I have relieved you of your hard work,
> I have imposed your load on man.
> You have bestowed noise on humankind.
> I have undone the fetter and granted freedom.'

This is of course the same 'noise of humankind' that, when it became excessive, caused the gods to destroy their creation – which we struggled to interpret in chapter 2. But if it was 'bestowed' on humans from the beginning, are we referring to the proper development of the power of speech and of intelligent communication? In any case the goddess then 'pinches off fourteen pieces of clay' and, with the assistance of the 'womb-goddesses', creates the first seven men and seven women.[11] Meanwhile the *Epic of Gilgamesh* contains a brief reference to the Mother Goddess' creation of humans, again involving 'purification' and 'clay':[12]

> She created a primitive man... offspring of silence...
> His whole body was shaggy with hair...
> He knew neither people not country; he was dressed as cattle are.
> With gazelles he eats vegetation,
> With cattle he quenches his thirst at the watering place.

The reference to him being the 'offspring of silence' is surely in direct opposition to the idea of bestowing noise on humankind. So, although the context of this composite text is completely confused, could this originally have been a reference to earlier human forms that *didn't* have the power to communicate properly?

THE MAKER, MODELLER, BEARER, BEGETTER

Moving over to the Americas, the Mayan *Popol Vuh* contains a lengthy description of how a variety of beings were created and destroyed before a successful human emerged, which is highly comparable to and yet in some ways very different from the world age traditions discussed in chapter 5.[13] It is thought to have been compiled by indigenous scholars in the middle of the sixteenth century, and the following extracts are taken from the translation by Dennis Tedlock.[14]

First, the creator deities referred to collectively as the 'Maker, Modeller, Bearer, Begetter' fashion various animals, but they're unable to speak properly to praise them:

And then the deer and birds were told by the Maker, Modeller, Bearer, Begetter:
'Talk, speak out. Don't moan, don't cry out. Please talk, each to each, within each kind, within each group', they were told – the deer, birds, puma, jaguar, serpent.
'Name now our names, praise us. We are your mother, we are your father... speak, pray to us, keep our days', they were told. But it didn't turn out that they spoke like people: they just squawked, they just chattered, they just howled. It wasn't apparent what language they spoke; each one gave a different cry.

So the deities experiment again:

Working with earth and mud they made a body, but it didn't look good to them. It was just separating, just crumbling, just loosening, just softening, just disintegrating, and just dissolving. Its head wouldn't turn, either. Its face was just lopsided, its face was just twisted. It couldn't look around. It talked at first, but senselessly. It was quickly dissolving in the water.

Accordingly this first 'human' creation is destroyed:

So then they dismantled, again they brought down their work and design. Again they talked:

'What is there for us to make that would turn out well, that would succeed in keeping our days and praying to us?' they said. Then they planned again.

After various further consultations, a new human is devised from wood:

The moment they spoke it was done: the manikins, woodcarvings, human in looks and human in speech.

This was the peopling of the face of the Earth.

They came into being, they multiplied, they had daughters, they had sons, these manikins, woodcarvings. But there was nothing in their hearts and nothing in their minds, no memory of their mason and builder. They just went and walked wherever they wanted. Now they did not remember the Heart of Sky.

And so they fell, just an experiment and just a cutout for humankind. They were talking at first but their faces were dry. They were not yet developed in the legs and arms. They had no blood, no lymph. They had no sweat, no fat. Their complexions were dry, their faces were crusty. They flailed their legs and arms, their bodies were deformed.

And so they accomplished nothing before the Maker, Modeller who gave them birth, gave them heart. They became the first numerous people here on the face of the Earth...

They were not competent, nor did they speak before the builder and sculptor who made them and brought them forth, and so they were killed, done in by a flood.

So again this race is destroyed, this time by the ubiquitous flood, and a detailed and gory description of the revenge taken on them by the deities they hadn't praised and the animals they hadn't respected ensues – followed by this highly suggestive passage:

Such was the scattering of the human work, the human design. The people were ground down, overthrown. The mouths and faces of all of them were destroyed and crushed. And it used to be said that the monkeys in the forests today are a sign of this. They were left as a sign because wood alone was used for their flesh by the builder and sculptor. So this is why monkeys look like people: they are a sign of a previous human work, human design – mere manikins, mere woodcarvings.

Manikins and woodcarvings that resemble monkeys: what can the authors have meant? We have already seen that the ancient texts and traditions place great emphasis on how the golden race paid due homage to their gods or, in more philosophical terms, appreciated and respected their spiritual roots. But here this idea is placed in an entirely different context, with an emphasis on early creations that are unable to speak so as to 'keep the gods' days and pray to them'. In purely practical terms the prerequisites for a golden race would have been sufficient *intelligence* to be able to think about and appreciate their spiritual roots, and the necessary corollary of *communication* that went far beyond the rudiments required for mere survival, allowing real culture to blossom for the first time. So were the Maya describing the idea that highly aware, individuated souls may have tried to incarnate *before* the human form was sufficiently advanced along the evolutionary path to make the experiment viable?

Let us return to the text to see if they give us any more clues. As a final resort, the creators decide to fashion humankind proper from corn:

'The dawn has approached, preparations have been made, and morning has come for the provider, nurturer, born in the light, begotten in the light. Morning has come for humankind, for the people of the face of the Earth', they said...

And then the yellow corn and white corn were ground, and Xmucane did the grinding nine times. Food was used, along with the water she rinsed her hands with, for the creation of grease; it became human fat when it was worked by the Bearer, Begetter, Sovereign Plumed Serpent, as they are called.

After that, they put it into words: the making, the modelling of our first mother-father, with yellow corn, white corn alone for the flesh, food alone for the human legs and arms, for our first fathers, the four human works.

This time the experiment was more of a success:

And these are the names of our first mother-fathers. They were simply made and modelled, it is said; they had no mother and no father. We have named the men by themselves. No woman gave birth to them, nor were they begotten by the builder, sculptor, Bearer, Begetter. By sacrifice alone, by genius alone they were made, they were modelled by the Maker, Modeller, Bearer, Begetter, Sovereign Plumed Serpent. And when they came to fruition, they came out human:

They talked and they made words.

They looked and they listened.
They walked, they worked.
They were good people, handsome, with looks of the male kind. Thoughts came into existence and they gazed; their vision came all at once. Perfectly they saw, perfectly they knew everything under the sky, whenever they looked. The moment they turned around and looked around in the sky, on the earth, everything was seen without any obstruction. They didn't have to walk around before they could see what was under the sky; they just stayed where they were.

As they looked, their knowledge became intense. Their sight passed through trees, through rocks, through lakes, through seas, through mountains, through plains. Jaguar Quitze, Jaguar Night, Not Right Now, and Dark Jaguar were truly gifted people.

Is this further eloquent description of the spiritual awareness humankind displayed in the golden age also telling us that this only came about after the first fully conscious, individuated souls were successful in incarnating in modern human form? If so it arguably adds weight to the suggestion that, underneath all the symbolism, the previous passages are describing unsuccessful earlier attempts.

THE DAWN OF CREATION

While the Maya appear to have merged the themes of multiple creations and of world ages, the Hopi tradition of world ages discussed in chapter 5 is preceded by a separate and complementary account of the creation of humankind that again involves multiple attempts:[15]

So Spider Woman gathered earth, this time of four colours, yellow, red, white, and black; mixed with *tuchvala,* the liquid of her mouth; moulded them; and covered them with her white-substance cape which was the creative wisdom itself. As before, she sang over them the Creation Song, and when she uncovered them these forms were human beings in the image of Sotuknang. Then she created four other beings after her own form. They were *wuti,* female partners, for the first four male beings.

When Spider Woman uncovered them the forms came to life. This was at the time of the dark purple light, Qoyangnuptu, the first phase of the dawn of Creation, which first reveals the mystery of man's creation.

They soon awakened and began to move, but there was still a

dampness on their foreheads and a soft spot on their heads. This was at the time of the yellow light, Sikangnuqa, the second phase of the dawn of Creation, when the breath of life entered man.

In a short time the sun appeared above the horizon, drying the dampness on their foreheads and hardening the soft spot on their heads. This was the time of the red light, Talawva, the third phase of the dawn of Creation, when man, fully formed and firmed, proudly faced his Creator.

'That is the Sun', said Spider Woman. 'You are meeting your Father the Creator for the first time. You must always remember and observe these three phases of your Creation. The time of the three lights, the dark purple, the yellow, and the red reveal in turn the mystery, the breath of life, and warmth of love. These comprise the Creator's plan of life for you as sung over you in the Song of Creation...'

The First People of the First World did not answer her: they could not speak.

This is clearly exactly the same concept as in the Mayan traditions. The account continues:

Spider Woman explained. 'As you commanded me, I have created these First People. They are fully and firmly formed: they are properly coloured; they have life: they have movement. But they can't talk. That is the proper thing they lack. So I want you to give them speech. Also the wisdom and the power to reproduce, so that they may enjoy their life and give thanks to the Creator.'

So Sotuknang gave them speech, a different language to each colour, with respect for each other's difference. He gave them the wisdom and the power to reproduce and multiply.

Then he said to them, 'With all these I have given you this world to live on and to be happy. There is only one thing I ask of you. To respect the Creator at all times. Wisdom, harmony, and respect for the love of the Creator who made you. May it grow and never be forgotten among you as long as you live.'

So the First People went their directions, were happy, and began to multiply.

The idea that once they'd been 'given the power of speech' it allowed them to 'respect the creator' is clearly the same as in the Mayan traditions too, again perhaps suggesting that humankind had at last advanced sufficiently along the evolutionary path to be ready to successfully receive the individuated souls that had been waiting in the wings. The account ends as follows:

> With the pristine wisdom granted them, they understood that the Earth was a living entity like themselves... Thus they knew their mother in two aspects which were often synonymous – as Mother Earth and the Corn Mother.
>
> In their wisdom they also knew their father in two aspects. He was the Sun, the solar god of their universe. Yet his was but the face through which looked Taiowa, their Creator.
>
> These universal entities were their real parents, their human parents being but the instruments through which their power was made manifest. In modern times their descendents remembered this...
>
> The First People, then, understood the mystery of their parenthood. In their pristine wisdom they also understood their own structure and functions – the nature of man himself.

What more eloquent expression of the dual lineage of our bodies from our earthly parents, and of our souls from the universal and ethereal, could we desire?

SILENT CREATIONS

Further examples of multiple creation attempts from the other side of the world can be found in the traditions of various Indonesian tribes, described by Roland Burrage Dixon in his Polynesian volume of *The Mythology of All Races*:[16]

> A somewhat different form of origin-myth describes a series of attempts at creation in which different materials are tried, the first trials being failures, although success is finally achieved. Thus the Dyaks of the Baram and Rejang district in Borneo say that after the two birds, Iri and Ringgon, had formed the earth, plants, and animals they decided to create man: 'At first, they made him of clay, but when he was dried he could neither speak nor move, which provoked them, and they ran at him angrily; so frightened was he that he fell backward and broke all to pieces. The next man they made was of hard wood, but he, also, was utterly stupid, and absolutely good for nothing. Then the two birds searched carefully for a good material, and eventually selected the wood of the tree known as Kumpong, which has a strong fibre and exudes a quantity of deep red sap, whenever it is cut. Out of this tree they fashioned a man and a woman, and were so well pleased with this achievement that they rested for a long while, and admired their

handiwork. Then they decided to continue creating more men; they returned to the Kumpong tree, but they had entirely forgotten their original pattern, and how they executed it, and they were therefore able only to make very inferior creatures, which became the ancestors of the Maias (orangutans) and monkeys.'

A similar tale is found among the Iban and Sakarram Dyaks, only reversing the order, so that after twice failing to make man from wood, the birds succeeded at the third trial when they used clay. Farther north, among the Dusun of British North Borneo, the first two beings 'made a stone in the shape of a man but the stone could not talk, so they made a wooden figure and when it was made it talked, though not long after it became worn out and rotten; afterwards they made a man of earth, and the people are descended from this till the present day'.

We can see even from such summaries that they contain similar themes, especially the pervasive idea of the inability of the earliest creations to talk.

UNUSUAL SOURCES

There are a couple of rather more unusual sources of support for my idea of experimentation with different hominid forms. I don't offer them as any sort of proof, and for those who are sceptical about such sources this section can be completely ignored without it detracting from my main argument. But I think they're interesting enough to merit inclusion here.

The first is the channelling work of American author JZ Knight, whose messages purportedly come from an ethereal entity called Ramtha:[17]

> The first men came forth only after much experimentation by a group of the Gods. At first only males were created, and they were not even created with loins. The loins were inside of them so that they could reproduce themselves through the process called cloning. Thus all man-embodiments looked alike when they were first created. And they were rather humble creatures who would be considered very grotesque to you today. But to the Gods in those times, they were very beautiful. Unfortunately, they were not very swift on their feet; thus they were continuously made a meal of by the animals about. So the Gods tried and tested and modified them for a long time until they were worthy of complete possession. Once the embodiment had been perfected, many of the Gods in great jubilation took possession of embodiments for a new adventure in the exploration of life.

The second is the hypnotic regression research of her countryman Michael Newton:[18]

> A few of my more advanced clients declare that highly advanced souls who specialise in seeking out suitable hosts for young souls evaluated life on Earth for over a million years. My impression is these examiner souls found the early hominid brain cavity and restricted voice box to be inadequate for soul development earlier than some 200,000 years ago.

CONCLUSION

In terms of orthodox opinion Joseph Campbell comments on the Mesopotamian creation texts and their biblical derivatives at some length.[19] Of course he discusses the simple symbolism of creation from mother Earth, and the gradual increase in emphasis on the role of male gods in the creation story as their society became increasingly patriarchal.[20] He also notes the marked change in attitude that results from the introduction of the idea that humankind was created as a servant of the gods.[21] These are all reasonable observations. More simply, it may be that all these creation-of-humankind traditions are nothing more than prosaic attempts to make humans seem special, or at least to provide some sort of answer to the question, 'What is it that really makes us human?' But somehow I doubt it. My strong suspicion is that again Campbell is failing to appreciate the deeper spiritual messages that I would argue lie beneath the surface of these creation accounts.

We should be clear that there are two separate but related themes that interest us here, and that some accounts contain both while others mainly concentrate on just one. The first is the simple idea that at some point 'successful' humans were created, and that broadly speaking their distinguishing features were their ability to 'talk' and 'see' properly, as well as to 'give thanks for their creation' and 'know who they were' – whether this was brought about by infusions from godly essence or in other more symbolic ways. My interpretation, using a typical, modern, spiritual perspective, is that these are veiled descriptions of the time when highly aware, individualised souls were first able to incarnate en masse – providing an incredible catalytic boost that paved the way for the development of advanced culture and, eventually, civilisation as we know it today.

This interpretation is reinforced by the other, related idea found in those accounts that describe multiple, *unsuccessful* attempts to create the human race. The related argument is that they refer to previous attempts by such souls to incarnate in human or protohuman forms that were insufficiently physiologically advanced to properly play host to them – and especially to house the golden race.

8
THE ORIGINS OF
THE WORLD

At the end of chapter 5 we discussed the idea of the conscious metaverse that underpins a series of progressively evolving universes, and saw how this might be what the Hindu universal cycle traditions are attempting to describe. More than this, though, it seems that at some point this idea was widely held, at least in terms of an understanding of how each universe emerges from its slumber at what we might call 'the Dawn of Brahma' – because this is the veiled message preserved in the sacred traditions of the origins of the world on every continent of the globe.

Of course, although the term *world* is used in most scholarly translations, we're making the assumption that this should really be taken to mean *universe* as a whole. This is just one of the inevitable distortions and contextual differences, regressively introduced by people who had lost sight of their original message, that we'll need to see through. It is also why it's arguably more appropriate to refer to them as *cosmogony* traditions. Indeed it's arguably here more than anywhere that the orthodox failure to appreciate the esoteric wisdom underlying supposed mythology is at its most glaringly obvious.[1]

IN THE BEGINNING

THE NEAR EAST

Let us first remind ourselves of the biblical narrative at the beginning of Genesis:

1. In the beginning God created the heaven and the earth.
2. And the earth was without form, and void; and darkness was upon the face of the deep. And the Spirit of God moved upon the face of the waters.

A 'formless void' that has connotations of water, depth and darkness, and which contains the 'spirit of God' – surely not a bad description of a boundless, timeless energy waiting to erupt into manifestation? Proof that this has as usual been condensed from more detailed sources is provided by the following wonderfully descriptive passage in the *Hermetica*:[2]

> In the deep there was boundless darkness and water and fine intelligent spirit, all existing by divine power in chaos. Then a holy light was sent forth, and elements solidified out of liquid essence.

This introduces us to the oft-expressed idea that this process is seen as 'creating order out of chaos' – a common source of confusion that seems likely to have pertained at least since the classical Greek era, and which has led many orthodox scholars down completely the wrong route. The key is that the name for the Greek god *Chaos* originally had nothing to do with disorder, but actually translated as 'chasm' or 'void'.[3] So, rather than this being some purely psycho-materialist concept of the creation of a universal order in the heavens that is mirrored in the ordered nature of the various new civilisations on Earth, the idea being conveyed is surely one of creation out of a chasm of formless nothingness.

In the meantime the same sense of awe pervades the *Hermetica's* multiple descriptions of the universal energy or consciousness that animates everything in the universe both seen and unseen, which as we saw in chapter 2 is often referred to simply as 'source':[4]

> The monad, because it is the beginning and root of all things, is in them all as root and beginning... the monad contains every number, is contained by none, and generates every number without being generated by any other number.

> God, who is energy and power, surrounds everything and permeates everything, and understanding of god is nothing difficult, my child... If matter is apart from god, my son, what sort of place would you allot to it? If it is not energised, do you suppose it is anything but a heap?

Despite their shortcomings the Gnostic texts too provide some fascinating material. For example *On the Origin of the World* commences as follows:[5]

> How well it suits all men, on the subject of chaos, to say that it is a kind of darkness! But in fact it comes from a shadow, which has been called by the name darkness. And the shadow comes from a product that has

existed since the beginning. It is, moreover, clear that it existed before chaos came into being...

When the ruler saw his magnitude – and it was only himself that he saw: he saw nothing else, except for water and darkness – then he supposed that it was he alone who existed. His [missing] was completed by verbal expression: it appeared as a spirit moving to and fro upon the waters.

This passage introduces us to two key ideas consistently expressed in origin traditions – that of the 'power of the Word' in the creation process, and that of the ultimate creative power recognising it is alone. In addition this power is described in the *Tripartite Tractate* as 'a spring which is not diminished by the water which abundantly flows from it', and as something that 'can't be grasped: nor is it possible for anyone else to change him into a different form or to reduce him, or alter him or diminish him... who is the unalterable, immutable one'.[6] How closely these intriguing descriptions mirror the scientific fact that energy – perhaps even underlying consciousness – can't be destroyed, it can only change its form.

MESOPOTAMIA

Unfortunately the Mesopotamian texts are somewhat deficient in this area, revealing only the faintest traces of any original wisdom. In part this may be explained by the fact that the only real origin tradition that survives is the relatively late *Epic of Creation*, which opens as follows:[7]

> When skies above were not yet named
> Nor earth below pronounced by name,
> Apsu, the first one, their begetter
> And maker Tiamat, who bore them all,
> Had mixed their waters together,
> But had not formed pastures, nor discovered reed-beds;
> When yet no gods were manifest,
> Nor names pronounced, nor destinies decreed,
> Then gods were born within them.

All we can really extract from this is that at one time there existed only the primeval waters of Tiamat, which are associated with chaos.[8] More generally orthodox scholars suggest that the Mesopotamians regarded the earth (Ki) as a flat disc that was separated from heaven (An) by the atmosphere (Lil), with the whole ensemble immersed like a gigantic bubble in the primeval waters of Tiamat.[9] Yet not only does this tend to ignore the esoteric significance of the primeval waters – which may or may not be a fair reflection of the Mesopotamians' own understanding – but also it's perhaps somewhat at odds with the astronomical knowledge they possessed.

EGYPT

These are the earliest verses of *The Story of Re* introduced in chapter 2:[10]

> In the beginning, before there was any land of Egypt, all was darkness, and there was nothing but a great waste of water called Nun. The power of Nun was such that there arose out of the darkness a great shining egg, and this was Re.
>
> Now Re was all-powerful, and he could take many forms. His power and the secret of it lay in his hidden name; but if he spoke other names, that which he named came into being.

To flesh this out let's again turn to John Baines and Geraldine Pinch, who provide an interesting summary of Ancient Egyptian cosmogony in their essay in *World Mythology* – even though it's a fine example of the way modern commentators tend to concentrate on prosaic descriptions of the various guises the gods take:[11]

> Before the gods came into existence there was only a dark, watery abyss called the Nun, whose chaotic energies contained the potential forms of all living things. The spirit of the creator was present in these primeval waters but had no place in which to take shape...
>
> The event that marked the beginning of time was the rising of the first land out of the waters of the Nun. This primeval mound provided a place in which the first deity could come into existence. He sometimes took the form of a bird, a falcon, a heron, or a yellow wagtail, which perched on the mound. An alternative image of creation was the primeval lotus, which rose out of the waters and opened to reveal an infant god. The first deity was equipped with several divine powers, such as Hu ('Authoritative Utterance'), Sia ('Perception') and Heka ('Magic'). Using these powers, he created order out of chaos. This divine order was personified by a goddess, Ma'at, the daughter of the sun god. The word Ma'at also meant justice, truth and harmony. The divine order was constantly in danger of dissolving back into the chaos from which it had been formed.
>
> The first deity became conscious of being alone and created gods and men in his own image and a world for them to inhabit. Deities

were said to come from the sweat of the sun god and human beings from his tears. The power of creation was usually linked with the sun, but various deities are also named as the creator [Ptah in the Memphite tradition, Ra-Atum in the Heliopolitan, and Amon-Ra in the Theban]. At the temple of the sun god in Heliopolis, the Benu bird... was said to be the first deity. Depicted as a heron, the shining bird was a manifestation of the creator sun god, and brought the first light into the darkness of chaos. When it landed on the primeval mound, it gave a cry that was the first sound.

As with the Near Eastern traditions we see from these two descriptions that the concept of darkness and waters is to the fore, with the added insight in the latter that these contain the *potential* for all forms of life. What is more we find the first deity being able to create by 'speaking names' or using the gift of 'authoritative utterance', suggesting again that the Word alone is sufficient to trigger the emergence and creation process. Meanwhile the symbolism of the primeval lotus clearly mirrors its use in the Indian cyclical worldview that we discussed in chapter 5.

INDIA

Moving farther east, the suggestion that the Indian *Vedas* are some of the finest philosophical texts known to humankind is nowhere more clearly demonstrated than in their conception of cosmogony. This is described with great eloquence in the *Rig Veda*:[12]

1. There was neither non-existence nor existence then; there was neither the realm of space nor the sky which is beyond. What stirred? Where? In whose protection? Was there water, bottomlessly deep?
2. There was neither death nor immortality then. There was no distinguishing sign of night nor of day. That one breathed, windless, by its own impulse. Other than that there was nothing beyond.
3. Darkness was hidden by darkness in the beginning; with no distinguishing sign, all this was water. The life force that was covered with emptiness, that one arose through the power of heat.
4. Desire came upon that one in the beginning; that was the first seed of mind. Poets seeking in their heart with wisdom found the bond of existence in non-existence.
5. Their cord was extended across. Was there below? Was there above? There were seed-placers; there were powers. There was impulse beneath; there was giving-forth above.
6. Who really knows? Who will here proclaim it? Whence was it

produced? Whence is this creation? The gods came afterwards, with the creation of this universe. Who then knows whence it has arisen?
7. Whence this creation has arisen – perhaps it formed itself, or perhaps it did not – the one who looks down on it, in the highest heaven, only he knows – or perhaps he does not know.

Could we ask for a finer description of the ineffable, unnameable, unknowable, infinite, immanent and transcendent life force of the universe, which slumbers in the dark, watery void that contains nothing and yet – at the same time – the seed of everything?

THE ORIENT

This theme is repeated in a somewhat cryptic extract from one of the Taoist *Essays from Huai Nan Tzu*:[13]

(1) There was the 'beginning': (2) There was a beginning of an anteriority to this beginning. (3) There was a beginning of an anteriority even before the beginning of this anteriority. (4) There was 'the existence'. (5) There was 'the non-existence'. (6) There was 'not yet a beginning of non-existence'. (7) There was 'not yet a beginning of the not yet beginning of non-existence'.

This extract is accompanied by a commentary that still forms part of the original text:

(1) The meaning of 'There was the beginning' is that there was a complex energy which had not yet pullulated into germinal form, nor into any visible shape of root and seed and rudiment. Even then in this vast and impalpable void there was apparent the desire to spring into life; but, as yet, the genera of matter were not formed.
(2) At the 'beginning of anteriority before the beginning' the fluid of heaven first descended and the fluid of earth first ascended. The male and female principles interosculated, prompting and striving among the elements of the cosmos. The forces wandered hither and thither, pursuing, competing, interpenetrating. Clothed with energy, they moved, sifted, separated, impregnated the various elements as they moved in the fluid ocean, each aura desiring to ally itself with another, even when, as yet, there was no appearance of any created form.
(3) At the stage 'There must be a beginning of an anteriority even before the beginning of anteriority', Heaven contained the spirit of harmony, but had not, as yet, descended: earth cherished the vivifying fluid, but had not ascended, as yet. It was space, still, desolate, vapoury

– a drizzling humid state with a similitude of vacancy and form. The vitalising fluid floated about, layer on layer.

(4) 'There was the existence' speaks of the coming of creation and the immaterial fluids assuming definite forms, implying that the different elements had become stabilised. The immaterial nuclei and embryos, generic forms as roots, stems, tissues, twigs and leaves of variegated hues appeared. Beautiful were the variegated colours. Butterflies and insects flew hither and thither: insects crawled about. We now reach the stage of movement and the breath of life on every hand. At this stage it was possible to feel, to grasp, to see and follow outward phenomena. They could be counted and distinguished both quantitatively and qualitatively.

(5) 'The non-existence' period. It was so called because when it was gazed on no form was seen: when the ear listened, there was no sound: when the hand grasped, there was nothing tangible: when gazed at, it was illimitable. It was limitless space, profound and a vast void – a quiescent, subtile [sic] mass of immeasurable translucency.

(6) In 'There was not yet a beginning of non-existence', implies that this period wrapped up heaven and earth, shaping and forging the myriad things of creation: there was an all-penetrating impalpable complexity, profoundly vast and all-extending; nothing was outside its operations. The minutest hair and sharpest point were differentiated: nothing within was left undone. There was no wall around, and the foundation of non-existence was being laid.

(7) In the period of 'There was not yet a beginning of the not yet beginning of non-existence', Heaven and Earth were not divided: the four seasons were not yet separated: the myriad things were not yet come to birth. Vast-like even and quiet, still-like, clear and limpid, forms were not visible.

Although the apparent order of these commentaries is somewhat confused, and there's perhaps a subtle suggestion that they ignore physical evolution, they do attempt to say something about the incredible complexities of the universe emerging into its various realms and forms, both nonphysical and physical. Another essay continues the theme:[14]

> The divinities Yin and Yang were separated... the hard and soft being mutually united... creation assumed form. The murky elements went to form reptiles: the finer essence went to form man. Hence, spirit belongs to Heaven and the physical belongs to Earth. When the spirit returns to the gate of Heaven and the body seeks its origin, how can I exist? The 'I' is dissolved.

The implication seems to be that during the Night of Brahma the void remains completely undifferentiated and unitary, whereas at the commencement of the Day of Brahma – or year, or life, the terminology really doesn't matter – the first thing the creative power does is split into two, in this case represented by the Yin and the Yang. These apparent dualities representing male and female, positive and negative, light and dark and so on are often misunderstood as opposites, but in fact they're better seen as complementary, unified principles that exist as contrasts on a single scale and have to be balanced. Indeed in this context it's useful to think of the Night of Brahma as a state of stasis or equilibrium that has to be knocked *out* of equilibrium if any sort of dynamic of creation and evolution is going to occur. In many traditions this is represented somewhat prosaically as the supreme creator recognising he's alone, and becoming so frustrated that he creates one or more companions for himself – as we saw, for example, with the Egyptian first deity as discussed earlier.

Perhaps unsurprisingly Japanese cosmogony follows a similar even if somewhat simplified line, perhaps partly due to it being more recently recorded. Compiled in the early part of the eighth century their two most sacred texts, the *Kojiki* or 'Record of Ancient Matters' and the *Nihongi* or 'Chronicles of Japan', each have similar content. The opening lines of the latter are as follows:[15]

> Of old, Heaven and Earth were not yet separated, and the In (Yin) and Yo (Yang) not yet divided. They formed a chaotic mass like an egg which was of obscurely defined limits and contained germs. The purer and clearer part was thinly drawn out, and formed Heaven, while the heavier and grosser element settled down and became Earth. The finer element easily became a united body, but the consolidation of the heavy and gross element was accomplished with difficulty. Heaven was therefore formed first, and Earth was established subsequently.

GREECE

In Greek cosmogony we find that, while many accounts contain the somewhat prosaic distortions we've come to expect, traces of the original wisdom still shine through in places. For example, here are the opening lines of Ovid's *Metamorphosis*:[16]

> Ere land and sea and the all-covering sky
> Were made, in the whole world the countenance

Of nature was the same, all one, well named
Chaos, a raw and undivided mass,
Naught but a lifeless bulk, with warring seeds
Of ill-joined elements compressed together.
No sun as yet poured light upon the world,
No waxing moon her crescent filled anew,
Nor in the ambient air yet hung the Earth,
Self-balanced, equipoised, nor Ocean's arms
Embraced the long far margin of the land
Though there were land and sea and air, the land
No foot could tread, no creature swim the sea,
The air was lightless; nothing kept its form,
All objects were at odds, since in one mass
Cold essence fought with hot, and moist with dry,
And hard with soft and light with things of weight.
This strife a god, with nature's blessing, solved;
Who severed land from sky and sea from land,
And from the denser vapours set apart
The ethereal sky; and, each from the blind heap
Resolved and freed, he fastened in its place
Appropriate in peace and harmony.
The fiery weightless force of heaven's vault
Flashed up and claimed the topmost citadel;
Next came the air in lightness and in place;
The thicker earth with grosser elements
Sank burdened by its weight; lowest and last
The girdling waters pent the solid globe.

This passage is guilty of the very confusion of linking the void with chaos – expressed in terms of 'warring seeds' and 'strife' – that we introduced at the beginning of the chapter. But if we remove these distorted elements and concentrate on the original 'undivided mass' that was self-balanced and 'equipoised', this is clearly in line with our current theme. In the meantime, as usual we might have expected to be able to turn to Plato for some rather better fare – but it seems cosmogony wasn't one of his strong points.

POLYNESIA

If we now turn to indigenous traditions from around the world, Roland Burrage Dixon provides the following entirely consistent overview of Polynesian cosmogony in *The Mythology of All Races*:[17]

The essential elements of this form of the myth may be stated as follows. In the beginning there was nothing but Po, a void or chaos, without light, heat, or sound, without form or motion. Gradually vague stirrings began within the darkness, moanings and whisperings arose, and then at first, faint as early dawn, the light appeared and grew until full day had come. Heat and moisture next developed, and from the interaction of these elements came substance and form, ever becoming more and more concrete, until the solid earth and overarching sky took shape and were personified as Heaven Father [Rangi] and Earth Mother [Papa].

So, for example, one Maori tradition reported by Dixon begins as follows:[18] 'Io dwelt within the breathing-space of immensity. The Universe was in darkness, with water everywhere. There was no glimmer of dawn, no clearness, no light.' Another is even more esoteric:[19]

From the conception the increase
From the increase the swelling
From the swelling the thought
From the thought the remembrance
From the remembrance the consciousness, the desire.
The word became fruitful...
From the nothing, the begetting,
From the nothing the increase
From the nothing the abundance,
The power of increasing, the living breath.

Meanwhile he reports that the cosmogony of the Society Islands, for example, follows similar lines:[20]

He existed. Taaroa was his name.
In the immensity
There was no earth, there was no sky,
There was no sea, there was no man.
Taaroa calls, but nothing answers.
Existing alone, he became the universe.
Taaroa is the root, the rock's foundation.
Taaroa is the sands.
It is thus that he is named.
Taaroa is the light.
Taaroa is within.
Taaroa is the germ.

Taaroa is the support.
Taaroa is enduring.

Again here we find the idea that the creative power in the void contains the potential germ or seed of all forms that will eventually emerge.

AMERICA

How do the indigenous traditions of the Americas compare? First let's hear once again from the Hopi Indians of the north:[21]

The first world was Tokpela, Endless Space.
But first, they say, there was only the Creator, Taiowa. All else was endless space. There was no beginning and no end, no time, no shape, no life. Just an immeasurable void that had its beginning and end, time, shape, and life in the mind of Taiowa the Creator.
Then he, the infinite, conceived the finite. First he created Sotuknang to make it manifest, saying to him, 'I have created you, the first power and instrument as a person, to carry out my plan for life in endless space. I am your Uncle. You are my Nephew. Go now and lay out these universes in proper order so they may work harmoniously with one another according to my plan.'
Sotuknang did as he was commanded. From endless space he gathered that which was to be manifest as solid substance, moulded it into forms, and arranged them into nine universal kingdoms: one for Taiowa the Creator, one for himself, and seven universes for the life to come.

This account typifies the Amerindian approach which, unlike that of the East, tends to anthropomorphise the power in the void, personifying it as a supreme creator. But it also describes the fundamental nothingness of the void, which is then differentiated into various 'universes' – or, in our terms, nonphysical and physical realms or planes.

Meanwhile the similarities of Mayan cosmogony can be seen in the following extract from the *Popol Vuh*:[22]

Now it still ripples, now it still murmurs, ripples, it still sighs, still hums, and it is empty under the sky.
Here follow the first words, the first eloquence:
There is not yet one person, one animal, bird, fish, crab, tree, rock, hollow, canyon, meadow, forest. Only the sky alone is there; the face of the earth is not clear. Only the sea alone is pooled under all the sky;

there is nothing whatever gathered together. It is at rest; not a single thing stirs. It is held back, kept at rest under the sky.

Whatever there is that might be is simply not there: only the pooled water, only the calm sea, only it alone is pooled.

Whatever might be is simply not there: only murmurs, ripples, in the dark, in the night. Only the Maker, Modeller alone, Sovereign Plumed Serpent, the Bearers, Begetters are in the water, a glittering light. They are there, they are enclosed in quetzal feathers, in blue-green.

Thus the name, 'Plumed Serpent'. They are great knowers, great thinkers in their very being.

This account continues by describing how 'the earth arose because of them, it was simply their *word* that brought it forth'.

AFRICA

In his essay on Africa in *World Mythology,* Roy Willis points out that many of its indigenous traditions tend to contain the idea of a 'cosmic egg' as also found in, for example, Egyptian and Japanese cosmogony. But what does this egg contain? The Dogon describe it as being 'the seed of the cosmos' that 'vibrated seven times, then burst open', so this is just another way of depicting the potential within the void.[23] He also suggests that their neighbours the Bambara have one of the most philosophical cosmogonies on the continent:[24]

In the beginning emptiness, *fu,* brought forth knowing, *gla gla zo*. This knowing, full of its emptiness and its emptiness full of itself, was the prime creative force of the universe, setting in train a mystical process of releasing and retracting energy.

MISSING THE POINT

The foregoing origin traditions are only those in which at least some of the original esoteric wisdom comes through, yet we've still managed to amass evidence from almost every part of the globe. Admittedly we've seen that some of them continue by describing how either the supreme deity – or various other deities created in their turn – proceed to separate heaven and earth from the waters, place the stars in their proper positions in the sky, arrange the seasons and so on. But these are the relatively prosaic or exoteric aspects that only serve to demonstrate how much the original wisdom had become lost or distorted by the time these traditions as we now have them were composed. Unfortunately these are the very aspects on which most modern scholars of mythology tend to concentrate – instead of properly examining, distilling and comparing the highly consistent underlying content and then placing it in what I would propose is its proper metaphysical, indeed spiritual, context.

It is perhaps to be expected that modern encyclopaedias and compendia of mythology should follow this route. They are, after all, aiming at a broad audience.[25] But it's somewhat surprising that the more in-depth studies of experts such as Joseph Campbell and Mircea Eliade should yet again fail to appreciate the true message of these traditions. For example, in *The Masks of God* the former suggests that all except the 'most rarefied' origin myths involve a creator, and that this is a by-product of the simple childhood response of regarding everything as being created by someone.[26] Not only are these most rarefied accounts not identified, but they don't seem to be discussed either. What is more, if we start with indigenous tribal cultures, the only American origin tradition he covers in any detail is that of the Apache Indians of New Mexico, which is one of the more prosaic anyway.[27] He doesn't comment on the far more interesting Hopi and Mayan versions, or on their African and Polynesian counterparts. Turning to the more complex early civilisations, for all that he seems to respect the high philosophy of Ancient India and China – discussing their general themes at some length – again nowhere does he cover their origin traditions in any depth.[28]

All we're left with, then, are Campbell's deliberations on the cosmogony of the Ancient Egyptians. He begins by appearing to praise the philosophical leap made by the Memphite priests of the Old Kingdom in according to the deity Ptah the power of creation via the Word – comparing this with the later, devolved Heliopolitan tradition in which the deity Atum's creative powers are more prosaically symbolised by his 'taking his phallus in his fist'.[29] But this is as far as he goes, and we're left uncertain about his real views on the extent of any true esoteric knowledge possessed by the Ancient Egyptians, or indeed other ancient cultures. Although we must clearly accept that Campbell's aim was not to concentrate on origin myths per se, and although I can only reiterate my support for the general admiration his work attracts, these omissions are somewhat dispiriting for anyone who devotes many weeks of study to his extensive but intricate and sometimes meandering work.

Eliade's most relevant book *Myth and Reality* is considerably shorter, so perhaps he can be rather more excused for failing to appreciate the subtleties of the various cosmogonies. In fact he does devote a whole chapter to them, but he concentrates solely on their magic and prestige in tribal cultures – for example how they're used to reinforce and celebrate the birth of a new chief, or the initiation of a young adult, by reference back to the original creation.[30] In none of his various works on mythology does he seem to investigate the more esoteric aspects of these indigenous traditions, or of those of the more complex ancient civilisations.

COMMON SOURCE

We have seen that in every part of the world there are origin traditions that contain a number of regularly repeated themes – even if some are heavily veiled, and even if each tradition doesn't contain full details of every theme. They can be summarised and elaborated on as follows:

- During the Night of Brahma the universe remains completely dormant. In the more sophisticated traditions it's conceptualised as a void, although it's often more prosaically described as a chasm, as an abyss, as the deep or as the primeval waters.

- The dormant creative power within the void is described in the more sophisticated traditions in abstract terms such as the One, the All, the Universal or the Absolute, although the more prosaic traditions anthropomorphise it into a supreme creator deity.

- This power contains the potential germ, embryo or seed of all forms that will be created in the universe when a new Day of Brahma commences.

- This potential is actualised by the mere will or Word of the creative power. The energisation process can perhaps be conceptualised as the blow of a hammer on an anvil, which scatters sparks and energy waves in all directions. Descriptions of light emerging from darkness are attempts to convey the same concept.

- The energy that's initially dissipated by this cosmic explosion starts to coagulate into a variety of vibrational states, creating the various dimensions or planes and the forms that inhabit them. Their vibrational state determines their level of physicality, varying from the purest energy form of the highest aspects of the ethereal realms right down to the dense physical plane exemplified, for example, by our own planet with all its myriad lifeforms.[31] Phrases such as 'separating heaven and earth' are an attempt to convey this in simple terms.

At this point it would be useful to return to the question of how this incredible consistency across huge geographic and temporal boundaries might have come about. We briefly saw in chapter 1 that the orthodox approach to mythology allows for two possibilities: geographical *diffusion* from a common original source, and separate but *parallel development* in each location. To the extent that the consistent traditions of a highly spiritual golden race who became debased and were destroyed represent a genuine human memory of former times, these would have been passed down orally by the survivors and by successive generations until they were first put into written form perhaps only around 5000 years ago. This is essentially diffusion at work.

But when we come to esoteric wisdom, the introduction of a spiritual worldview gives an additional slant to parallel development. This is because certain people in any given community tend to be able to tap into higher sources of such wisdom – whether spontaneously or during meditation and so on doesn't really matter here – and to introduce it to their community. Having said that, even this form of parallel development isn't exempt from a certain degree of distortion, depending on the quality and understanding of the human medium. What is more, of course, any such wisdom can be smothered and all but eradicated by the all-too-human political motive of replacing a broad spiritual understanding with organised, state-sponsored religion to achieve power and control.

In this context, it's interesting to note that the same 'degeneration' of spiritual awareness that arguably infected our forgotten race seems to have occurred at various times in the post-catastrophe epoch too. Or, at the very least, there have been regressive influences. What is more, in most cases these seem to have coincided with the development of supposedly more sophisticated civilisations right from their inception. Why was this? Apart from the obvious desire of some people to control their fellows, there was a far more practical issue. If the new city-states were to survive with their specialisms of labour and so on, they had to have a guaranteed source of food. So the whole process of agriculture needed to be brought under central control. Of course it could be argued that in more matriarchal societies this could be achieved in an entirely fair and cooperative way. But in the apparently power-obsessed, patriarchal environment found in many of these first civilisations of the post-catastrophe epoch, a degree of coercion would have been required. Physical force was one way, but in the long run that's hard work and a constant investment. Far better to win control of minds using sophisticated, purportedly religious mechanisms. The threat of everlasting torment in hell, for example, can be a pretty effective deterrent for the bulk of poorly educated people.

More specifically, as suggested in chapter 2, much early Vedic philosophy seems to display a relatively unspoiled sophistication compared to the arguably more regressive traditions of, for example, Mesopotamia. This is very much Campbell's view, as can be seen in the quote from *The Masks of God* reproduced in chapter 6 when he discusses the 'devolution of tradition' that must have occurred at some point in early Mesopotamian history – *before* the earliest texts we've found so far were compiled. The same argument for a regression in quality can surely be made about Ancient Egypt too, however much that may be more controversial.[32]

CONCLUSION

It would appear that, while various scholars of mythology have noted certain similarities between certain origin traditions, they've nevertheless tended to concentrate on their more prosaic aspects at the expense of the esoteric. As a result it's my view that they've completely failed to appreciate their true meaning and importance. In fact arguably the consistency of the profound spiritual understanding displayed in cosmogonies from across the globe has never before been properly appreciated, and it's high time that it was.

Furthermore we'd do well to remind ourselves that the theme of a forgotten race who became debased and were destroyed was in many cases recorded by the same authors in the same documents. Admittedly we know that some of the versions we now have were cobbled together from multiple sources. Yet the depth of esoteric wisdom they display, particularly in their opening sections dealing with cosmogony and the golden age, surely suggests that it would be simplistic and reductionist to write off their entire contents. Indeed the position adopted by most modern scholars – that they all derive from a mixture of superstitious nonsense and sophisticated yet purely psychological constructs – is surely untenable in the face of the evidence we've collated in Part 1.

Not only that, but maybe other more concrete disciplines such as archaeology and geology are able to provide evidence that supports our ancestors' version of events. It is to this we'll now turn in Part 2.

PART TWO

CORROBORATION

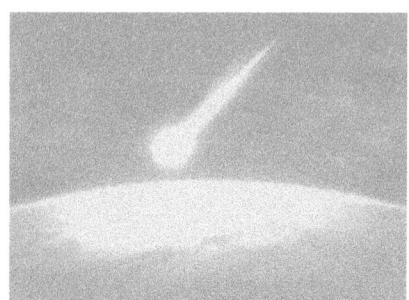

9

ARCHAEOLOGY

There are a number of ways in which we can investigate whether physical and other evidence bears out the various themes developed from the worldwide texts and traditions in Part 1. In this chapter we're interested in examining the archaeological evidence for when the modern human race emerged, and indeed what we mean by 'modern'. More specifically we'll be looking for signs of two main events: on the one hand, when the first wave of individuated souls might have successfully incarnated en masse; on the other, when our forgotten race might have reached the height of its cultural and spiritual sophistication. We will also allow ourselves to speculate on the realistic level of technology they might have achieved.

PHYSICAL EVOLUTION

Although it's not directly relevant to this quest, we could do worse than to start by taking a brief journey through the orthodox view of planetary and human evolution – not least to act as a counterbalance to various alternative theories that, as so often, simply don't stand up to close scrutiny.

Of course preceding even this is the whole issue of whether life here evolved from a purely fortuitous chemical cocktail, or was seeded from other parts of the galaxy via meteor impact. Or, indeed, whether the process of evolution has sometimes been deliberately nudged in the right direction by our higher selves or supersouls operating in higher planes of awareness. For what it's worth, and given that I've already expressed a degree of support for the idea of an intelligently guided metaverse in chapter 5, my money would be on a combination of seeding and guidance. For me pure materialistic chance is out.

Yrs Ago	Era	Period	Epoch	Evolutionary Steps
4.5bn	Proterozoic			Earth formed
4bn				Single-cell life forms
3.5bn				Multi-cell life forms
541m	Palaeozoic	Primary	Cambrian	Marine invertebrates
485m			Ordovician	
443m			Silurian	Marine vertebrates
419m			Devonian	Amphibians
359m			Carboniferous	
299m			Permian	Land reptiles
252m	Mesozoic	Secondary	Triassic	Sea reptiles
201m			Jurassic	Air reptiles
145m			Cretaceous	Birds
66m	Cenozoic	Tertiary	Palaeocene	Mammals
56			Eocene	
34			Oligocene	Primates
23m			Miocene	Hominids (c. 8m ya)
5m			Pliocene	
2.6m		Quaternary	Pleistocene	*Homo* genus (c. 2.5m ya) *Homo sapiens* (c. 300k ya)
12k			Holocene	

Figure 4: Evolution in the Geological Ages [1]

In any case, current orthodox thinking is that, while the universe itself burst into manifestation nearly 14 billion years ago, the Earth was formed around 4.5 billion years ago during the birth of our solar system. It is estimated that primitive single-cell life forms developed in the primeval chemical cocktail about 0.5 billion years later, and that the first multi-cell forms emerged around 0.5 billion years after that. It then took nearly 3 billion more years for life forms of any significant size and complexity to appear during the Cambrian explosion. This shows that, although there can be sudden periods of 'punctuated equilibrium' during which significant changes occur rapidly, with new species evolving and old ones dying out, evolution is normally an extremely slow and laborious process.

Is there any serious challenge to this orthodox view of evolutionary timescales? Not really, unless we give credence to the Christian creationist view that all life was given form by God simultaneously in 4004 BCE – an idea that is pretty much universally rejected as entirely at odds with the available evidence. But if we now turn specifically to *human* evolution, an alternative challenge was mounted by Hindu Creationists Michael Cremo and Richard Thompson in their 1993 work *Forbidden Archaeology*. Their argument was that supposedly anomalous *modern* human remains dating back many millions of years had been incorrectly categorised or even deliberately covered up by the orthodox 'establishment'. It is fortunate that, although their work enjoyed a fair degree of initial exposure, it's now rarely mentioned – because as usual their material is selective and severely lacking in credibility.[2] So again there's every reason to suppose that the orthodox archaeological view of human development is broadly correct – even if its timescales are subject to constant refinement with the discovery of new species, sub-species and so on.

Although it's now a relatively old publication, for a non-specialist work such as this we could do worse than to consult Richard Leakey, one of the most influential paleoanthropologists of modern times who has carried on the pioneering work of his parents Louis and Mary in East Africa. He opens his 1994 work *The Origin of Humankind* with a general warning concerning the paucity of evidence:[3]

> My anthropological colleagues face two practical challenges in addressing these problems. The first is what Darwin called 'the extreme imperfection of the geological record'. In his *Origin of Species,* Darwin devoted an entire chapter to the frustrating gaps in the record, which result from the capricious forces of fossilisation and later exposure of bones. The conditions that favour the rapid burial and possible fossilisation of bones are rare. And ancient sediments may become uncovered through erosion – when a stream cuts through them, for instance – but which pages of prehistory are reopened in this way is purely a matter of chance, and many of the pages remain hidden from view. For instance, in East Africa, the most promising repository for early human fossils, there are very few fossil-bearing sediments from the period between 4m and 8m years ago. This is a crucial period in human prehistory, because it includes the origin of the human family.

Even for the time period after 4m years we have far fewer fossils than we would like.

The second challenge stems from the fact that the majority of fossil specimens discovered are small fragments – a piece of cranium, a cheekbone, part of an arm bone, and many teeth. The identification of species from meagre evidence of this nature is no easy task and is sometimes impossible. The resulting uncertainty allows for many differences of scientific opinion, both in identifying species and in discerning the interrelatedness of species. This area of anthropology, known as taxonomy and systematics, is one of the most contentious.

In fact back in 1859, when *On the Origin of Species* was first published, Charles Darwin assumed that humankind had split off from the apes at a very early stage and quickly developed the traits we associate with human life – a view that mollified him as a committed Christian in that it allowed our species to retain a degree of special status. The three most important of these human traits were bipedalism, technology in terms of tools and weapons, and an enlarged brain – and Darwin argued they were all linked together in a self-inflating chain reaction.

He was writing in an era when the only fossil evidence of our ancestors consisted of relatively late Neanderthal remains from Europe, but this thinking predominated even as increasing numbers of older specimens were uncovered. In India in 1932 a part of the upper jaw of a small apelike creature labelled *Ramapithecus* was discovered in Tertiary sediments around 15m years old, and was immediately reported to have more hominid than ape characteristics. But because this would mean our earliest ancestors weren't like us at all it was left in relative obscurity – while other far less ancient discoveries hogged the limelight. Yet that all changed in the early 1960s when Elwyn Simons of Yale University shocked the establishment by speculating that it was indeed our earliest human-like forebear, and his view that this species marked the divergence of the first proto-humans from our ape cousins was soon widely accepted.

This view was in turn challenged in the late 1960s when Allan Wilson and Vincent Sarich, two biochemists at Berkeley University, adopted the revolutionary approach of comparing the blood proteins of modern humans and apes, arguing that the rate of mutation of their molecular structure acted as a clock. This suggested that the divergence occurred no more than 5m years ago. Paleoanthropologists were slow to accept this new technique, but similar experiments continued to confirm its findings.

Then the decisive discovery of new and more complete *Ramapithecus* remains in Pakistan and Turkey in the early 1980s indicated that it had continued to live in trees and wasn't bipedal at all.

More recent genetic tests have now pushed the date for the divergence of hominids from apes back to a universally accepted figure of somewhere between 6m and 8m years ago. However the issue of what *caused* it remains highly contentious. Darwin's 'linkage' has proved false because, while the earliest signs of stone tools appear around 2.3m years ago, and this does coincide with brain expansion sufficient to differentiate the genus *Homo* for the first time, this still leaves a gap of several million years back to the time when our earliest ancestors descended from the trees and became bipedal. This latter characteristic, with its associated advantage of freeing the upper limbs and allowing the hands to develop to cope with more intricate tasks, has therefore become the defining marker for hominid–ape divergence.

There is also a broad consensus about *where* this occurred. When the Great Rift Valley formed down the spine of Africa around 20m years ago it created a natural barrier that separated the east and west sides of the continent and their ape populations. The climate and ecology of the eastern side dramatically changed, with dense forest being replaced by more sparse woodlands, then by grasslands and savannah, meaning running rather than swinging in the trees became essential. However there's less consensus about *why* bipedalism acted as such an impetus to hominid evolution. Perhaps the freeing of the arms allowed males to collect more food for females, whose improved nutrition and diet produced better offspring. Perhaps in the hot climate this form of locomotion, although not as swift, was more energy-efficient and required less food. Or perhaps it allowed our ancestors to operate more efficiently in water when crossing the increasingly abundant swamps, or when catching fish in inland lakes and shallow seas.

Given that *Ramapithecus* was more apelike, the genus that has now been accorded the status of the first bipedal hominid is *Australopithecus*. The extensive fossils uncovered in the Hadar region of Ethiopia include the almost complete skeleton of the infamous 'Lucy', and they were originally categorised as a single species, *Australopithecus afarensis,* dating from around 3.5m years ago. But further discoveries in South and East Africa have confirmed that a number of other australopith species developed, the earliest around 4m years ago. In fact the latest classifications include a new although similar genus, *Ardipithecus,* which is thought to be slightly older still, and one tentatively classified as *Kenyanthropus,* which dates to at least 3.5m years ago and may or may not represent our closest hominid ancestor.

Although these various hominids are thought to have died out by about 1m years ago, another branch of the family tree had been developing. Remains first discovered by the senior Leakeys at Olduvai Gorge in East Africa show that around 2.3m years ago an entirely different genus had emerged. While *Homo habilis* had a significantly thinner cranium, indicating a slighter overall build, the major reason for classifying it as the first of the genus *Homo* was its significantly increased cranial capacity – which had nearly doubled from the average for australopiths of around 450cc. Another contemporary species that has since been classified is *Homo rudolfensis.*

Associated with this emergence of the genus *Homo* are the first stone tools, signifying the start of the Palaeolithic or Old Stone Age. Initially these merely comprised small flints with sharp edges classified as Olduwan technology, although they still required significant skill to produce, and may have been used not just for butchering meat but also to cut saplings and reeds for shelters. Indeed it does seem that the shift from vegetarian to meat eater had a significant impact on our ancestors' survival prospects. Then about 1.6m years ago a new type of Acheulean technology emerged, involving larger flints shaped into hand axes, cleavers and picks – which not only required even more skill and patience to produce, but also indicated a more developed and not merely opportunistic awareness of the differentiated shapes required. These tools are associated with a species known as *Homo erectus,* which first emerged around 2m years ago and had a cranial capacity of between 900 and 1100cc, and with *Homo ergaster* – although there's some dispute about whether this is really a separate species. Another huge step would have been the ability to control fire, which seems to have first been mastered around 1.5m years ago.

Then from around 0.6m years ago several different species began to emerge that are even closer to our own and often classified under the general heading *archaic Homo* – although modern DNA evidence is revealing such complexities in the relationships between them that the way in which they spawned our own species may forever be shrouded in mystery. These include *Homo heidelbergensis, Homo rhodesiensis,* the

Denisovans and the better-known *Neanderthals*, who all had a larger cranial capacity of between 1200 and 1400cc, which saw them introduce a further expansion of the toolkit into Mousterian technology around 250,000 years ago.

Emergence (Yrs Ago)	Genus or Species	Cranial Capacity (cc)
4.4m	Ardipithecus	?
4.0m	Australopithecus	375–550
2.3m	Homo habilis	800
2.0m	Homo erectus	900–1100
0.6m	archaic Homo	1200–1400

Figure 5: Cranial Development

In fact modern human brains are slightly smaller on average, but we should remember that improved neural networking – possibly as a result of more evolved thought processes and so on – mean size isn't everything. So *when* did our species emerge? Discoveries in 2017 in Morocco have now pushed the emergence of *Homo sapiens* right back to around 300,000 years ago.[4] This date is somewhat out of kilter with further genetic testing conducted by Wilson, who in 1987 used mitochondrial DNA that is passed on only by women to establish that the most recent common female ancestor, 'mitochondrial Eve', lived around 150,000 years ago in Africa – a finding that has done much to shape the now widely accepted 'out of Africa' model.[5]

As for the first *fully* modern humans, or *Homo sapiens sapiens*, genetic evidence seems to be consistent with this model, tracing a group that apparently left the African continent and crossed the mouth of the Red Sea into the Arabian Peninsula somewhere between 70,000 and 50,000 years ago.[6] From here it appears they continued in different directions. One group followed the coast eastwards towards Southern Asia, from where they managed to cross the sea to Australia. The other group moved north into the Near East and Central Asia, from where some – referred to as Cro-Magnons or 'European Early Modern Humans' – continued to migrate westward.

However we'll have cause to question the reliability of these various genetic tests later in this chapter.

THE EVOLUTION OF CULTURE AND CONSCIOUSNESS

We should start this part of the investigation by heeding another general warning from Leakey:[7]

> We have to remember that the vast preponderance of human behaviour in technologically primitive human groups is archaeologically invisible. For instance, an initiation ritual led by a shaman would involve the telling of myths, chanting, dancing, and body decoration – and none of these activities would enter the archaeological record. Therefore we need to keep reminding ourselves, when we find stone tools and carved or painted objects, that they give us only the narrowest of windows onto the ancient world.

This, then, brings us on to trying to tackle the first of the questions this chapter set out to answer: when did the first wave of individuated 'human-type' souls incarnate successfully? Of course we can't answer this without being more specific about what we mean by 'human', and what is it about our level of culture and consciousness that *really* differentiates our species. For example, while the bipedalism and tool use of *Homo habilis* and *Homo erectus* increased their cultural sophistication sufficiently for them to be categorised as part of our genus, the quality of their consciousness was clearly a long way short of that of modern humans.

For some time the orthodox view persisted that it was when early humans first developed self-awareness that their consciousness started to diverge substantially from that of their ape cousins. That changed in 1970, however, when psychologist Gordon Gallup came up with an ingenious test.[8] He placed a red spot on the forehead of various primates, and stationed them in front of a mirror. He then waited to see whether they'd investigate by touching the curious anomaly on the reflected image, thinking that they were confronted with another animal, or by touching it on their own forehead, which would indicate they recognised the image as their own. Contrary to the conventional wisdom of the time he found that chimpanzees and orang-utans tended to touch themselves, although gorillas tended to touch the reflection – although in more extensive tests the latter too have now been found to pass.

Of course modern studies, often shown in popular documentaries, have also revealed that primates living in large groups have an advanced social network and awareness of group politics – which requires not only some sense of self, but also of one's allies and enemies, of *their* allies and enemies, of how these alliances change over time, and even of the need to deliberately and consciously change them to one's own advantage. All of this tends to indicate a sufficient degree of self-awareness in certain other primates that it can't be the major differentiating factor of human consciousness.

Some commentators have instead suggested that the difference in humans is our ability not only to predict how others will behave, but also to empathise with how they feel. Yet again primates living in groups have been seen to exhibit altruistic behaviour, while anyone with a domestic cat or dog will be aware that they can sense mood changes in humans and that their empathy *can* be far more than just manipulation to gain food. Meanwhile film footage of, for example, elephants cooperating to save one of their kin from drowning in a bog reinforces the view that this too can't be the main distinguishing factor.

Is it possible to look for more clues in the link between consciousness and language? It seems that species such as *Homo heidelbergensis* and *neandertalensis* were probably the first to develop a primitive spoken language of any consequence.[9] But there remains much debate about whether a more developed consciousness would have precipitated this development, or vice versa. Whatever the mechanism it seems likely that in protohumans these two gradually evolved as part of an interlinked process that probably commenced as much as several million years ago, and went hand in hand with advances in social interaction and tool use. Yet modern research is increasingly revealing just how many animal species have highly developed forms of communication too, so nor is this a clear differentiator.

The one area that may be more definitive is our awareness of our own mortality. Admittedly there's now evidence that elephants display signs of group grief when one of the herd dies. Moreover this is backed up by, for example, heart-rending footage of a male sparrow feeding his mate who had been run over by a car, and then exhibiting signs of serious agitation and grief after she dies.[10] But what certainly *is* clear is that we're the only species that decided long ago to ritually bury our dead. This represents a huge milestone in the development of consciousness and sophisticated thought.

While new discoveries are pushing back the dates for cultural firsts all the time, so far some of the earliest significant evidence for it comes from the Twin Rivers Cave in Zambia, where the use of various coloured pigments dates to some time between 400,000 and 200,000 years ago – and certainly suggests body painting and rituals, as well as some degree of language.[11] But perhaps an even more definitive landmark for our current purposes is that the earliest definitive proof of ritual burial comes from excavations carried out in the Qafzeh Cave in Israel, dating back to around 92,000 years ago.[12] Skeletons had been deliberately laid on their side in pits, sometimes with animal bones placed in their hands (see Plate 1). Meanwhile the earliest symbolic art so far discovered comes from the Blombos Cave in South Africa, which yielded an engraved piece of ochre dated to anywhere between 100,000 and 70,000 years ago. It has evenly spaced, diagonal lines forming a series of diamond or lozenge shapes (see Plate 2).[13] A number of shells with worked holes, which probably allowed them to be strung together as a necklace, were also found in the cave. Another example dated to around 54,000 years ago comes from the Quneitra site in Israel's Golan Heights, in the form of a flat piece of stone inscribed with nested semicircles and vertical lines (see Plate 3).[14] Meanwhile a plank of wood *manufactured* from mulberry, discovered at Nishiyagi in Japan, has been given the same approximate date.[15]

Because of this evidence some experts argue that 'behavioural modernity' developed gradually over a long period.[16] However they don't seem to make the distinction between 'primitive culture' and 'culture proper' as defined in the Preface. The use of fire, deliberate ritualised burials, and the production of simple jewellery, pigments for body painting and primitive art, can all surely be classified under the former. But around 50,000 years ago something extraordinary seems to have happened. A quantum leap forward into culture proper signalled the start of what has come to be known as the 'Upper Palaeolithic Revolution'.

This began in the Levant and then spread west into Europe.[17] For example, the first carved figures begin to appear, including stylised 'Venus Figurines' indicating the matriarchal nature of these cultures (see Plates 4 and 5). This is coupled with even more elaborately ritualised burials – the Sungir Cave in Russia, dating to around 30,000 years ago, being a wonderful example (see Plate 6). Over 13,000 small, drilled, ivory beads and over 250 perforated fox teeth were found herein, which would have been used to adorn clothing and as part of necklaces and other jewellery. It also seems that these developments were widespread and relatively standardised in the Aurignacian cultures of the Near East, Europe, Asia and Africa by at least 40,000 years ago, suggesting the existence of a shared system of communication and probably trading links over wide geographic areas.[18]

Yrs Ago	Era	Culture	Developments
2,300,000	Lower Palaeolithic	Olduwan	Small flints
1,600,000		Acheulean	Stone tools – c. 12 main types
1,500,000			Use of fire
250,000	Middle Palaeolithic	Mousterian	More advanced stone tools – c. 60 main types
100,000-50,000			Isolated ritual burials, shell necklaces, first abstract art, worked wooden plank
50,000	Upper Palaeolithic	Emiran Ahmarian (Near East)	More complex tools; regular ritual burials; stylised and realistic animal/human figurines; finely drilled beads/teeth for body adornment; bone flutes
43,000		Aurignacian (Europe)	
33,000		Gravettian Solutrean	Pottery; advanced Venus figurines; cave paintings
17,000		Magdalenian	Advanced cave art; geometric art; sophisticated figurines; crop management
12,000	Neolithic		Agriculture; stone buildings; urbanisation; protowriting
6,000			City-states
5,000			Pictographic writing

Figure 6: Major Cultural Advances

As for pottery, although it's normally only associated with the advent of the Neolithic, the Gravettian culture that first emerged around 33,000 years ago was the first to use fired clay to make artifacts and figurines.[19]

Meanwhile recent discoveries in China show that by at least 17,000 years ago it was being used for pottery itself.[20] But the magnificent sculpted artifacts and gorgeous cave paintings with which we're most familiar tend to be associated with the Magdalenian culture that emerged around the same time (see Plates 7 and 8).[21] These show a marked shift to a more hunter-based and patriarchal society, possibly because of the climatic upheavals associated with the last glacial maximum around 22,000 years ago.[22] They also indicate engagement in what we now refer to as shamanic practices.[23]

One other development during the Upper Palaeolithic is the widespread use of geometric patterns in rock art. These include dots within circles, grids, chevrons, curves, zigzags, nested curves, rectangles and, in one isolated case, a swastika.[24] This abstract form of art was clearly a progression from the earlier finds mentioned above from the Blombos Cave and Quneitra sites; and it would go on to become even more conspicuous on the megaliths associated with Neolithic temples and burial mounds all over Western Europe, by which time it had developed to include cups and rings, spirals, linked spirals, mazes and lozenges.[25] There is every reason to suspect these patterns had an esoteric significance, possibly connected to shamanic trance states that may or may not have been induced by the use of hallucinogens, and they reveal just how spiritually aware our Palaeolithic and Neolithic ancestors were.[26]

FARMING AND URBANISATION

For a long time the Neolithic Revolution was regarded as having begun in the Near East about 12,000 years ago, ushering in the hugely significant switch from nomadic hunter-gathering to farming and urbanisation.[27] But discoveries in the last few decades have changed this picture significantly.

Evidence of earlier farming has come from, for example, the Natufian culture who were living in sizeable permanent settlements in the Levant; not only were they hunting and fishing, but from at least 14,500 years ago they were also cultivating wild strains of cereal crops.[28] Abundant agricultural tools have been found on these sites, including flint-bladed sickles for harvesting, grinding stones and storage pits. Similar finds have been made at various sites in the Nile Valley dating from around the same time.[29] More recently evidence of trial cultivation of plants at a far earlier time has been found at a site on the shore of the Sea of Galilee – dated to some 23,000 years ago.[30] This is a good example of how earliest dates for various cultural firsts keep being pushed further and further back as we explore more sites with better technology – and there is no reason to suppose this marked trend won't continue.

But eventually these earlier settlements turned into urbanisation proper, marked most obviously by building more permanent structures in stone. For many years the earliest such example was the infamous town of Jericho in Palestine, a 'walled city' with interior houses and courtyards first developed as long as 10,300 years ago. But we now know it has precursors. To the northwest in Anatolia the settlement of Catal Hoyuk was first excavated in 1958, followed by a number of nearby sites such as Nevali Cori and Gobekli Tepe.[31] They are all roughly contemporaneous with Jericho and contain multiple stone buildings, often including communal and ceremonial structures, sometimes along with elaborately carved stone columns bearing animal and other motifs. Each site shows some signs of crop management too.

Yrs Ago	Name	Location	Details (all construction in stone unless stated otherwise)
11,600	Jerf el Ahmar	Syria	Up to 40 round then rectangular houses; communal buildings; terracotta plaquettes
11,100	Gobekli Tepe	Turkey	20 roughly circular, sunken structures, each housing a ring of c. 8 T-shaped pillars up to 6m high with elaborately carved reliefs, with benches for seating
10,400	Nevali Cori	Turkey	Various long, rectangular buildings split into parallel houses with mezzanine floors and underfloor ducting; communal structures containing 3m high T-shaped pillars with reliefs
10,300	Jericho	Palestine	Large site with multiple circular, mud-brick houses and 8.5m high tower, all surrounded by 3.6m high walls
9100	Catal Hoyuk	Turkey	Large number of rectangular, mud-brick, 2-room houses with decorated walls built close together and accessed via holes in rooftops that formed plazas

Figure 7: Details of Early Urban Settlements [32]

Then in 1995 a discovery in Syria pushed the earliest stone settlements back even further. Led by Danielle Stordeur, who kindly sent me a number of previously unpublished photographs (see Plates 9 to 12), a Franco-Syrian team spent several years excavating at Jerf el Ahmar and dated its earliest buildings to a full 11,600 years ago.[33] Not only did they find evidence of crop cultivation and of domestication of grain but also, in only slightly more recent levels, a number of small terracotta plaquettes bearing what they speculate may be mnemonic symbols – these etchings being twice as old as the first pictographic writing developed in Sumer around 5000 years ago (see Plates 13 to 15). Then in 2008 a site with a similar communal structure was uncovered some way away at Wadi Faynan in Jordan, and was given precisely the same early date.[34] To counteract these new finds, though, sadly the construction of new dams in the 1990s left both Jerf el Ahmar and Nevali Cori submerged.

The dates for these settlements reaching a point of true urbanisation are given in Figure 7, showing that its onset was relatively rapid, even if simpler, less permanent versions do exist from previous millennia. Meanwhile their widespread distribution around the Mesopotamian 'fertile crescent' can be traced in Figure 8.

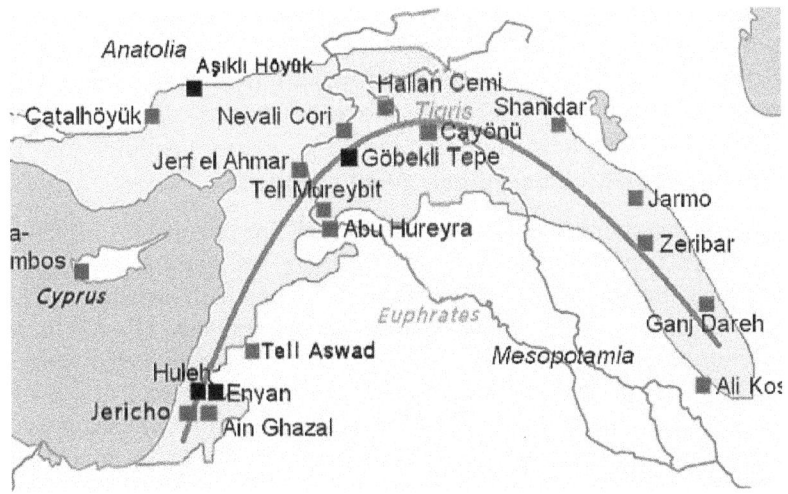

Figure 8: Map of Early Urban Settlements [35]

It seems there may have been something of a lull after this initial period of urbanisation, until from around 5500 years ago new, larger and more imposing developments began to spring up that are arguably the first major cities. Not only were they far larger but they had more varied communal buildings such as temples, bakeries, breweries and potteries. The best-known are the early examples from Mesopotamia proper, such as Uruk, Eridu, Ur and Lagash, but they're again found in the wider area – for example in Syria, where excavations at Tel Hamoukar have unearthed an impressive city of similar age.[36] Then within the next few millennia they spread well to the east, to the celebrated sites of the high Indus culture at Harappa and Mohenjo-daro.

MAVERICKS

The foregoing is a largely orthodox analysis of human emergence and cultural development, but we should be clear that this doesn't in any sense make it infallible. New evidence, techniques and theories are emerging all the time; and although the speculations of most alternative researchers can be dismissed because they demonstrate no proper knowledge of the orthodox evidence that invalidates them, there are some highly qualified specialists whose currently unorthodox views at least deserve an airing.

We have already seen that genetic research has led to the widespread acceptance of the 'out of Africa' model of modern human emergence. But some dispute this theory, and apparently with good reason. One such is the Australia-based and peer-reviewed experimental archaeologist and Palaeolithic art specialist Robert Bednarik, who questions the basic assumptions underlying the various genetic models:[37]

> Assumptions about a neutral mutation rate and a constant effective population size are completely unwarranted, and yet these variables determine the outcomes of all the calculations. For instance, if the same divergence rate as one such model assumes (2%-4% base substitutions per million years) is applied to the human-chimpanzee genetic distance, it yields a divergence point of 2.1m to 2.7m years, which we consider to be unambiguously wrong. Nei (1987) suggests a much slower rate, 0.71% per million years, according to which the human-chimpanzee separation would have occurred 6.6m years ago, which is close to the estimate from nuclear DNA hybridisation data, of 6.3m years. But this would produce a divergence of Moderns [modern humans] at 850,000 years ago, over four times as long ago as the favoured models, and eight times as long ago as the earliest fossils of

Moderns ever found... Instead of unambiguously showing that Moderns originate conclusively in one region, Africa, all the available genetic data suggest that gene flow occurred in the Old World hominids throughout recent human evolution (Templeton 1996).

As for the development of culture itself Bednarik sides heavily with the idea of a slow and lengthy development, but also argues that earlier species were far more advanced than is normally assumed. In particular he pinpoints stone tool finds at various sites on the island of Flores in Southern Indonesia dating to around 800,000 years ago, although no skeletal remains of their makers have yet turned up.[38] Sea levels were much lower during the last ice age, with far greater quantities of the Earth's water trapped in massive ice sheets, but it's known that Flores remained disconnected from the main Asian coast throughout this period. So, argues Bednarik, a pre-sapien species of *Homo* must have been using some sort of raft.[39] This suggests a shared and reasonably complex language allowing for sophisticated cooperative working. It also means that, as well as producing roughly appropriate lengths of tree trunk or bamboo, they were using some sort of vines, sinews or fibres to lash them together, and making knots too – although, of course, none of this survives in the archaeological record. To prove his theories he has conducted numerous seafaring experiments in the area, replicating the technology he believes was used – with the key one in 2004 being sponsored by National Geographic.[40]

But he goes much further than this. He also describes how, despite the scant and usually ignored evidence of tools and other artifacts made from *wood* dating to the Lower and Middle Palaeolithic, microscopic wear surveys of the cutting edges of early stone tools seem to show that the majority were used to work wood. Similarly he maintains that a small number of bone and ivory artifacts from these eras are largely ignored. We will pick up on this crucial evidence shortly.

By contrast Bednarik has personally examined hundreds of artifacts that are commonly reported as showing evidence of early human artistic working, and has rejected the vast majority of them as resulting from natural phenomena:

> By far the most common examples are objects of bone, limestone, ivory and ostrich eggshell, which I have shown to bear mycorrhizal grooves [from fungi] that may resemble engravings... bones can be

perforated by animal teeth and corrosive agents, gastropod shells are commonly bored through by parasitic organisms. Similarly, natural surface markings on rock have often been archaeologically misinterpreted, and again I have corrected numerous such instances.

Nevertheless he contends that some authentic examples of exactly this kind of manmade 'palaeoart' *have* been found, and he highlights several isolated but very early examples. These include two drilled pendants from Austria, one a tooth and the other a piece of bone, dating to 300,000 years ago; and three drilled ostrich-shell beads from Libya, probably used for necklaces, dating to 200,000 years ago. With respect to the latter, he has concluded from extensive personal experiments that the beads were deliberately manufactured in the smallest possible size that wasn't too fragile; that huge amounts of extra effort were put in to ensure they were perfectly spherical; and that the holes were drilled right at the centre. All of this, he says, shows a desire to make something that was perfect, indeed a status symbol designed to show that the wearer – or his of her tribe – were 'pushing the available technology to its very limits'. As a result of all this he makes a wonderful concluding observation:

> How would an interstellar visitor interpret the carved ivory figurines of an incomplete chess set? If his anthropology were as simplistic as ours he may well explain its knights as evidence of an equine cult. It is at this level that most interpreting of Pleistocene symbolism has occurred, which I find quite unsatisfactory.

Bednarik and others often mention two of the more controversial finds to come from professional archaeological digs, both excavated in Israel by teams led by Naama Goren-Inbar, who also led the work at the Quneitra site mentioned earlier. The first is a lump of volcanic rock found at a site in the Golan Heights in 1982 that is claimed to be the world's earliest-known sculpture at 250,000 years old – although it has to be said that, even if it was worked by human hand, the 'Berekhat Ram figurine' is extremely primitive.[41] The second, and arguably far more important, is a fragment of plank made from willow uncovered at a site in the Northern Jordan Valley in 1989, which was reported to be highly polished on one side – because no tool marks were evident – and as having one completely straight and deliberately bevelled edge. The team estimate its date to be an absolute minimum of 240,000, and possibly as much as 750,000, years old.[42] If their analysis is correct it represents a major breakthrough in our understanding of just how far back in time serious craftsmanship in wood – which, of course, doesn't normally survive in the archaeological record – can be traced. It also ties in with Bednarik's findings above.

At this point I should mention that for the last few centuries alternative researchers have repeatedly written about a variety of other anomalous or 'out-of-place' artifacts – OOPARTS for short – purporting to show high levels of advanced culture and technology dating back hundreds of thousands, even millions, of years. Indeed they still do to this day. These include, for example, ancient boats, pestles and mortars, iron nails and cups, copper coins and various pieces of artwork – often found in deep mines and well shafts. Although some of these are still available for inspection, and for most of those found in the last century pictures are freely available, not a single one stands out as proper evidence of advanced culture before the Upper Palaeolithic.[43] In some cases this is because the evidence is centuries old and purely anecdotal; in some because the archaeological context was never properly established at the time of the find; in some because there's clear misidentification – for example of what is clearly a decorated, bell-shaped, Victorian candle-stick holder that was supposedly blasted out of a quarry; and in some because it's a clear piece of fakery – such as the local newspaper editor whose mother reported that she found a silver necklace inside a lump of coal. Little wonder then that orthodox archaeology pays these supposed anomalies no attention at all.

But to return to mavericks operating *within* the scholarly community, there are others who concentrate on more recent prehistory. For example two books by British authors, both published in 1999, argue that at the very least protofarming was common throughout the Upper Palaeolithic – *Neanderthals, Bandits and Farmers* by biologist Colin Tudge, and *Lost Civilisations of the Stone Age* by anthropologist Richard Rudgley. What is more some of the more recent discoveries mentioned above tend to back up this view. Indeed there can surely be little question that farming would have developed in stages, and that the process would have at least commenced in the Upper Palaeolithic. Although local climate in different places at different times would have had a significant impact, we can construct a typical, general scenario. It commences with nomadic hunters gathering increasing quantities of wild grasses, buries, nuts and other naturally occurring foodstuffs, and storing and transporting whatever would last through the winter. They would then have developed seasonal settlements, deliberately managing the wild food resources in their chosen sites in spring and summer months before following the animal herds during the winter. The major breakthrough would have come when they discovered how to deliberately plant wild seeds, and in time to cultivate and accumulate sufficient crops to get them through the winter without leaving en mass – because at this point more permanent settlements would have emerged, even if some of the hunters might still have had to follow the migrating herds during winter. Coupled with this, dependent on where they were, would have been the possibility of developing parallel skills in animal husbandry and fishing. The final stage would have been the deliberate domestication of both animals and crops by breeding desirable strains, coupled with further skills development in areas such as irrigation and food storage.

We might note that some scholars postulate a reverse causality, and argue that farming developed *as a result* of hunter-gatherers deliberately deciding to adopt a more settled lifestyle, even though they had known *how* to farm for a long time.[44] Whichever is true, the universally accepted fact is that the mastery of agriculture allows a society to produce food for far greater numbers of people than need to be involved in its production, freeing the rest up to perform other communal tasks – and this is arguably *the* key element in the development of a settled, urbanised culture.

Rudgley also ascribes a great many other firsts to the Upper Palaeolithic – for example arguing that a rudimentary symbolic script was used throughout – and proposes that protowriting existed in a variety of forms in the early Neolithic.[45] This latter conjecture is perhaps now supported by the discovery in 2007 of numerous examples of a pictographic script carved into cliffs at Damaidi in China, dated to between 7000 and 8000 years old.[46]

CONCLUSION

Is there anything about early human evolution that suggests more than just a mechanistic, evolutionary impetus? Certainly it would be a mistake to claim there's anything *definitive* that supports a more spiritual take on the process, but we might suggest that the orthodox arguments about how and why we diverged from our ape cousins aren't entirely conclusive. For example, if bipedalism conferred such an evolutionary advantage, why did all the other hominid species with that trait die out while other primate species that lacked it carried on perfectly happily? Similarly if tool use expands the brain and leads to evolutionary leaps in consciousness, how come the various primates and other animals that use primitive tools – for example to crack open nuts – haven't developed as serious rivals to our human dominance? Ditto with spatial awareness, which birds building nests and beavers building dams show in abundance. Meanwhile we've also seen that communication and even language is sophisticated in a number of other species, as is the ability to cooperate and play politics within a group context, and even to show empathy and mourn the dead. One could argue that all of these developments should have allowed these species to evolve much more than they have – yet only we humans have actually done so. Was there indeed some degree of energetic nudging and guidance from higher planes, as discussed at the outset?

What is more we've seen that *Homo sapiens* emerged at least 300,000 years ago. So do we have any clues as to when the first individuated souls incarnated – any signs of the sort of evolutionary leap that would surely have been the outcome of such a significant spiritual catalyst? It seems that in the early stages human consciousness and culture did evolve relatively gradually, progressively pulling us clear of other members of our genus. But as we've seen one of the most significant milestones that differentiates us from other species is an awareness of our own mortality. Moreover, in contrast to so many of the other issues under discussion, there's one very clear archaeological indicator of this awareness – deliberate, ritualised burial, the earliest example of which dates to 92,000 years ago in Israel.

Such behaviour isn't *definitive* proof of a belief in some sort of afterlife – our early ancestors *could* just have been 'honouring' their dead – but personally I'd argue that it's far more likely they were using ritualised burial ceremonies to mark the end of one journey and the beginning of another. No mechanism is more likely to have provided this catalyst than a newly acquired appreciation of the temporary nature of physical life, and of the eternal nature of the soul – an appreciation that would surely have arisen when for the first time individuated souls successfully incarnated in a physical body that possessed the appropriate mental capabilities.

The problem with this evidence is that it appears to be a relatively isolated incident, because the practice doesn't appear again in the archaeological record in any widespread sense for tens of thousands of years. Almost certainly this reflects a degree of incompleteness. But we're still led to the conclusion that the experiment in Israel, which didn't involve fully modern humans, didn't usher in any widespread change in culture. Of course it might have been deliberately designed as one of a series of small-scale experiments, most of which we've not yet discovered.

What we can say is that by 50,000 years ago we have a major breakthrough with the onset of the Upper Palaeolithic Revolution. It is from this point on that culture *proper* at the very least seems to emerge. But we must surely allow for the fact that the successful incarnation of individuated souls who remembered anything about their true spiritual nature would have taken some time to take hold in any widespread way, as this new kind of 'spiritual human' really learned to master the art of survival and to *fully* develop the *primitive* culture – including sophisticated language and so on – that had already been emerging for tens, even hundreds, of thousands of years. If we take these two dates as boundaries, then, we can reasonably suggest that individuated souls must have started incarnating in serious numbers some time between around 100,000 and 50,000 years ago.

What about the other question we set out to answer in this chapter? Can we say that the Upper Palaeolithic Revolution marks the start of the golden age? Not necessarily. Again the cultural developments at this point may well have taken some time to really take hold. This would certainly be true of any sizeable, permanent, coastal settlements showing evidence of genuinely *advanced* culture for the first time. So the question of how long it would have taken for our forgotten race to really flourish to the point where the golden age proper commenced, and of how widely they then spread their net, remains extremely difficult. What we can say is that at some point there would have been previously unseen population growth in the settled communities that had spread to the most advantageous parts of the globe and had properly mastered the art of survival. This in turn would have allowed for the *mass* incarnations of individuated souls for the first time, which in its turn would have provided the strongest impetus yet for the development of genuinely advanced culture – far stronger, perhaps, than the gradual development of bipedalism, tool use, language and so on all thrown in together. In other words I'm suggesting that it was a self-inflating spiral deriving from a primarily *spiritual* impetus that produced the greatest surge in cultural growth in human prehistory.

But we know that the physical prerequisite for all this is the mastery of agriculture and possibly of animal husbandry too. So if new evidence is increasingly suggesting that our ancestors were successfully farming far earlier than has hitherto been accepted, how long was it before they started to build seriously large settlements with all their associated specialisms of labour – along with time for nonessential, cultural endeavours? Tudge in particular argues that early farmers found themselves in a vicious spiral, because the more successful their farming the more their population grew and the more they needed to produce, and so on. Such a dynamic would soon lead to genuine urbanisation. What is more, once they had started down this route, how long was it before they began to look further afield for trading partners, and to navigate the seas that separated them?

We have seen that the first evidence of sizeable settlements built from stone comes from the start of the Neolithic. Yet, although he's referring to far earlier artifacts, Bednarik makes a hugely important point:

> If the earliest found representatives of a class of material evidence are among the most deterioration-resistant types of that class, then the probability of significantly older, less resistant types is very high indeed.

In other words such developments don't spring from nowhere, they normally have a series of precedents showing gradual development. So if such advanced settlements suddenly appear in the Neolithic, it's highly likely that similar settlements built from less durable materials would have been gradually developing in size and sophistication for a long time beforehand. Because the dates for all the major cultural firsts are being continually pushed further and further back, it may even be that – despite the needle-in-a-haystack problem – proper evidence for our culturally advanced forgotten race will finally emerge over the coming decades.

In the meantime the key question remains. Is it reasonable to suggest that people who were capable of taking the time to produce stunning and sometimes intricate works of art, jewellery, musical instruments, tools and weapons, and of organising highly elaborate ritual burials, would *all* continue to struggle to survive as nomads for tens of thousands of years? Or is it far more likely that what we see in the archaeological record from at least 40,000 years ago, which mainly comes from Europe and the Near East, is only the tip of the iceberg of the level of culture, maybe even civilisation, that some of our other ancestors had developed elsewhere. Present, perhaps, in settlements that we have yet to uncover because we've not yet looked in the right places on the globe; or, even more likely, in settlements we'll never discover because they were catastrophically destroyed before being permanently submerged.

So, despite the lack of physical evidence, the *contextual* archaeological evidence, coupled with that of the texts and traditions, arguably means our hypothesis of a culturally and spiritually advanced forgotten race that flourished perhaps for most of the Upper Palaeolithic starts to gain some serious credibility.

10

SUPPOSED LOST CONTINENTS

Legends of the supposed lost continents of Atlantis and Lemuria have proliferated massively in the last few centuries, and they show little sign of abating. But do they have any sort of solid foundations, and if so do they have anything of value to offer us in our search for our forgotten race?

PLATO'S ATLANTIS

The common starting point for any piece on Atlantis is the oldest account as provided by Plato in his *Timaeus* and *Critias*. We have already seen in chapter 4 that he provides a remarkable description of the original spirituality and subsequent debasement of the inhabitants, which is completely consistent with our main theme. He also continues from where we left off in chapter 5 by providing a clue as to when the 'greatest of all destructions by water' actually occurred:[1]

> Solon was astonished at what he heard and eagerly begged the priests to describe to him in detail the doings of these citizens of the past. 'I will gladly do so, Solon', replied the priest... 'The age of our institutions is given in our sacred records as eight thousand years, and the citizens whose laws and whose finest achievement I will now briefly describe to you therefore lived nine thousand years ago; we will go through their history in detail later on at leisure, when we can consult the records.'

Of course many alternative researchers have seized on this assuming that, if Solon really did visit Egypt it would have been around 500 BCE, meaning the flood must have occurred some time before 9500 BCE. Nevertheless the aspect of Plato's work that has tended to captivate them most is the tantalising but equally prosaic one of Atlantis' original location.[2]

Their search has typically involved trying to match a variety of sites to his lengthy descriptions not only of its general whereabouts – that is, beyond the 'Pillars of Hercules' or Straits of Gibraltar – but also of its layout.[3] The main acropolis apparently comprised a vast palace with several temples surrounded by concentric rings of land and water, forming a complex network of bridges, canals and docks encircled by a huge outer wall with dense adjacent housing. All this lay on a large flat plain surrounded by mountains, but the entire island was much larger and split into ten districts, each ruled by a separate governor. The buildings were constructed from stone as well as timber, and their walls were covered with metals such as gold, silver, bronze, tin and 'orichalc'.[4] The temples were full of gold statues, there were public baths and gardens and an elaborate water system, the docks contained large trireme ships and were a hive of activity, and there was even a horseracing track. Plato concludes by providing details of the military and political organisation of the island. It is of course all this that sowed the seeds of the idea that the Atlanteans had a relatively high level of technology, at least equivalent to anything that existed in his own time.

Although much of this is consistent with the general idea of a culturally but not technologically advanced civilisation, suggestions of the widespread use of stone and metal in art and architecture may owe more to Plato's vivid imagination than to ancient records of what's now prehistory. We also saw previously that his whole account is placed within the artificial political context of the supremacy of the pre-flood Athenians. But this doesn't have to mean it's entirely fictitious, because we already know how common it is for old traditions to be expediently edited to suit the political needs of the time.

Yet even if we limit ourselves to the general location, it's clear that most contenders for Plato's Atlantis are seriously flawed. The Greek island of Santorini or Thera is one of the favourites because it's a volcanic caldera that suffered a massive eruption around 1500 BCE, which had disastrous consequences for both itself and Minoan Crete.[5] Yet not only is it within the Mediterranean rather than beyond its entrance, but nor does it fit with the 9500 BCE timescale. The suggestion that a landmass named 'Atland' or 'Aldland' in the North Sea disappeared under the waves around 2200 BCE suffers from similar shortcomings.[6] Meanwhile the idea that the continent of Antarctica was in what's now the Southern Atlantic, and therefore largely free of ice until it was moved to its present location by a crustal shift at the end of the Pleistocene, is not borne out by geological or other evidence – as we'll see in the next two chapters.[7] A more recent suggestion is a submerged landmass in the Caribbean Sea in the vicinity of Cuba, but the physical evidence for this is less than convincing.[8]

Of course a large, submerged continent within the Atlantic Ocean itself is the best known of all the suggestions.[9] What is more, as we'll shortly see, this idea has tended to be accompanied by the similar suggestion that an earlier Lemurian civilisation inhabited a former continent in either the Indian or the Pacific Oceans. However the relatively recent confirmation of the long-standing theory of continental drift via the understanding of plate tectonics has tended to leave both these ideas very much on the fringes.[10] That is not to say that the idea of sunken landmasses is entirely rejected by professional geologists, it's just that the major ones they do accept – such as the Kerguelen Plateau in the far south of the Indian Ocean, and the Zealandian Continent that surrounds New Zealand – were submerged tens of millions of years ago.[11] As we'll see in chapter 13, however, there is one whose conventionally accepted submergence date *does* fit into reasonable timescales for the destruction of our forgotten race.

In any case, for the moment what is arguably more interesting than the locations of Atlantis and for that matter Lemuria – and has been less well documented in recent decades – is the body of work that follows up on Plato's ideas about the nature of the inhabitants and the reason for their destruction. Much of this material is not only old, but has also supposedly been channelled from ethereal sources by human mediums. Although the reliability thereof can vary considerably from source to source and from medium to medium, I don't believe it should be rejected out of hand. Indeed it will be instructive to see whether it sheds any interesting light on our central theme.

FOUNDING FATHERS

In his excellent 1954 compilation of Atlantis traditions, *Lost Continents*, Lyon Sprague de Camp chronicles the various references to Plato's account in the work of his mainly Greek and Roman successors. Then as now they were clearly split between believers and sceptics, but they added nothing new from any other ancient source.[12]

Then from about the sixth century all discussion of Atlantis seems to have disappeared, until it began to be resurrected after the Spanish conquest of South America in the sixteenth century. Initially the favoured suggestion was that the Americas themselves were Plato's target, but it became increasingly clear that in many indigenous American traditions their ancestors were reported as having arrived from the East after their home continent sank – so the focus shifted to the Atlantic Ocean. These traditions were first recorded by Diego de Landa, a Spanish priest who became bishop of Yucatán after the conquest. In a disaster for historians as well as the local population his religious fervour led him to seek out and burn as many original Mayan books and codices as he could find. Yet almost schizophrenically he also spent a great deal of time learning and recording as much as he could about Mayan customs and religion, leaving an invaluable legacy. However he seems to have frightened two Mayan assistants into furnishing him with a completely false alphabet for supposedly translating each Mayan glyph into its equivalent in the Roman alphabet, and it was not until the twentieth century that scholars realised each glyph is a whole syllable.[13]

In fact de Landa's false alphabet remained lost until the 1860s anyway, but then French historian Charles-Etienne Brasseur de Bourbourg rediscovered it and attempted to use it to translate the *Troano Codex*.[14] He coupled it with a hugely fertile imagination to produce a mangled tale of a lost continent from a work that, as we saw in chapter 5, is now known to be largely divinatory. Far worse, according to Sprague de Camp he found there were two glyphs he couldn't translate that vaguely resembled de Landa's *m* and *u* and, with a massive leap of logic, concluded they spelled out the name of said sunken continent. This is how the name *Mu* entered modern folklore, so we should be clear it has no sound basis whatsoever – and one could argue that any communication mentioning it is equally suspect. It was also around this time that the name Lemuria was coined by the zoologist Philip Sclater. Contemporary geologists believed there had once been a landmass connecting India and Madagascar, and he proposed that this accounted for lemurs being found in those two countries but not in Africa. The name has stuck ever since, even though it's now more often associated with the Pacific.[15]

Not long after this the Jersey-born antiquarian Augustus Le Plongeon entered the fray. He managed to compound Brasseur de Bourbourg's errors in translating the *Troano Codex* by combining it with various other inscriptions from the ruined city of Chichen Itza to conjure up a tale of 'Queen Moo' of Atlantis or Mu – who fled from the devastation of her homeland to Egypt, where she had the Great Sphinx built as a memorial.[16] He even quoted the work of various contemporary 'pyramidiots' who insisted that the Great Pyramid had also been erected when Atlantis sank. We saw briefly in chapter 3 that all this flies in the face of the sound archaeological evidence that these edifices are only around 4500 years old but, because such ideas retain a significant degree of popular support, we'll return to them properly in the next chapter.

But from an exoteric perspective at least it was former US politician Ignatius Donnelly who really resurrected the Atlantis tradition in the modern era, with the publication of *Atlantis: the Antediluvian World* in 1882. He follows the line that it was a lost continent in the Atlantic, and asserts that the survivors of its demise went on to found the earliest historic civilisations on each side of that ocean. Yet we've already seen that this location is suspect. What is more he discusses the supposedly sudden emergence of the Ancient Egyptian civilisation, and the supposed similarity between its pyramids and hieroglyphs and those in South America.[17] These observations too are highly suspect but again, because they're still repeated by modern alternative researchers, we'll return to them in the next chapter.

HELENA BLAVATSKY

By contrast it was the infamous Russian-born Madame Helena Petrovna Blavatsky who fired up the more occult or esoteric side of the Atlantis legends at around the same time.[18] She travelled extensively in India and the Far East, although in her later years she split her time between England and America. She founded the Theosophical Society in 1875, and not long afterwards released her two best-known works, *Isis Unveiled* in 1877 and *The Secret Doctrine* the following year. Both are massive, two-volume compilations stretching to more than fifteen hundred pages each, and they're well referenced – but use a grammatical style that makes them particularly hard going. She has often been accused of plagiarism, not without some cause. Indeed she herself admitted in later life that some of her channelling – including the apparent mid-air materialisation of letters from the 'masters', who were its main source – was faked.

Nevertheless in her case I'd argue that it would be a mistake to reject the entirety of her huge and massively influential corpus on these grounds alone.[19] In particular for our current purposes some of the most interesting aspects of her work are the stanzas reproduced from a supposed 'archaic manuscript' to which she claims to have had access called the *Book of Dzyan*. Needless to say some argue that these are just fakes too, but recent research by theosophical scholar David Reigle reveals the possibility that they formed part of a closely guarded commentary on the *Books of Kiu-te* – the more common form of which is the *Kala Chakra*, the first tantra of a portion of the Tibetan Sacred Canon known as the *Kanjur*.[20] If so they *may* be relatively untainted by Blavatsky's own extensive commentaries thereon, which as we'll shortly see contain clear faults. On that basis It's worth reproducing in full those stanzas that describe the five 'root races' of humanity:[21]

Stanza 5

18. The First were the sons of Yoga. Their sons the children of the Yellow Father and the White Mother.
19. The Second Race was the product by budding and expansion, the asexual from the sexless. Thus was, O Lanoo, the Second Race produced.
20. Their fathers were the Self-born. The Self-born, the Chhaya from the brilliant bodies of the Lords, the Fathers, the Sons of Twilight.
21. When the Race became old, the old waters mixed with the fresher waters. When its drops became turbid, they vanished and disappeared in the new stream, in the hot stream of life. The outer of the First became the inner of the Second. The old Wing became the new Shadow, and the Shadow of the Wing.

From the stanzas themselves it appears that these first and second races, described as 'self-born' and 'sweat-born' respectively, were only energetic beings with no physical body.[22] The third 'egg-born' race was the first to become fully physically manifest:

Stanzas 6 to 8

22. Then the Second evolved the Egg-born, the Third. The sweat grew, its drops grew, and the drops became hard and round. The Sun warmed it; the Moon cooled and shaped it; the wind fed it until its ripeness. The white swan from the starry vault overshadowed the big drop. The egg of the future race, the Man-swan of the later third. First male-female, then man and woman.
23. The self-born were the Chhayas: the Shadows from the bodies of

the Sons of Twilight.

24. The Sons of Wisdom, the Sons of Night, ready for rebirth, came down, they saw the vile forms of the First Third. 'We can choose', said the Lords, 'we have wisdom.' Some entered the Chhaya. Some projected the Spark. Some deferred til the Fourth. From their own Rupa they filled the Kama. Those who entered became Arhats. Those who received but a spark, remained destitute of knowledge; the spark burned low. The third remained mind-less. Their Jivas were not ready. These were set apart among the Seven. They became narrow-headed. The Third were ready. 'In these shall we dwell', said the Lords of the Flame.

25. How did the Manasa, the Sons of Wisdom, act? They rejected the Self-born. They are not ready. They spurned the Sweat-born. They are not quite ready. They would not enter the first Egg-born.

26. When the Sweat-born produced the Egg-born, the twofold and the mighty, the powerful with bones, the Lords of Wisdom said: 'Now shall we create.'

27. The Third Race became the Vahan of the Lords of Wisdom. It created 'Sons of Will and Yoga', by Kriyasakti it created them, the Holy Fathers, Ancestors of the Arhats.

28. From the drops of sweat; from the residue of the substance; matter from dead bodies of men and animals of the wheel before; and from cast-off dust, the first animals were produced.

29. Animals with bones, dragons of the deep, and flying Sarpas were added to the creeping things. They that creep on the ground got wings. They of the long necks in the water became the progenitors of the fowls of the air.

30. During the Third Race the boneless animals grew and changed: they became animals with bones, their Chhayas became solid.

31. The animals separated the first. They began to breed. The two-fold man separated also. He said: 'Let us as they; let's unite and make creatures.' They did.

32. And those which had no spark took huge she-animals unto them. They begat upon them dumb Races. Dumb they were themselves. But their tongues untied. The tongues of their progeny remained still. Monsters they bred. A race of crooked red-hair-covered monsters going on all fours. A dumb race to keep the shame untold.

These stanzas are confusing at best and self-contradictory at worst, but in general they seem to be describing a race with different strains or 'subraces', some good, some not so good. What is more they seem to bear out the theory, proposed in chapter 7, of multiple and initially unsuccessful incarnation attempts by individuated souls. In particular there seems to be uncertainty about whether the available forms are 'ready' for such souls to incarnate into, and a decision by some to 'defer til the fourth'; plus a description of some of the race as 'dumb', reminding us of the traditions in which unsuccessful humans are 'silent' or 'can't speak to praise their creators'.

Stanza 9
33. Seeing which, the Lhas who had not built men, wept, saying: –
34. 'The Amanasa have defiled our future abodes. This is karma. Let us dwell in the others. Let us teach them better, lest worse should happen.' They did.
35. Then all men became endowed with Manas. They saw the sin of the mindless.
36. The Fourth Race developed speech.
37. The One became Two; also all the living and creeping things that were still one, giant fish-birds and serpents with shell-heads.

This fourth must surely be the golden race, not least because the theme of their subsequent debasement rings out loud and clear:

Stanzas 10 to 11
38. Thus two by two on the seven zones, the Third Race gave birth to the Fourth-Race men; the gods became no-gods; the sura became a-sura.
39. The first, on every zone, was moon-coloured; the second yellow like gold; the third red; the fourth brown, which became black with sin.[23] The first seven human shoots were all of one complexion. The next seven began mixing.
40. Then the Fourth became tall with pride. We are the kings, it was said; we are the gods.
41. They took wives fair to look upon. Wives from the mindless, the narrow-headed. They bred monsters. Wicked demons, male and female, also Khado (dakini), with little minds.
42. They built temples for the human body. Male and female they worshipped. Then the Third Eye acted no longer.
43. They built huge cities. Of rare earths and metals they built, and out of the fires vomited, out of the white stone of the mountains and of the black stone, they cut their own images in their size and likeness, and worshipped them.
44. They built great images nine yatis high, the size of their bodies.

Inner fires had destroyed the land of their fathers. The water threatened the Fourth.

45. The first great waters came. They swallowed the seven great islands.

46. All Holy saved, the Unholy destroyed. With them most of the huge animals, produced from the sweat of the earth.

Despite the likely distortion that this race bred with inferiors to produce monsters, and the debatable suggestion that they were erecting huge cities containing huge stone statues, these stanzas contain all the traditions with which we're already familiar: the preoccupation with the material, the loss of the third eye of spirituality, and the eventual destruction by flood, which also eliminates most large animals. So what was the aftermath?

Stanza 12

47. Few men remained: some yellow, some brown and black, and some red remained. The moon-coloured were gone forever.

48. The Fifth produced from the holy stock remained; it was ruled over by the first divine Kings...

49 ...who re-descended, who made peace with the Fifth, who taught and instructed it.

This fifth race, then, are the survivors of the catastrophe who went on to found our current race. We even find the first 'divine kings' seemingly reincarnating to instruct their fellows, which has clear echoes of the more spiritual form of knowledge transfer we discussed in chapters 3 and 8. So, plenty to ponder here that may or may not be seen to augment and reinforce some of the themes – and my interpretation thereof – from Part 1. But if we now turn to the current topic of lost continents, while there's no explicit mention of them in the stanzas, Blavatsky's commentaries suggest the following context:[24]

- The *First Race,* although ethereal, inhabited the 'Imperishable Sacred Land' of which 'little can be said', although 'the pole star has its watchful eye upon it'.

- The *Second Race* resided in Hyperborea, named after the Greek traditions of a continent in the north, which at one time 'stretched out its promontories southward and westward from the North Pole' and 'comprised the whole of what's now known as Northern Asia'.

- The *Third Race* inhabited Lemuria, following Sclater's terminology, although Blavatsky identifies the continent with the entirety of the present Indian Ocean, right across to Indonesia and on down to Australia.

- The *Fourth Race* then migrated to *Atlantis,* which is implied to have been somewhere in the Atlantic and originally, somehow, an extension of Lemuria.

Blavatsky provides plenty more detail on these lost civilisations, but much of it is confusing and contradictory. Fundamentally this aspect of her work is undermined not only by the proposed location and extent of the Lemurian and Atlantean continents, but even more by her dates for when they flourished. She asserts that the former emerged sometime before 18m years ago and sank about 5m years ago, while the bulk of the latter was submerged in stages between 2m and 1m years ago – although the last remnants didn't disappear until 9564 BCE. As we saw in the last chapter all of this is totally at odds with modern, orthodox archaeology.

To make matters worse she insists that various ancient monuments should be redated, and that the Lemuro-Atlanteans were highly technologically advanced – a stance that, as we'll see in the next chapter, continues to be maintained by many modern alternative researchers despite substantial evidence to the contrary. For example, she too commits the fatal mistake of proposing that the Great Pyramid was built by the last remnants of the Atlantean civilisation around 78,000 years ago.[25] She also suggests they may have been responsible for the pyramids at Angkor Wat in Cambodia and in Central and South America too, whereas we now know that all these structures are only a few thousand years old at most.[26] But she's at her most imaginative as one of the first to suggest, even in the 1880s, that the Indian epics contain descriptions of aeronautics – a skill supposedly taught to their ancestors by the Lemuro-Atlanteans.[27] Finally we might note that she places the root races within the overall context of the Hindu world cycles of Manvantaras and so on that we discussed in chapter 5.

So much for Blavatsky's distortions. As to her sources for the Atlantean and Lemurian material, it's clear that she drew extensively on a number of contemporary works. From a prosaic perspective these include Donnelly's *Atlantis*, and Louis Jacolliot's interpretations of Hindu traditions that posit a former continent in the Pacific rather than Indian Ocean called Rutas.[28]

From an esoteric perspective one of the major sources she openly and repeatedly references is her fellow theosophist Alfred Sinnett's *Esoteric Buddhism*, published in 1883 – even though she can't help but proclaim that she taught him everything he knew.[29] As to the extent to which her more occult speculations about Lemuria and Atlantis may have been genuinely channelled, this is almost impossible to determine. In fact arguably it's even harder to establish the real provenance of this material than that of the stanzas of the *Book of Dzyan*.

THEOSOPHICAL EVOLUTION

The next major player in the development of occult Atlantism was the theosophist William Scott-Elliot, who broadly follows Blavatsky's narrative in *The Story of Atlantis* and *The Lost Lemuria*, published in 1896 and 1904 respectively – although he does manage to further exaggerate a few of her distortions. If we commence with the most obvious he suggests, for example, that the two large Giza pyramids were erected by Atlantean evacuees just before a catastrophe that occurred as long as 200,000 years ago, 'partly to provide permanent Halls of Initiation, but also to act as treasure house and shrine for some great talisman of power during the submergence which the Initiates knew to be impending'.[30] He also adds considerable detail about the construction and power sources of the 'aerial boats' used by more important Atlanteans for transport.[31]

We are also told that he was 'allowed access to some maps and other records physically preserved from the remote periods concerned'; and that the Atlantean maps consisted of 'a globe, a good bas-relief in terracotta, and a well-preserved map on parchment, or skin of some sort', while those of Lemuria consisted of 'a broken terracotta model and a very badly preserved and crumpled map'.[32] Six reproductions of these maps are included in his work: two purporting to show the positioning of the major continents of the world at the time when Lemuria was 'at its greatest extent and then somewhat smaller in a later epoch'; and four the continent of Atlantis as it was progressively destroyed by supposed catastrophes 800, 200, 80 and 11.5 thousand years ago.[33] The detailed contours of these landmasses and islands are superimposed on the current world map for comparison, but this only helps to emphasise that their positioning is totally at odds with modern geological theory. Not only that but his timescales too are totally unrealistic, especially with respect to his report that Lemuria was *wiped out* before the *start* of the Eocene, which we now date to 55m years ago.

In his Preface to Scott-Elliot's *Story of Atlantis* Sinnett explicitly reveals the method by which much of it was supposed to have been composed:

> There is no limit really to the resources of astral clairvoyance in investigations concerning the past history of the Earth, whether we are concerned with the events that have befallen the human race in prehistoric epochs, or with the growth of the planet through geological periods which antedated the advent of man... Meanwhile the present volume is the first that has been put forward as the pioneer essay of the new method of historical research... Every fact stated in the present volume has been picked up bit by bit with watchful and attentive care, in the course of an investigation on which more than one qualified person has been engaged, in the intervals of other activity, for some years past.

In modern parlance 'astral clairvoyance' is a form of channelling information from other planes by going 'out-of-body', and it was certainly pioneered by Scott-Elliot's theosophical colleagues Charles Leadbeater and Annie Besant – indeed the former is argued to be the source of much of Scott-Elliot's work.[34] While I have made some constructive references to Leadbeater and Besant's research in my more spiritual books, most of the material under discussion is way too outlandish from the perspective of archaeology and geology to garner my support.

Yet is that all? It just might be worth recording what Scott-Elliot has to say about the root races because, despite the clear flaws and distortions elsewhere, there just may be some gems mixed in – and the advantage is that his work is far shorter and easier to analyse than Blavatsky's.[35] He describes the first root race as 'ethereal' and the second as 'astral', presumably denoting a lowering or densening of the energetic vibration of the second – although he indicates that neither would be visible to us. Then he comes to the third or Lemurian race:

> Lemurian man, during at least the first half of the race, must be regarded rather as an animal destined to reach humanity than as human according to our understanding of the term; for though the second and third groups of Pitris, who constituted the inhabitants of Lemuria during its first four subraces, had achieved sufficient self-consciousness in the Lunar Manvantara to differentiate them from the animal kingdom, they had not yet received the Divine Spark which

should endow them with mind and individuality – in other words, make them truly human.

This latter is surely an even more explicit reference to the transition from group to individuated soul consciousness discussed in chapter 7. But by contrast Scott-Elliot's subsequent reports on the traits of the various Lemurian subraces enter into the world of complete fantasy – with the earliest, for example, being giants with no bone structure, while others supposedly domesticated dinosaurs. To make matters even more complex and bewildering the development of the various subraces is intertwined with the same evolutionary patterns on other planets and star systems. So in summary, like Blavatsky and other theosophists, his work seems to be broadly unreliable but with a few possible gems thrown in.

His successor, the more celebrated Rudolf Steiner, also used some form of channelling to compile his *Atlantis and Lemuria,* first published by the Theosophical Society in 1911 then republished in broadly similar form in 1923 by the Anthroposophical Society – a breakaway movement he formed after various disagreements. In the introduction he discloses that 'such history as this is written in very different letters from those which record the everyday events of past times, for this is Gnosis – known in anthroposophical speech as the Akashic Records'.[36] But however impressively esoteric this may sound, in this work at least he broadly follows the lead and apparent distortions of his predecessors. Yet a few comments about the mental capacities of the various races are probably worth mentioning briefly: he suggests the Lemurians used something akin to telekinesis to control nature, while the Atlanteans achieved this by more occult means – including mastering the magical power of words.[37]

In summary these reflections of the early theosophists continue to exert great influence in occult circles, for all that they appear to contain manifest and multiple distortions interspersed, perhaps, with the odd gem. Moreover it would appear they've exerted a strong influence on a number of other lost-continent theorists who have no direct connection with theosophy – as we'll now see as we review the most influential contributions to the debate in subsequent years.

THE COLONEL

James Churchward, who designated himself 'Colonel' in later years, left it until he was in his seventies before producing a number of now well-known works – including *The Lost Continent of Mu* and *The Sacred Symbols of Mu*, published in 1926 and 1933. The latter is a treatise on the common origin and universal meaning of a number of symbols, that he argues function as archetypes operating via universal or collective consciousness. But the earlier work describes the pre-Atlantean lost continent of Mu, which he not only shifts away from Le Plongeon's Atlantic location into the Pacific, but also dates to between 50,000 and 12,000 years ago – a far more sensible timeframe than those adopted by various theosophists.[38] But that is, unfortunately, the end of the good news.

Churchward provides no source references but his works are apparently based on two sets of ancient tablets. The 'Naacal' set were supposedly composed in Burma or even in Mu itself, and were shown to him by a temple priest in India after which the two of them proceeded to decipher them together – Churchward having studied the 'dead language' with the priest for two years before. From his interpretations they appear to contain little more than a basic esoteric view of world origins that is common to most Eastern and Western traditions, as we saw in chapter 8, and they certainly contain no obvious references to Mu.[39] The other set of tablets, which he came across subsequently and incorporated into a second edition of *The Lost Continent* in 1931, are described as having been discovered not long before by William Niven in Mexico. These were supposedly lost at sea towards the end of Niven's life, but from Churchward's selected reproductions they appear to contain relatively standard Mayan glyphs, which wouldn't date to more than 12,000 years ago as he suggests.[40] In any case he appears to use these only as vague support for his far heavier reliance on Le Plongeon's distorted interpretations of the *Troano Codex* and other Mayan inscriptions as discussed previously.[41]

THE ARCANE TRADITION

Lewis Spence's work on Atlantis is in many ways more sensible than that of most other commentators in that his timescales are practically short and he attempts to pay at least some attention to the realities of orthodox archaeology. In his 1926 work *History of Atlantis* he proposes the gradual destruction of two landmasses in the Atlantic, Antillia in the east and Atlantis in the west.[42] He also suggests that the Aurignacian and Azilian cultures, which ushered in the Upper Palaeolithic and Neolithic eras respectively, were two successive strains of Atlantean refugees who colonised Europe – with the first wave being *more* advanced than its degenerate successor.[43] This latter is an interesting proposition, but we've already seen that the Atlantic is an unlikely location, while his suggestion that there's no evidence they emerged from the East is also highly suspect. Then in his 1932 work *The Problem of Lemuria* he too moves the earlier civilisation from Blavatsky's Indian Ocean into the Pacific – where he asserts *two* landmasses existed. But again, although his timescales are more reasonable, modern geology doesn't support the continents he proposes.[44]

In fact it's arguably in his 1943 work *The Occult Sciences in Atlantis* that Spence makes his most useful contributions. His sources for this too aren't ethereal, but reported to be a combination of ancient texts and traditions – and in particular a set of manuscripts belonging to what he refers to as the 'Arcane Tradition' of an anonymous secret fraternity of which he was supposedly a member.[45] Indeed he suggests such records are kept by all such fraternities and all initiates are allowed to inspect them, although they can't make notes or copies. Whether or not this is correct, the most interesting aspect of this work is his description of Atlantean occult practices. These are said to have included astrology, alchemy, prophecy, necromancy and divination – this information coming from what appear to be medieval French and Spanish manuscripts.[46] He also describes how these practices were primarily restricted to the higher priestly and royal class – except that at some point the lower castes began to practice their own degenerate 'black magic', which is what led to the downfall of the civilisation.

What then are we to make of these latter contributions from Spence? He certainly doesn't appear to take everything he reads in his sources at face value. What is more he shows discernment when he discusses what he regards as clear distortions that were introduced every time the material was recompiled or translated – from what he believes to be, originally, Egyptian sources. So, despite the fact that his most interesting material can't be referenced or checked by outsiders, his suggestion that it was the misuse of occult practices that led to the downfall of the Atlanteans just *may* be an interesting possibility for our understanding of the fate that befell our forgotten race.

THE AUTOMATIC AUTHOR

Hugh or 'HC' Randall-Stevens supposedly had no previous history of channelling and 'little interest in occult matters' when he received his first communication from two Ancient Egyptian initiates who called themselves Osiraes and Oneferu in 1925.[47] He recorded these communications using 'automatic writing'.[48] They were published in a number of works known as the *Osirian Scripts,* the first of which appeared in 1928. These were then bundled together along with some new material and commentary in *From Atlantis to the Latter Days,* published by his own 'Knights Templars of Aquarius' in Jersey in 1954.

His supposed sources provide detailed reports of Atlantis, and even a genealogical tree of humankind's earliest ancestors.[49] But again his material doesn't pass the 'Giza test', because like various theosophists before him he suggests all three pyramids were erected in great antiquity after the destruction of Atlantis.[50] He even describes a network of underground passages and chambers under the Sphinx that, as we saw in chapter 3, is almost certainly a complete fabrication.[51] Not only that but there's a possibility that his detailed drawings of the underground temples in the vicinity of the Sphinx were plagiarised from a Rosicrucian source.[52] Accordingly, although his work is still occasionally quoted, it's surely insufficiently reliable to merit further consideration here.

THE SLEEPING PROPHET

In the early twentieth century Joseph Benja Leslie supposedly interviewed a variety of 'Atlantean spirits' via a medium, and collated this material into his two-volume work *Submerged Atlantis Restored*, published in 1911. This includes copious details of 'its mountain ranges, valleys, seas, lakes, bays, rivers, sections or states, cities, convulsions, submergence, geographic, geologic, ethnographic and ethnologic conditions, languages, alphabets, figures, cardinal and ordinal numbers, punctuation marks, calendar, money, the six flags of the nation, religion, enterprises, government, and much, much more'.[53]

While Leslie's material is now hardly ever mentioned, his contemporary Edgar Cayce – the American seer often referred to as the 'sleeping prophet' – managed to forge a worldwide reputation as a psychic, healer and clairvoyant. While in a meditative trance he performed thousands of verbal 'readings' for his subjects and, although he remained unaware of their contents in real time, they were invariably transcribed by an observer. They spanned five decades until his death in 1945, and much of his reputation was gained as a result of his holistic medical diagnoses – which subsequent developments have proved to be reasonably accurate.[54] But around 20 percent came in the form of 'life readings' that repeatedly suggested his subjects had enjoyed previous incarnations in Atlantis. These were collated by his son Edgar Evans in *Edgar Cayce on Atlantis*, published in 1968.

The information divulged has much in common with theosophical material, although the timescales are somewhat more realistic.[55] It can be summarised as follows. The Earth was first populated 10.5m years ago by spiritual entities who only gradually took physical form and then split into males and females. Meanwhile the Atlantean civilisation, which emerged at least 50,000 years ago, was repeatedly destroyed – its history defined by conflicts between the 'Sons of the Law of One' who attempted to remain true to the 'righteous path', and the 'Sons of Belial' who indulged themselves in the material world and abused their power and technology. The latter gradually gained the upper hand until, aware of imminent destruction, a number of the more enlightened Atlanteans made their escape to various parts of the globe. It was these refugees who brought civilisation to, for example, Egypt – where, it will come as no surprise, they built the Great Pyramid and Sphinx in about 10,500 BCE.[56] They also set up a number of Halls of Records around the world to preserve their ancient wisdom and to warn humankind of the fate that had befallen Atlantis. Indeed Cayce himself was supposed to be the reincarnation of one of the more important of these escapees, a priest by the name of Ra-Ta. His readings are also replete with advanced technology, including reports of aerial and submarine craft, and the 'terrible mighty crystal' or 'firestone' whose misuse led to the last destruction.

Cayce's timescales for the emergence and destruction of Atlantis, and his clear message of debasement, fit well with our main theme. However we can also see that unfortunately his readings contain all the distortions we've come to expect of the genre, as well as a few additions. Many of his supporters have tended to stress the objectivity of his messages, suggesting he had no interest in or exposure to theosophical material – indeed that as a devout Christian he was often troubled by the way they tended to revolve around the concepts of reincarnation and karma.

However we should now bring in Kenneth Paul Johnson, a former theosophist and also member of the organisation founded to preserve and promote Cayce's work, the 'Association for Research and Enlightenment' or ARE. In his 1998 work *Edgar Cayce in Context* he reveals that the Atlantean material only started to emerge in 1923 when Arthur Lammers, a prosperous printer who was well versed in theosophy, visited Cayce for a reading.[57] Indeed one of the Association's own biographers, Thomas Sugrue, reports that Cayce then stayed with Lammers for several weeks – during which time they discussed such things as 'the cabala, the mystery religions of Egypt and Greece, the medieval alchemists, the mystics of Tibet, yoga, Madame Blavatsky and theosophy, the Great White Brotherhood, the Etheric World'.[58]

The association with Lammers was apparently short-lived, but at about this time Cayce also struck up a close friendship with the financier Morton Blumenthal who, according to Johnson, was also an avid theosophist.[59] This collaboration lasted for seven years, and Blumenthal was closely involved in both the running and financing of various Cayce projects. Johnson even reveals that Cayce had given a lecture to the Birmingham Theosophical Society in 1922, the year *before* he met Lammers, although admittedly on medical rather than Atlantean matters. If we also consider that his readings were not monologues but were prompted by questions from his subjects – some of whom may themselves have had theosophical and similar leanings – we have the very real possibility that Cayce was merely regurgitating from his subconscious information that had already entered his conscious mind, with the few additions and distortions that would inevitably arise.

This isn't to suggest in any way that Cayce was a fraud. He tirelessly devoted the bulk of his life to trying to help thousands of men and women who came to him for help, almost certainly to the detriment of his own health. What is more he too provides support for our general theme of a forgotten race who became debased and were destroyed, all within sensible timescales. But it's important to recognise the high probability that at least some elements of his readings on the topic of Atlantis were influenced by information received by perfectly normal means.

CONCLUSION

A question that naturally follows on from discussion of the stanzas in the *Book of Dzyan*, and of Arcane Traditions, Halls of Records and so on, is whether we're ever likely to find a hidden cache of records of what currently remains human *pre*history? Or whether any hitherto closely guarded ancient texts will ever be made public? My own assumption is that our forgotten race, though culturally advanced, didn't develop writing or feel the need to draw up historical records. If that were true then, even if the answer to either of the above questions was yes, we'd only be working from much later written versions that had survived millennia of oral transmission and geographical diffusion – meaning the possibility of significant distortions already having crept in is high.

As for current accounts, many, many writers have followed in the footsteps of the Lemuro-Atlantean trailblazers we've discussed in this chapter – indeed far too many to mention. But once we get past the early part of the twentieth century it's impossible to accurately determine the value of any channelled information about these lost civilisations, simply because any medium with the slightest interest in the subject will almost certainly have been consciously exposed to a whole plethora of books or discussions thereon. That is not to say they their messages will be completely without value – indeed, as we've seen several times in this chapter, there may be important gems therein. But it's nearly always impossible to argue that their messages are 'clear', or untainted by the copious previous distortions that are still widely peddled.

One major objective of this work is to bring these distortions to light in the hope that future alternative researchers may work from a rather more grounded platform. In fact, in the interests of raising the levels of discernment amongst the alternative community generally, let's recap the major distortions that really ought to ring alarm bells whenever they're encountered. They include the idea that physically modern humans date back many millions of years; that our more recent ancestors possessed advanced technology such as aerial machines; that they lived on now-submerged landmasses in the Atlantic, Indian or Pacific Oceans; and that the Giza pyramids and Sphinx were built in a remote epoch by Atlantean survivors.

While we're at it, though, are there any *alternative* interpretations of the seemingly more outlandish material we've reviewed in this chapter that *do* stand up to scrutiny? For a start, the common theme of Lemurians being less physical than modern humans might make sense if viewed as a sort of stepping-stone experiment between existing purely on the 'astral plane' – which is similar to an Earth-based experience but typically with a higher level of vibration – and full 'physical' incarnation in a modern human body. A sort of halfway house whereby they would have inhabited the same Earth 'space' that we do, but in a less dense or 'physical' form – perhaps in a similar way to how some 'spirits' or 'ghosts' can remain trapped in this plane. Another option is that there are almost certainly huge numbers of other planets in this galaxy and others housing intelligent lifeforms both more and less advanced than us, and sometimes less physical than us – and some, even many, of these might involve human or humanoid lifeforms operating in environments that look and feel similar to Earth.

But now let's really open our horizons. Although it's not an *essential* aspect of the Supersoul Spirituality I referred to on a number of occasions in Part 1, my favoured 'big picture' view is that in fact we live in a digital universe – indeed that ours is just one out of a huge variety of such universes that can be compared to a series of computer games.[60] Further that each of us has free will to navigate our way through the particular version of the game we happen to be involved in, within the fundamental constraints imposed by that game. This means that the 'human life on planet Earth' game would be just one of a huge number of alternatives that our supersouls can create and then project aspects of themselves into. Not only that, but there would probably be many different versions even of our Earth game.[61]

In these, of course, all sorts of different scenarios may have played out, involving far earlier and different civilisations, different evolutionary and geological developments and timescales, and so on. In this context the sky is the limit – and it may be that much theosophical and other material on lost continents should be viewed in this light. However in this chapter and work generally I'm trying to limit my interpretations to the context of the evolution of Earth and the lifeforms thereon in *this* version of the game we're all engaged in.

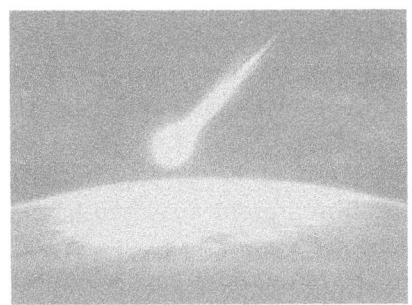

11

PSEUDO ARCHAEOLOGY

We have seen that many alternative researchers both ancient and modern have tended to place the emphasis on advanced technology, while others concentrate more on redating ancient monuments to more distant epochs and various related issues. We have only summarily dismissed these ideas so far, so now it's time to examine the supposed evidence properly to show exactly why it collapses under any sort of real scrutiny.[1] We will consider the technological and dating 'non-mysteries' in order, before turning to the more reliable evidence for the sort of skills our forgotten ancestors may have genuinely possessed.

TECHNOLOGICAL NON-MYSTERIES

ANCIENT WEAPONS AND AIRCRAFT

We saw in the last chapter that even the theosophists of the late nineteenth and early twentieth centuries were discussing how the Atlanteans had aeronautic vehicles, and their ideas of technological advancement were then reinforced by Edgar Cayce. Since then many alternative researchers have attempted to interpret passages in ancient texts as descriptions of aerial and other advanced warfare, even of extraterrestrial craft. They particularly cite Mesopotamian texts involving the god of war Ninurta, which we'll review in chapter 12;[2] certain biblical passages;[3] and above all Indian epics such as the *Mahabharata* and *Ramayana*. Indeed this is the main theme of David Hatcher Childress' 1991 work *Vimana Aircraft of Ancient India and Atlantis*. Although this topic doesn't merit the reproduction of detailed quotes, suffice to say that as usual there's no contextual support for these interpretations, and it's far more appropriate to look at such passages from the perspective of symbolism and literary creativity.

Nevertheless many alternative researchers insist these texts are indeed backed up by physical evidence. For example, a small wooden model in the Cairo Museum, which was found in a tomb at Saqqara and dates to around 300 BCE, is held to represent a glider.[4] With a wingspan of eighteen centimetres it has supposedly proved to be aerodynamically sound. But contextually it's far more likely to represent a stylised bird – indeed its head is very much that of a falcon, a guise used by both Ra and Horus. The only real enigma is that unlike any bird it does have a vertical tail. Yet if it *was* a scale model of a glider, why have we found no evidence of a full-size, fully operative version? As for other suggestions that certain artifacts from South America represent powered aircraft, these too are clearly symbolic representations of birds.[5]

On the face of it the most fascinating find is an Egyptian relief in the Temple of Seti I at Abydos, which really does appear to show the clear profile of a modern helicopter.[6] But in fact the picture circulating on the internet was almost certainly doctored by the removal of a cartouche at the supposed craft's nose, whereas in fact the whole relief was built up in stages by recarving, a common practice in Ancient Egypt. In other words the admitted similarity of the doctored end result to a helicopter is just a coincidence, similar to simulacra. Moreover even if these doubts didn't exist we can surely rule out the helicopter interpretation on the grounds that, again, no hint of such technology has turned up in the pre- or post-flood archaeological record; and let's nor forget that even if a glider can be made of perishable materials, a powered helicopter or other aircraft certainly can't. Nor is such an artifact small and easily overlooked.

THE DOGON

In his popular 1976 work *The Sirius Mystery* Robert Temple suggested that we were visited by beings from the Sirius star system around 5000 years ago. The major foundation of this theory was the supposed traditions of the Dogon tribe of West Africa, revealed to French anthropologist Marcel Griaule in the mid-twentieth century, suggesting that they knew Sirius had an invisible companion star that was only discovered by telescope some time later.[7] But not only had the existence of Sirius B been mathematically postulated a century earlier, but more recent interviews with the Dogon cast doubts that they were talking about Sirius at all.

To make matters worse Temple too discusses the Great Sphinx of Giza, and in particular the erosion of the walls of the limestone bedrock enclosure from which it has been sculpted. This is the feature that recent alternative researchers have used to suggest it should be redated, as we'll shortly see. But Temple goes as far as to suggest that the erosion occurred when the enclosure was originally filled with water by these extraterrestrial visitors, because they were amphibious.[8] Some of his more recent work is rightly praised as we'll also see shortly. But not only does this earlier work show a woeful ignorance of the commonplace symbolism of composite, hybrid beings and especially of fish, it also defies logic when one understands the context of the layout of the Sphinx enclosure and the Giza Plateau in general.[9]

COMPUTERS, BATTERIES AND SPARK PLUGS

In 1958 Derek de Solla Price became the first person to properly investigate the 'Antikythera computer' in the Athens museum.[10] It was found in the wreck of a Greek ship off Crete, and its inscriptions date it to the first century BCE. He estimated that when complete it consisted of between 20 and 40 interlocking bronze gears; those that survive are only 2 millimetres thick, while the largest has 240 teeth each only just over a millimetre high. Moreover, he established beyond doubt that it was an astrolabe that would have been used to predict the positions of the planets – although, somewhat ironically given its wonderfully technical nature, it was designed based on the Ptolemaic system whereby they all revolved around the Earth not the sun. This device is fascinating for its uniqueness, with nothing of comparable complexity having yet been found from the Classical period. Yet it's commonly accepted that the use of gears was understood in this era, and above all this is a relatively recent piece of technology that proves nothing about earlier civilisations.

The 'Baghdad batteries' are a similar enigma. The first, discovered in 1938, consisted of a clay vase about fifteen centimetres high into which a copper tube and an iron rod had been inserted.[11] Other similar artifacts were subsequently found. Archaeologists came to the conclusion that these were simple batteries and one, Arne Eggebrecht, built a replica containing nothing more than an acidic grape-juice solution that produced half a volt of electricity. He even went as far as to suggest that a number of Ancient Egyptian statuettes have such a thin layer of gold plating that it couldn't have been administered by hand, but more recently this has been questioned. Indeed, although this collection of vases was looted from the

Baghdad Museum in 2003 and their whereabouts are now unknown, apparently the tops of the originals were completely sealed with asphalt, so it's perhaps hard to see how an electric current could have been extracted.

Laying such concerns aside, it's quite stunning to think the Parthians *might* have developed a rudimentary electrical device some 2000 years ago. But even if they *had*, what would this really mean? Just as the Antikythera device was dubbed a 'computer' to enhance the effect for the general public, alternative researchers discussing these 'batteries' give the impression that our forebears were running around with power tools and goodness knows what else. But they clearly weren't, because yet again no such contextual evidence has been found. Far more interesting is the fact that, *if* these artifacts were being used to produce a small electrical current, their inventors failed to see the broader applications – and it would be another two millennia before the phenomenon was *re*discovered.

By contrast a supposedly anomalous artifact that has led many researchers a merry dance – and still does, despite having been proved totally erroneous – is the 'Coso artifact'.[12] Three mineral hunters discovered an apparently ancient geode near Olancha, California in 1961, and when they cut the specimen in half the interior revealed what appeared to be a replica of a spark plug. But subsequent investigation has proved this to be no great surprise – because this was no ancient geode but a recently formed conglomerate, and its enigmatic contents have now been matched perfectly to a plug made by the Champion Company in the 1920s.

MAPS AND PORTOLANS

This section is less about advanced technology, and more about attempts to prove that our ancient forebears were sufficiently advanced to have sailed to and mapped the continent of Antarctica *before* it was icebound. This suggestion was originally made in 1956 by Captain Arlington H Mallory after he'd investigated the infamous Piri Re'is map of 1513. It was then expanded upon by Charles Hapgood in his 1966 work *Maps of the Ancient Sea Kings,* in which he examined a number of other medieval maps and portolans, including the Oronteus Finaeus map of 1531.[13]

In the last chapter we briefly mentioned the theory that Atlantis was located in Antarctica *before* it was shifted southward by a crustal displacement at the end of the Pleistocene – and that this isn't born out by geological evidence. We will revisit this in the next chapter, but for now it's commonly understood that the continent has been completely icebound for at least the last 15m years.[14]

But does Hapgood nevertheless have a strong basic case about the maps? Unfortunately the answer is again a resounding no, because a casual perusal reveals that the relevant portions don't match the Antarctic coastline – glaciated or unglaciated – to anything like the degree Hapgood proposes. In addition it's often overlooked that classical Greek scholars theorised there must be a landmass in the Southern Seas to act as a counterbalance to the known ones that lay predominantly in the northern hemisphere. Aristotle was the first to coin the term Antarctica for it, but Ptolemy referred to it as Terra Australis Incognito or the 'unknown southern land', which is highly similar to the label we find on some of these medieval maps.[15]

So although our forgotten race may well have been fine seafarers and possibly even cartographers, as we'll shortly see, it's clear that the evidence provided by Hapgood and his followers in support of this claim is seriously flawed.

ANCIENT HIGH TECH

The various artifacts that are supposedly indicative of ancient advanced technology are still generating huge interest, alongside new ones that continue to emerge. Witness the fact that the reputable publishing house Simon & Schuster will shortly be releasing the UK version of Frank Joseph's *Ancient High Tech*. He was the editor of *Ancient American* magazine for many years, and more recently has published books on Atlantis and Lemuria among other topics.[16]

A glance at the marketing blurb and various extracts reveals that it contains some fascinating discoveries. For example, a self-igniting match from Babylon; a coin-operated holy-water dispenser from Alexandria; a form of 'tin can and string' telephony device from pre-Columbian South America; and supposed sex robots from Ancient Troy, Greece and China. But these are all relatively recent civilisations, and the tech isn't exactly high. What is more, unfortunately all this is combined with evidence of 'robotics and other forms of artificial intelligence', and of 'ancient Egyptian aircraft'. This, I'm afraid, is where I switch off – for all the reasons given above.

ANCIENT ASTRONAUTS REVISITED

As we saw in chapter 2 theories about ancient aircraft have diversified into the whole Ancient Astronaut genre, fuelled in part by the massive interest in UFOs since the 1950s. The idea is that extraterrestrials have visited the Earth at various times in the past, seeding technology, erecting monuments and even, according to Interventionists, genetically creating humankind.

In fact the British journalist Harold Wilkins was arguably the founder of this school in the 1950s, but in the 1960s a number of writers followed a similar line to that of Erich von Däniken and Zecharia Sitchin already discussed in chapter 2. For example, in his 1968 work *Gods and Spacemen in the Ancient East* W Raymond Drake reinterpreted a great deal of the ancient textual material that Sitchin subsequently used, and in fact his work is better referenced; but his disclosure of sources is still woefully inadequate, and on close inspection much of his material too appears to have been somewhat manipulated and distorted.

Meanwhile the early 1970s saw a plethora of similar books from, for example, Peter Kolosimo with *Not of this World* and *Timeless Earth,* and from Andrew Tomas with *We Are Not the First* and *On the Shores of Ancient Worlds*, among others. Perhaps unsurprisingly both writers showed a similar lack of scholarship by failing to provide proper references for much of their material, and an excellent flavour of these books is provided by chapter headings from Thomas' first offering: 'Electricity in the remote past', 'Did the ancients master gravitation', 'Prehistoric aircraft', 'They conquered space long before we did' and 'First robots, computers, radio, television and time-viewing machines'. Not long afterwards in *Worlds Before Our Own* the prolific Brad Steiger wrote about the supposed textual and physical evidence of ancient aviation, nuclear holocausts and other advanced technology – although at least he didn't follow the extraterrestrial route of his contemporaries, preferring instead to postulate a forgotten race of indigenous giants who developed this technology.

In the 1990s Alan Alford followed Sitchin's lead with *Gods of the New Millennium*, but to his credit subsequently abandoned the Intervention hypothesis; while Laurence Gardner's *Genesis of the Grail Kings* also partly followed Sitchin's interpretation of the Mesopotamian texts. The 2000s provided some hope that maybe this genre was finally disappearing, but it was a false one – because the last decade has seen a reigniting of the flame, similar to that of ancient advanced technology generally. As the title indicates without any hint of shame, Michael Tellinger's *Slave Species of the Gods* took the Interventionist hypothesis to whole new levels of human subjugation, as did Jan Erik Sigdell's *Reign of the Anunnaki*. Meanwhile, after a number of years of relative silence, von Däniken too has burst back into life with a plethora of new books all repeating the same old ideas – including *History Is Wrong*, *Twilight of the Gods*, *Odyssey of the Gods*, *Evidence of the Gods*, *Astronaut Gods of the Maya*, *The Gods Never Left Us* and *Impossible Truths*. It is sad but true that if the letters 'un' were inserted before the second word of the latter it would accurately sum up the majority of his entire corpus.[17]

Perhaps most surprising of all has been Robert Bauval teaming up with British astronomer Chandra Wickramasinghe in 2018 to produce *Cosmic Womb: The Seeding of Planet Earth*. Having insisted for many years that he was really only interested in more conventional, albeit-alternative ideas about ancient civilisations, Bauval has now revealed himself to be a fully fledged member of the Ancient Astronaut school. In Part 1 his co-author tends to concentrate on the panspermia theories for which he's renowned, and which aren't particularly outlandish. But sadly, though perhaps not surprisingly, the quality of Bauval's contribution in Part 2 is questionable at best – particularly his concentration on and insistence that the construction and mathematics of the Great Pyramid cannot be of terrestrial origin, of which more shortly.

DATING AND OTHER NON-MYSTERIES

We have seen that the early theosophists were not averse to ascribing very early dates to ancient monuments such as the Great Pyramid and Sphinx, and that trend continued right through the twentieth century with many of the Ancient Astronautists and other alternative authors who were also somewhat obsessed with ancient technology. But as we saw in chapter 2, alternative researchers such as Bauval, Graham Hancock, John Anthony West and Boston geologist Robert Schoch have more recently come to the forefront of the modern Redating movement.

To be fair to them, not only have they done a great deal to raise public awareness of ancient civilisations and their accomplishments but – with the exception of Bauval's recent admission as above – they've also moved away from the more outlandish high technology and other claims of their predecessors. For all of this they deserve full credit. Modern alternative researchers have also learned to follow their lead and give their research a fine veneer of scholarly respectability, with copious endnotes and so on. Unfortunately, despite this, their underlying scholarship remains questionable. So let's look more closely at their arguments to see why this is the case.

NO OVERNIGHT DEVELOPMENT

West's best-known work remains *Serpent in the Sky*, first published in 1979. In general it represents a fine attempt to follow up on the work of radical Egyptologist René Schwaller de Lubicz, who explored the esoteric symbolism of the Ancient Egyptians in his 1961 work *Sacred Science*. West suggests in his introduction that he regards their 'science, medicine, mathematics and astronomy' as being of 'an exponentially higher order of refinement and sophistication than modern scholars will acknowledge'. It is a moot point whether this statement was true even in its day, as is whether West and others like him have had any significant influence on the course of more orthodox Egyptology over the last few decades. But one thing that stands out is his view that such sophistication had no real development period – indeed that 'Egyptian civilisation was not a development, it was a legacy' that 'proves Atlantis'.[18]

This is, of course, a very particular version of the 'no overnight development' theory that continues to form part of the bedrock for the work of many alternative researchers. But, as already suggested in the Preface, the general idea is invalidated in a number of ways. First, by a simple look at the technological progress made in the modern world in just a handful of centuries. Second, by its failure to acknowledge the period of gradual development that clearly *does* exist in the archaeological record – for example, the 80 years or so of pyramid building that preceded the work at Giza, which produced among others Djoser's Step Pyramid at Saqqara and Sneferu's Bent and Red Pyramids at Dashur.[19] Third, if the Redaters are wrong about the age of various Egyptian monuments, as we'll discuss below, then what they're actually proposing is a thoroughly punctuated development – with an original Atlantean stage, then a hiatus of many thousands of years, and then a re-emergence; although they might have had to wait for the climate to settle and so on after the catastrophe, would survivors who retained this advanced knowledge not have put it to good use again rather sooner?

THE AGE OF THE GIZA MONUMENTS

Arguably the most stubborn and enduring element of West's work, which forms another part of the bedrock for the entire Redating school, is his attempt to ascribe a far earlier date to the Great Sphinx than the roughly 2500 BCE suggested by Egyptologists. The main evidence at the centre of this debate is the water weathering on the walls of the bedrock enclosure out of which this great monument was carved, and West relied heavily on Schoch's work in this area. The full evidence is presented in a 1993 update of *Serpents* and in a number of more recent papers by both men. Suffice to say this issue is considered in detail in Volume 1 of the 'Prehistoric Truth' series, *Giza: The Truth*, in which our conclusion was that there's no truly compelling evidence that the Sphinx is older than the orthodox date – and certainly not by the eight or so millennia that most Redaters proposed.[20] Indeed Schoch originally parted company with West when he argued that it dates back as far as 10,500 BCE, preferring a far more conservative date – but by 2012 he had completely changed his tune with a similar date in *Forgotten Civilisation*, reinforced in 2017 when he teamed up with Bauval for *Origins of the Sphinx*.

This date seems to have been arrived at in conjunction with Hancock and Bauval, who supported it in their hugely popular 1996 work *Keeper of Genesis*, their choice being heavily influenced by Cayce's readings on the subject, as discussed in the last chapter. It was bolstered with a highly suspect astronomical argument involving precession and the position of Orion's belt stars and of the star Regulus in the constellation of Leo at the time – which they refer to as the 'first time', the dubious provenance of which we've already discussed in chapter 4. To make matters worse, after this West suggested that – given the supposedly inhospitable climate in Egypt at the end of the last ice age – the Sphinx should actually be dated to the *previous* precessional age of Leo around 36,000 BCE.[21]

If we turn now to the age of the Great Pyramid itself, and if we ignore the horribly exaggerated distortions of the early theosophists and others that we discussed in the last chapter, it was Sitchin who really set the modern ball rolling with a totally groundless accusation that Colonel Richard Howard Vyse faked the 'quarry marks' in the so-called 'Relieving Chambers' above the King's Chamber.[22] In fact I investigated this in great detail in *Giza: The Truth*, and the evidence is overwhelming that they're genuine – and prove beyond all reasonable doubt that the edifice was built by the Fourth Dynasty king Khufu, again around 2500 BCE. Indeed, although Bauval has now changed his tune as mentioned above, he and Hancock did originally accept this date – despite their somewhat confusing argument that the *ground plan* of the three Giza pyramids was laid out to reflect the position of Orion's belt stars in 10,500 BCE, at the same time as the Sphinx was built.[23] This confusion was made worse by their apparent support for Sitchin's assertions, which seems to have been incorporated – with scant regard for the logical flow of their arguments – merely to bolster their regrettable hostility towards orthodox Egyptologists.[24] Whether this attitude itself was genuine or merely adopted for commercial reasons, it was extremely unhelpful and, more to the point, largely unwarranted.

PYRAMID AND TEMPLE CONSTRUCTION

Although less outlandish in their views, all these members of the Redating school do ascribe a *relatively* high level of technological advancement to their lost civilisation – and nowhere is this better demonstrated than in their attitude toward the construction of the Egyptian and Mesoamerican pyramids, and various other megalithic structures around the world.

If we take the Great Pyramid as the prime example, even before Bauval's recent change of allegiance he and Hancock suggested that it would have been impossible for the Ancient Egyptians to have constructed the edifice with nothing more than simple stone and copper tools and a plentiful supply of labour – the inference being, of course, that they used a technology handed down by the survivors of a lost civilisation.[25] But I spent considerable time examining the logistics of the Great Pyramid's construction in *Giza: The Truth*, and I reached the same conclusion as professionals who have examined the evidence properly.[26] Although it represents an incredible piece of engineering, modern experiments have proved beyond reasonable doubt that it was nevertheless achievable with the relatively simple tools and labour the Ancient Egyptians possessed. Its project management, though, was comparable with anything attempted today – in fact possibly superior – as was the dedication of the builders to the cause. All pyramid building represented a national project to which virtually everyone was fully committed – almost certainly not as slaves, even though there may well have been some press-ganging – but because they were all successfully brainwashed by the idea that it was essential for the very survival of their religion and of their civilisation itself.

As for the techniques used, a number of modern construction experts with a passion for the edifice have come up with some detailed and highly plausible theories about the combinations of ramps and levers that could be sensibly and efficiently used to lift the huge numbers of blocks into place within the time available.[27] They even include estimates of the numbers of workers needed, based on detailed plans of how many were required to haul or lift each block of stone, how many teams could use the ramps and so on at any one time, how long the shifts would need to be, and so on. These experts *absolutely* give the lie to any casual suggestion that the construction of the edifice involved 'impossible engineering'.

These models also take into account the fact that the largest blocks in the Great Pyramid, used to construct the floors and ceilings of the previously mentioned Relieving Chambers, weigh in at a sizeable 70 tonnes. But even these are dwarfed by the blocks used to construct all levels of the walls of many of the ancillary temples at Giza, which weigh as much as 200 tonnes. Yet recent research into the mechanics of their construction suggests that even these could have been dragged up and placed in position using sand ramps. As to the question of *why* the blocks should be so large if this made the builders' task much more difficult, a perfectly sensible suggestion is that their size would reduce the likelihood of serious earthquake damage.[28]

Another oft-touted example of 'impossible' construction is that of the Trilothon, the three massive 800-tonne blocks in the walls of the Roman Temple of Jupiter at Baalbek in the Lebanon. But again the fact that this looks impossible to a layperson with no proper knowledge of ancient construction techniques doesn't make it the work of a lost civilisation with forgotten technology, or especially of extraterrestrial visitors. In fact this was one of the easier projects undertaken by the Romans because they only had to drag the blocks downhill from the quarry – whereas on other, more difficult projects they still used similar size blocks and the same system of winches and sleds that is depicted in paintings and reliefs.[29]

While we're on this topic Bauval and Hancock were delighted to support the findings of American engineer Chris Dunn in his 1998 work *The Giza Power Plant*. If we stick to his speciality in the first instance, he used the evidence of the striations on one particular 'drill core' in the Petrie Museum in London to argue that the Ancient Egyptians used ultrasonics to drill hard stone like granite. Yet in *Giza: The Truth* I show that a number of books and papers include period drawings of the use of weighted tubular drill-borers and coring drills, while modern experiments prove that identical drill cores can be produced using nothing more than a hand-turned bow drill incorporating a copper tube – with a sand slurry acting as the cutting agent.[30]

THE GREAT PYRAMID'S PURPOSE

All sorts of ideas have been put forward concerning purpose of this amazing edifice over many decades, one particularly popular one being that the internal dimensions of the structure encode biblical and other timelines. Again I have written about all this at length in *Giza: The Truth*.[31] But because it gained a fair bit of exposure at the time we must briefly consider one of the more outlandish modern suggestions, which again came from Dunn – the 'power plant' theory that provides the provocative title for his book. I engaged in lengthy correspondence with him about this and his ultrasonics ideas.[32] In fact I did the same with a number of other researchers too, such as Bauval concerning his Orion Correlation theory, all of which is published on my website.

To summarise my arguments for anyone tempted to question why the Great Pyramid was built, the key word is *context*. If it had been built in glorious isolation in a long distant epoch then it might be perfectly reasonable to question, and wax lyrical about, its true purpose. But even Dunn accepts that it's contemporary with the other Fourth Dynasty pyramids and associated temples, tombs and other structures at Giza and elsewhere – all of which show beyond any shadow of a doubt that these complexes had a ritual and indeed funerary context. What is more this fact stands, irrespective of the debate about whether or not kings like Khufu ever actually allowed their bodies to be buried inside their pyramid for fear of looting – which is known to have taken place despite the increasingly sophisticated security precautions built into pyramid designs, suggesting it may even have occurred shortly after internment as an 'inside job'. Although during the Fourth Dynasty the fashion was to leave internal pyramid walls free of reliefs, hieroglyphic texts or other decoration, nowhere is this context more clearly demonstrated than in the *Pyramid Texts* found inscribed on various kings' burial chamber walls from the Fifth Dynasty onward.

It would be wrong not to admit that there may still remain some unexplained enigmas relating to this fascinating edifice. For example, we were originally baffled by the purpose of the two pairs of narrow, so-called 'air' or 'star shafts' that run off from behind the walls of the King's and Queen's Chambers and upwards through the mainly solid masonry – particularly since the pair coming from the latter don't run right through to the outer casing, so air would never have got in.[33] What is more the idea they align with certain stars is somewhat weakened by the fact the two northern shafts contain a number of significant kinks. Yet, again, more recent research into construction has provided an ingenious yet highly plausible solution to these conundrums. If we assume the Queen's Chamber was an insurance policy in case Khufu died earlier than expected, the shafts may then have had a dual purpose. The first was indeed to provide ventilation during the burial process, meaning once the Kings and Relieving Chambers were complete the Queen's Chamber shafts could be blocked off. But for ventilation only it would have been far easier to make them horizontal. The second purpose, therefore, was to act as a primitive intercom system linking workers on the north and south sides – and if the shafts sloped upwards the system would last much further into the construction.

Another possible enigma is the discovery in 2016 of what appear to be two previously unknown 'voids' in the structure, one large and possibly representing a second 'Grand Gallery'.[34] For various reasons as yet there's been no official word on further investigation.

But does any of this change our fundamental understanding of why the monument was erected? No, it doesn't.

COMMON ORIGINS

Moving farther afield, Hancock in particular has always had a broader scope than just Ancient Egypt. The book that launched him into the spotlight of alternative history in 1995, *Fingerprints of the Gods,* contains a great deal of discussion about, for example, Mesoamerican pyramids and other ruins. It will come as no surprise that he suggests some of these are far older than the orthodoxy allows, and were built by an advanced pre-catastrophe civilisation. However American archaeologists are as insistent about their dates of between 500 and 2000 years old for these structures as their Egyptologist counterparts, and there's every reason to trust the professionals in this instance too.

Indeed because the weight of evidence is so strong Hancock is also forced to accept that many of these structures may *not* have been built in a remote epoch. So in one of his typically fleet-footed but not entirely logical moves he changes tack and resurrects Ignatius Donnelly's 'common origins' argument from more than a century ago. This runs that the pyramidal shape of the edifices on both sides of the Atlantic indicates their builders must have learned their skills from a common source – the survivors, of course, from a prior civilisation. This argument tends to be used alongside that of no overnight development, and is equally flawed. Just using basic common sense, the square-based pyramidal shape is an obvious choice for a large and imposing structure – but that's where the similarity ends. Whereas the Mesoamerican pyramids are all 'stepped', the only Egyptian pyramid that corresponds to this design is the first, that of Djoser at Saqqara; all its successors had smooth, shiny sides formed from high-quality casing stones that have in most cases been looted – although, for example, they're still visible at the top of the second pyramid at Giza, erected by Khafre. Moreover the external shapes tend to be far more complex in Mesoamerican structures – in fact they more closely resemble the ziggurats of Ancient Mesopotamia. It is also highly relevant that the impressive, large-scale sites of the Indus culture at Harappa and Mohenjo-daro – which are of similar age to, for example, the Giza monuments – don't contain pyramid structures at all.

Hancock attempts to reinforce the idea of common origins with the fact that the Maya too had a hieroglyphic form of script – but, again, this is totally unlike any Egyptian script. Meanwhile the use of pictorial symbols in early writing is hardly so unusual or surprising as to warrant such an explanation.

One interesting theme that has only come to the fore relatively recently, and *is* very clearly repeated on both sides of the Atlantic, is that of the 'handbag' or 'purse' found in the hands of deities or sages in myriad pieces of ancient art.[35] These come mainly from Ancient Mesopotamia – for example, in statues of Gilgamesh and Adapa; and from the Olmec culture of South America – for example, in statues of Quetzalcoatl. However the same symbol is also found in Indonesia, Armenia and even somewhat earlier and *sans deity* at the top of one of the stone columns at Gobekli Tepe. One interpretation is that they indicate spiritual wisdom or knowledge, which would fit nicely with the central theme of this book. Another is that the semi-circle of the handle represents the sphere of heaven and the immaterial, while the square or rectangle of the bag itself represents the materiality of the Earth. However a significant number of free-standing, sculpted equivalents have also been found, again *sans deity* – which, despite their often elaborate carvings, were almost certainly used as measured weights on a balancing scale. One interesting parallel that has been drawn is with the theme of the sages who introduced weights and measures as part of civilisation, as discussed in chapter 3. However sadly a more prosaic and quite possibly better interpretation is that whoever takes over as the ruler of any country or culture automatically tends to impose their own system of weights and measures – which are the fundamentals of any trading economy.

OTHER PYRAMIDS AND STRUCTURES

Before we leave the subject of pyramids, their previously little-known existence in a number of other countries has been widely reported in recent decades. For example, on a trip to central China in 1994 German visitor Hartwig Hausdorf stumbled upon a number of them on the Guanzhong plains in Shaanxi Province, not far from where the famous Terracotta Warriors were found. Although they'd been known about even in the West for some time, his reports caused a sensation when he suggested they were possibly of great antiquity – and linked them with ancient texts that supposedly described 'emperors descending from heaven in flying dragons'.[36] But in fact professional research into the 38 that have so far been documented shows them to be really quite recent constructions.[37] That is not to say they're not imposing, despite being constructed using clay and earth rather than stone. Indeed the largest is around 350 metres square at the base compared to the 230 metres of the Great Pyramid of Giza, although with an original height of around 75 metres it's only about half the height of its Egyptian counterpart. It does also seem that the Chinese authorities have sometimes been reticent about discussing them, or even acknowledging their existence. But on balance it doesn't appear there's any great mystery to them.

Even less mysterious were the reports of the largest pyramid ever discovered, first released by Bosnian-American businessman Semir or 'Sam' Osmanagić in 2005.[38] These detailed what he supposedly found when excavating certain structures clustered around the central Bosnian town of Visoko. However it appears that most if not all of their contents were pure fabrication. Moreover, amid subsequent outrage at the widespread publicity given to what they perceived to be ridiculous claims, local geologists revealed details of why they believed them to be perfectly natural features of the landscape. Apparently this hasn't stopped Osmanagić from continuing to artificially alter the natural structures, and to develop the whole site as a sort of New Age Disneyland.

Before we leave this section, it's worth briefly mentioning a number of stunning and extensive underground cities that have been discovered in Cappadocia in Central Turkey, for example at Derinkuyu and Kaymakli.[39] As amazing as these are, though, archaeologists are clear that they were only fully developed in the second half of the first millennium, particularly to protect their Christian populations during the Arab-Byzantine wars.

UNDERWATER SITES

To complete this section we'll turn to various underwater sites that have been investigated around the world in the modern era. The most celebrated is the 'Bimini Road' first reported as lying in shallow waters off the island of the same name by J Manson Valentine in 1968 – although it may or may not be a coincidence that this was exactly when and where Cayce predicted, many decades earlier, that Atlantis would first 'rise again'.[40] As yet none of the alternative researchers who have dived on the site seem to have produced any sort of *conclusive* evidence of human working.[41] By contrast most geologists, including Schoch, seem to believe the apparently symmetrical fissures in the bedrock to be a perfectly natural formation.[42]

Meanwhile in 1987 large structures supposedly resembling temples with platforms and giant stairs were located in the waters off Yonaguni, the most southerly of the Japanese Ryukyu island chain.[43] The marine geologist Masaaki Kimura, the first to properly explore it, initially argued that it would last have been above sea level at least 10,000 years ago – but has since accepted it may have been submerged by volcanic activity, and revised his estimate to between 2000 and 3000 years old. However he still insists it's man-made. By contrast Schoch, who was invited by a documentary team to dive on the site alongside Hancock and West, believes it to be totally natural – describing the bedrock as 'criss-crossed by many joints and fractures running vertical to the bedding planes'.[44] Nevertheless it's quite stunning that the right-angled and apparently regular shapes, which to the uninitiated appear so clearly fabricated, can be caused by natural processes.

The most recent such discovery occurred in 2001 when oceanographers carrying out pollution checks for India's National Institute of Ocean Technology reported they'd found a 'grid of geometric structures thought to be the foundations of two cities', each more than eight kilometres wide and lying at a depth of around 40 metres in the Gulf of Cambay – now Khambat – some 30 kilometres off the coast of Gujarat.[45] Indian officials went public with sensational claims of the earliest-known civilisation without the site ever having been properly investigated by marine archaeologists because the waters are so cloudy – and with a date of 9500 years old based on a single fragment of wood retrieved by dredging. Yet critics insist that this method extremely unreliable from an archaeological perspective, while supposed pottery fragments were so small that there is some doubt whether they're man-made at all. To make matters worse supposed 'structures' were only revealed by side-scan sonar – which, for various reasons, gives only the vaguest of outlines of what's going on under the water, and can easily be misinterpreted.

Accordingly there's nothing at all definitive related to our forgotten race in these underwater sites.

REALISTIC SKILLS

A number of orthodox and alternative authors are now concentrating on revealing the less fanciful but previously underrated skills developed by our earliest-known civilisations, and this approach has undoubtedly led to a more balanced view of their significant cultural achievements. Indeed it *may* shed useful light on the realistic skills that *could* conceivably have been possessed by their pre-catastrophe forebears.

ASTRONOMY AND NAVIGATION

We are increasingly aware of just how astronomically sophisticated the early civilisations of the modern epoch were. For this we can be thankful to pioneers like Sir Norman Lockyer, who set the tone in his 1894 work *The Dawn of Astronomy*. He suggested that the layout of a variety of ancient monuments around the world indicated they'd been deliberately aligned to the sun or to certain stars at one of the equinoxes or solstices, thereby acting as extremely accurate calendars. Furthermore he realised that these alignments could be used to date the monuments, particularly using the phenomenon of precession discussed in chapter 5. His conclusive proof came when he established that amendments to the layout of many ancient monuments were clearly introduced to allow for changes in the position of heavenly bodies over time.[46]

Although in itself Lockyer's work didn't prove that ancient astronomers completely understood the full precessional cycle, subsequent pioneering research based primarily on a symbolic interpretation of various ancient texts and reliefs has provided strong support for this argument. Carl Jung and Schwaller de Lubicz were pioneers of this approach, but it was brought to full fruition by Giorgio de Santillana and Hertha von Dechend in their 1964 work *Hamlet's Mill*.

However as usual a health warning is needed. Nowhere is this more apparent than in, for example, Hancock's attempts in his 1998 work *Heaven's Mirror* to apply knowledge of precession – and in particular the 'marker' of the 'first time' date of 10,500 BCE – to the layout of every monument he encounters. This includes, for example, the many temples at Angkor Wat in Cambodia, which were actually constructed around the twelfth century.[47] Meanwhile Rand Flem-Ath and Colin Wilson's suggestion in their 2000 work *The Atlantis Blueprint* that all the major sacred sites of the ancient world were laid out to a global geometric blueprint, indicating advanced geodesic and other knowledge, is also likely to be a step too far.

Nevertheless we can say with some certainty that the astronomer-priests of our historical ancient civilisations, in the Near and Far East and the Americas, did have an advanced knowledge of astronomy – as did their Celtic counterparts, even though their monuments at first sight appear less sophisticated. The ancient megalithic site of Stonehenge clearly has a combined ritual and calendrical function, while much recent attention has been focused on sites such as Maes Howe in the Orkneys and New Grange in Ireland. For example, in their 1999 work *Uriel's Machine* Christopher Knight and Robert Lomas suggest that these too were developed by the Grooved Ware people of the fifth to third millennia BCE as sophisticated calendars that used Venus' highly accurate eight-year cycle.[48]

All of this indicates that these ancient astronomers knew the Earth was round and orbited the sun. Yet this knowledge apparently became lost to the Christianised Western world, in which the primitive idea predominated that the Earth was flat and physically as well as symbolically at the centre of the universe – with everything else revolving around it. Indeed the truth was only *re*discovered in the West by Nicolas Copernicus at the beginning of the sixteenth century, and even then he only agreed to publish his work on his deathbed. Meanwhile his successor Galileo was put under house arrest for the last years of his life. This amply proves, as if we didn't have enough evidence already, just how distortive and destructive an influence dogmatic religious orthodoxy can be.

All of this also suggests that our forgotten ancestors may well have had a good understanding of astronomy, although whether precession would have been included in that is a moot point. We can conjecture that this would have been developed not only to aid with the planning of the seasons for agriculture and so on, but also because it would have been extremely useful for ocean navigation.

This theory is strengthened by Crichton Miller in his 2001 work *The Golden Thread of Time*. He provides persuasive arguments that our forgotten race mastered the use of a simple, bob-weighted, angle-measuring dial attached to a right-angled cross for determining their position from the stars and sun with astonishing accuracy (see Plates 16 and 17). This device would of course confer great power on anyone who knew how to use it both on land and at sea – and his argument continues that our ancestors in the modern epoch commemorated it in the archetypal symbol of the Celtic cross, even though they no longer understood its original purpose. He adds that anyone out at sea at the time of a major catastrophe would have been least affected by any tsunamis, which cause only a swell in deep ocean rather than the breaking, destructive waves experienced on the shore. Further that the most advanced astronomers of our forgotten race may even have predicted the impact of an extraterrestrial body and set sail accordingly, which gives a whole new slant to the traditions of the flood. Was the redoubtable Noah less of a farmer and more of an expert navigator?

In fact early seafaring is increasingly posited by orthodox archaeologists. Robert Bednarik's suggestion in chapter 9 that *Homo erectus* managed to cross a significant stretch of sea to reach Flores will probably remain controversial for some time to come. But the idea that some sort of rafts or simple craft were used to reach Australia by 40,000 years ago at the latest is now entirely accepted.[49] This is potentially backed up by the 'Solutrean Hypothesis' supported by, for example, Smithsonian archaeologist Dennis Stanford.[50] Although not without its critics, based on the similarity of Clovis and Solutrean technology it proposes that Atlantic crossings were made some time after 20,000 years ago by following the edge of the ice pack westwards in the North Atlantic. So, while the idea would probably remain anathema to most conventional archaeologists, it's not a huge leap of logic to posit that our forgotten ancestors *could have been* expert boat builders, seafarers and navigators.

CRYSTAL AND MAGNIFICATION TECHNOLOGY

Channelled material regularly suggests that the Atlanteans were using sophisticated crystal technology for a variety of purposes. Sometimes this idea is associated with energy generation and travel, and with information storage. In this latter context enigmatic 'crystal skulls' are often mentioned. A number of these are already known to exist, all supposedly of Mesoamerican origin, but most have proved to be of relatively recent manufacture using powered tools – effectively, therefore, fakes.[51]

In the first edition of this work I originally concluded that one skull in particular was perhaps not so easily dismissed – the enigmatic Mitchell-Hedges skull. This was reputedly discovered in a Mayan temple at Lubaantun in Belize in 1924 by Anna Mitchell-Hedges, the stepdaughter of the famous explorer Frederick. It is life-sized, anatomically detailed, visibly far superior to all the others and, unique among all the skulls known to exist, has a detachable jaw. Even the crystal experts from Hewlett-Packard's Santa Clara laboratories, who spent two days testing it in 1970, were not a little bemused by its quality.[52] Sadly, however, more recent tests conducted at the Smithsonian's National Museum of Natural History in 2008 have conclusively proved that it had been manufactured using a 'high-speed, hard-metal, rotary tool coated with a hard abrasive such as diamond'.[53] To make matters worse we now know too that it wasn't found in Lubantuun, but bought by Mitchell-Hedges at a Sotheby's auction in 1943.

On a more prosaic note a number of optical lenses that have been precision ground from rock crystal have now been located in museums all over the world. Although a few of these were being discussed at least in von Däniken's time, Temple has exhaustively tracked down a large number over several decades, presenting the results in 2000 in *The Crystal Sun* – which is a considerable improvement on his earlier work mentioned previously. The oldest so far found dates to the Old Kingdom in Egypt, and almost certainly *wasn't* manufactured using the soft-metal tools available at the time, but using hard stone and a grinding paste. So could our forgotten race have been using lenses to produce rudimentary telescopes for astronomical observation and especially ocean navigation? It is surely a possibility, although such items *would* of course be expected to survive in the archaeological record.

It may also be relevant at this point to consider the research of geoscientist Ivan Watkins, who like many others has studied the stonemasonry of the Incas.[54] Not only did they use large granite blocks that were often fitted together using intricate shapes, but also the joints are so accurate that even a slip of paper can't be inserted into them. In the 1980s Watkins considered all the methods that had been proposed to date – for example, hammering, grinding and polishing, wedging and even chemical processes – and concluded that none properly explained these remarkable feats. But he did notice a glazing on the surface of some of the Incan stones, and further research revealed that this is exactly the effect achieved when modern producers of granite tiles finish them using a high temperature flame. Two other factors influenced him. First, he had heard descriptions of a 'great golden dish two men across' that was reported to have been melted down by Conquistadores. Second, he had come across the research of David Lindroth of the US Bureau of Mines, who had found that 100 watts of light focused to a point about two millimetres in diameter will cut any rock to the same depth – meaning that accurate, repeated passes would produce a much deeper cut. Putting all this together he proposed that the Inca stonemasons had used large, concave, gold dishes to concentrate the rays of the sun to cut and shape rock.

This is a fascinating theory that again doesn't postulate high technology per se. Admittedly if our forgotten ancestors weren't building in stone or using metal then it's not directly relevant to our current study, but it's conceivable that they may have been able to use smaller crystal lenses to concentrate the sun's rays for other purposes.

CONCLUSION

In the course of this chapter we've seen that the physical evidence normally presented in support of claims of advanced technology in any former epoch crumbles under the slightest of scrutiny. It is important to reemphasise that the main yardstick that should be used when evaluating this evidence is that of *context*. If the Great Pyramid stood alone without an accompanying complex laid out for clearly ritual and funerary purposes, and without other pyramids inscribed with ritual and funerary texts, it might be reasonable to suggest it had some other function. But it doesn't. Similarly if all the ancient paintings, reliefs and artifacts interpreted as indicative of aerial, electrical and other advanced technology were backed up by proper physical evidence that such technology really existed, then we should perhaps be prepared to consider a literal rather than a ritual, stylistic or symbolic interpretation. But, again, they're not.

Of course it's not *entirely* impossible that our forgotten race *could* have been using advanced technology, which *might* even have been transferred to them by extraterrestrial visitors, for example, but all such evidence was destroyed in the catastrophe. Yet there's really nothing *substantive* that points us in that direction – apart perhaps from predominantly channelled messages usually relating to Atlantis and Lemuria, which, if they have any substance at all, may well relate to other planes, planets or even other versions of the Earth game, as discussed in the last chapter. So as long as that remains the case we should surely keep our conjectures about the forgotten race discussed in the ancient texts and traditions as grounded and realistic as possible. On that basis we do have some pointers to the sort of realistic, low-technology skills they *might* have possessed in addition to those in building and construction, tool and utensil making, agriculture and so on that any cultured, settled society requires – and to which we'll return in the final chapter. These might have included a fair knowledge of astronomy and navigation, for example. But even then we should be clear there's no definitive argument that, just because these skills are evident in the earliest civilisations of the current epoch, they *must* have been present beforehand too.

The corollary to this approach is, as always, a requirement for discernment. We need to be able to stand back from any evidence and assess it and its implications calmly, without diving in and resorting to massive and ill-founded leaps of faith and logic. Of course if we're to be realistic we can't escape the fact that, unfortunately, some such leaps made by alternative researchers may owe more to a desire to exploit the understandable yearning for mystery that dwells within most of us, rather than to pure ignorance and poor scholarship. One might have hoped that, whatever the cause, we've been bombarded with enough materialistically oriented pseudoarchaeology over the last century and a half to satiate the hungriest of sensationalist appetites. Sadly, though, it shows no signs of disappearing. If anything, the opposite is the case.[55]

Some modern alternative researchers have led the way in reining in the more outlandish claims and materialistic obsessions of their predecessors, and in focusing more on the importance of symbolism and on the more metaphysical preoccupations of our ancient ancestors; and it's worth reemphasising that for all this they're to be applauded. But there's also no escaping the fact that their attempts to redate a variety of ancient monuments, along with theories of no overnight development and common origins, suffer from glaring defects. I merely hope that the current work will help towards a concentration on what are arguably even more grounded scenarios – whose true *spiritual* message may one day be seen as far more exciting and relevant to us today than anything that has gone before.

Bearing that in mind, our search for some sort of physical grounding to back up what we learned from the texts and traditions in Part 1 must now start in earnest – with an examination of any potential geological evidence of a global catastrophe towards the end of the Palaeolithic.

12

GEOLOGY

In reviewing the geological evidence for a major catastrophe at the end of the Palaeolithic, we must first understand something of the general theory of ice ages. We will then need to review and also dismiss many of the alternative theories that have abounded in this area for decades, before considering certain more recent evidence that does stand up to close scrutiny. We can then turn to a review of possible textual echoes of such an event, before closing with a discussion of the most likely locales in which our forgotten race may have flourished.

ICE AGES

The idea that the Earth has been rocked by major catastrophes has been around for a long time. Christian scholars of the seventeenth and eighteenth centuries used primitive geological studies to support the biblical notion of a global flood not long after God created the world. But by the early part of the nineteenth century a more rational view of an Earth that had been repeatedly ravaged over a far more prolonged timeframe had begun to emerge. The leading exponent of this new 'catastrophist' school was the gifted French scientist Georges Cuvier, who reached his conclusions by studying the various geological strata that had been laid down in the environs of the Paris basin.

Yet by the mid-nineteenth century this view had in turn been challenged, with Charles Lyell at the forefront of the new 'uniformitarian' or 'gradualist' school. They proposed that many huge boulders found all over the world had been carried to their current locations not by a worldwide flood but by gradual glacial movement over prolonged periods, and the theory of ice ages was born.

We now know that here have been many ice ages during the Earth's history with the most recent, referred to as the Pleistocene epoch, thought to have started around 2.5m years ago.[1] Analysis of ocean-floor sediments and of ice cores has revealed that it was dominated by as many as 11 major cycles of glacial encroachment of the polar ice caps towards more temperate zones, followed by interglacial retreat. The extent of glaciation differed in each cycle, as it did on each continent in each cycle, but North America and the northern parts of Europe and Asia were most affected, being considerably closer to the North Pole than South America, Africa and Australasia are to its southern counterpart.

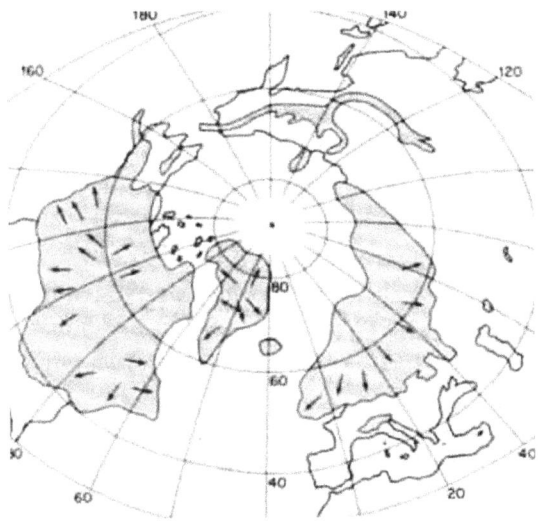

Figure 9: Maximum Glaciation in the Late Pleistocene [2]

For our purposes the most important phase of the Pleistocene is the 'last glacial period' that began around 110,000 years ago, reaching its height at the 'last glacial maximum' around 20,000 years ago. Figure 9 reveals that at this point glaciation reached down as far as the 50th parallel in most parts of Northern Europe and Western North America, and even further down to the 40th parallel on the latter's Eastern side – while sea levels were 100 metres or more lower than they are now.[3] Then a significant retreat took us into the current interglacial, known as the Holocene epoch, which began around 12,000 years ago.

So much for the universally agreed *effects*. By contrast geologists are far less united about the *causes* of ice ages and their fluctuations. Probably the most widely accepted theory is that of Milankovitch cycles, which combines the effects of various underlying cycles relating to Earth's orbit and axial tilt, but this is far from providing a complete explanation for the observed variations.[4] We also know from modern research into global warming that any models of worldwide climate have to consider huge numbers of variables that interact with each other in hugely complex ways, even before human factors come into play. Above all we know that the Earth's climate is in fact extremely sensitive, and easy to knock out of equilibrium.

QUESTIONABLE EVIDENCE OF DESTRUCTION

Gradualism remained dominant for more than a century, but challenges to it started to emerge in the mid-twentieth century. For some time the pioneers were left pretty much on the fringes, but in recent decades catastrophism has made such a dramatic recovery that the two theories now tend to coexist and combine. The turning point came in 1980 with the publication of a landmark paper by Walter and Luis Alvarez, proposing that the impact of a huge asteroid caused the mass extinction of the dinosaurs around 66m years ago, at the Cretaceous-Tertiary boundary.[5] When the massive Chicxulub crater was located in the Yucatan ten years later, measuring around 150 kilometres across and dated to the same timeframe, the theory rapidly gained acceptance – while the body that created it is estimated to have been anywhere from 11 to 81 kilometres in diameter.[6] Since then analysis has shown there to have been four major extinction events before this that typically wiped out anything from 60 to 75% of all species – although one eliminated a massive 96%.[7] None of these has been put down to extraterrestrial bodies, but rather to a variety of other factors.

All this means that in contemporary academic circles the work of leading catastrophists such as Richard Huggett and Trevor Palmer is now widely respected.[8] But some real controversy remains, and it surrounds the idea that a major, relatively recent catastrophe occurred at the end of the Pleistocene – and perhaps even brought it about.

MASS EXTINCTIONS

Although most animal species had managed to survive the Pleistocene relatively unscathed, somewhere between 13,000 and 11,000 years ago a significant number of North American species disappeared from the archaeological record.[9] These were predominantly large mammals such as mammoths, mastodons and native cats, and there's similar evidence of megafauna extinction in Northern Eurasia at much the same time. This much is not controversial, but again what's less clear is the cause – and the key factor that has a major bearing on that is the timeframe over which these extinctions occurred.

Those who insist they were spread over at least several thousand years are currently in the orthodox majority, and they offer three main explanations. First, relatively rapid climate and associated habitat changes that didn't suit these large mammals; second, the contemporaneous arrival of 'Clovis people' in the Americas, who hunted them to extinction; and third, the introduction of lethal diseases by these people and the domesticated animals they brought with them. Because on their own these explanations face problems in explaining the entirety of the evidence, a combination thereof is usually preferred.

Yet some catastrophists reference a body of physical evidence that, in their view, tells a very different story.

SIBERIAN MAMMOTHS

Perhaps the most celebrated is the large numbers of supposedly flash-frozen mammoths found in the permafrost of Northern Siberia in the eighteenth and nineteenth century. Some of these were supposed to have been in such a fine state of preservation that their meat was apparently eaten with no ill effects.

Cuvier was one of the first to write about these discoveries, pointing out not only that the Siberian climate must have been sufficiently temperate for such animals to live there *before* the end of the last ice age, but also that they no longer live there *despite* the fact that the global climate has generally become warmer. Yet they were really brought to the public's attention by probably the most celebrated leader of the resurgent catastrophist movement, Immanuel Velikovsky, in his 1955 work *Earth in Upheaval*. In this he gathers together a multitude of old and new evidence for the first time and, as far as the mammoths are concerned, suggests that some had surviving red-blood corpuscles that seemed to indicate death by drowning or suffocation, possibly by poisonous gas.[10]

The other major catastrophist to emerge at this time was Charles Hapgood, who we met in the last chapter and whose *Earth's Shifting Crust* was first published in 1958 and republished under the title *The Path of the Pole* in 1970. With respect to the mammoths he adds that as many as 20,000 pairs of tusks were exported from Siberia in the last few decades of the nineteenth century alone, and emphasises that both meat and ivory must be frozen swiftly and permanently in order to remain edible and workable respectively.[11] He further provides a table of radiocarbon dates on a selection of mammoth and other animal remains found predominantly in the US, which place a significant proportion of their deaths in the period from 13,000 to 9,000 years ago.

Velikovsky and Hapgood, although by training a psychoanalyst and a science historian respectively, both use geological sources for their evidence. But some of these were relatively old and unreliable even in their day, and further professional studies of same have been undertaken more recently with far better understanding of geological layers, and far more accurate dating technology. Unfortunately for many alternative researchers these tend to cast serious doubt on catastrophic interpretations. With respect to the Siberian mammoths, apart from questioning the assertion that they were suddenly flash-frozen, and the numbers of animals involved, modern research also indicates that the dates of the remains vary considerably – falling into two main periods from 45,000 to 30,000 and from 17,000 to 10,000 years ago.[12] This of course suggests their demise wasn't the result of a sudden, one-off event.

ALASKAN MUCK

Velikovsky and Hapgood both cite reports that twentieth-century gold mining in Alaska revealed a similar tale of sudden destruction of mammoths and other animals – their bones well preserved but thrown about in a catastrophic melee within a layer of muck deposits that in some places reached 45 metres in depth.[13] Many of the bones were reported to be relatively recent in that they weren't fossilised, and partial skeletons were apparently jumbled together, dismembered and disarticulated; nor were there any teeth marks or other signs of them having been the victims of predators. To cap it all the muck was reported to contain masses of twisted and splintered trees to bear witness to the ferocity of a catastrophe that affected a huge area.

Hapgood reproduces an extensive quote from the contemporary archaeologist Frank C Hibben of the University of New Mexico, who visited the sites himself. It is full of dramatic descriptions of 'earthshaking volcanic eruptions of catastrophic violence', 'toxic clouds of gas from volcanic upheavals' and vivid descriptions of the remains themselves:[14]

> Mammoth and bison alike were torn and twisted as though by a cosmic hand in Godly rage. In one place, we can find the foreleg and shoulder of a mammoth with portions of the flesh and the toenails and the hair still clinging to the blackened bones. Close by is the neck and skull of a bison with the vertebrae clinging together with tendons and ligaments and the chitinous covering of the horns intact. There is no mark of a knife or cutting instrument. The animals were simply torn apart and scattered over the landscape like things of straw and string, even though some of them weighed several tonnes. Mixed with the piles of bones are trees, also twisted and torn and piled in tangled groups; and the whole is covered with fine sifting muck, then frozen solid.

But, again, more modern studies cast doubt on catastrophic interpretations of this evidence.[15] Apparently they reveal not a jumbled, chaotic mass but rather a series of seven, well-defined geological layers dating back as far as 3m years ago. What is more the tree remains are limited to three specific layers only, and the dislocated state of the animal remains has been somewhat exaggerated. In particular it would appear that landslides and mudflows created by the melting of the permafrost have created a confused picture in places – something the original investigators failed to appreciate or to place in the clearly stratified broader context.

OTHER ANIMAL REMAINS

Velikovsky chronicles similar evidence of jumbled animal remains from other countries. First from various caves in Britain and France explored by geologist William Buckland in the early nineteenth century.[16] He continues by discussing various British, European, American and even Asian sites investigated in the late nineteenth century, where rock fissures and other crevices and pits were apparently filled with similar debris.[17] As usual, though, there are problems with this evidence. Buckland himself changed his mind about what he'd found in, for example, Kirkdale cave, deciding instead that it was used by hyenas who dragged in the carcasses of various other animals and devoured them; indeed by 1840 he'd completely forsaken catastrophism for the gradualist approach of glaciation.[18] Meanwhile much of the other evidence is questionable at best.[19]

Velikovsky's final body of evidence involves supposedly anomalous marine remains.[20] He describes how the relatively recent skeletons of whales and other large sea animals have been discovered north of Lake Ontario, in Michigan, in Vermont and near Montreal. There is little modern material available about these discoveries, but what there is indicates that dating is problematic.[21] Not only that but sperm whales are a well-known attraction in the fresh waters of Lake Michigan today, so perhaps this isn't the enigma that Velikovsky suggests.[22]

Overall then we can see that pretty much all of the material cited by Velikovsky and Hapgood contains substantial flaws, even though it continues to be unquestioningly reproduced by some alternative researchers. So is there any other evidence of a major catastrophe at the end of the Pleistocene?

SUPPOSED EXTRATERRESTRIAL BODIES

We have seen that one of the most obvious causes of major catastrophes in Earth's history is the impact of some sort of extraterrestrial body, typically a comet or asteroid. Velikovsky firmly believed in this idea before it was generally accepted;[23] and we now have plenty of evidence that bodies smaller than the ten-kilometre object that ended the dinosaurs' reign have regularly impacted with devastating consequences. For example, evidence suggests that bodies of between two and five kilometres in diameter impacted in the Southern Ocean southwest of Chile, and somewhere in Indochina, some 2m and 800,000 years ago respectively.[24]

What are the effects? Of course these depend heavily on the location and size of the impact. Broadly speaking if it occurs on land it causes general tectonic upheaval, activates volcanoes and has two, competing, knock-on effects: the mass emission of carbon dioxide from volcanoes tends to produce global warming via the greenhouse effect, counteracted by a blanket of dust and debris being thrown into the atmosphere that tends to blank out sunlight for considerable periods. By contrast an impact in the ocean causes massive tidal waves and, while the immediate consequences for the quality of the atmosphere are less, the knock-on effects of ocean warming and of both initial and longer-term sea water evaporation can be considerable. In addition there's a third option, which is the explosion of such a body in the air – that is, after it has entered the Earth's atmosphere but before it can hit land or sea – the shockwaves from which can still have devastating consequences.

If we now concentrate on the idea of an impact at the end of the Pleistocene, right back in the seventeenth century the astronomer Sir Edmund Halley proposed that such an agent may have been the cause of the biblical flood.[25] He was most notably followed in 1883 by Ignatius Donnelly, who followed a similar path in *Ragnarok: The Age of Fire and Gravel*. But arguably the first proper scholarly research into the possibility came in 1990 with the publication of astronomers Victor Clube and Bill Napier's *The Cosmic Winter* – in which they suggest that the modern orbits of the Comet Encke, the asteroid Oljato and the Taurid meteors derive from the disintegration of a giant comet. In particular they report on ice-core studies indicating that a significant quantity of dust was deposited in the last years of the Pleistocene, which has been found to have the same chemical content as that deposited in the Tunguska region of Russia by the impact of an extraterrestrial body in 1908. Napier has separately pointed out that even a 200-metre-diameter body would produce devastating tidal waves if it hit the ocean.[26] Nevertheless, they provide a date of 9500 years ago for this event, which as we saw in chapter 9 is a full two millennia *after* the building of the first stone settlements in the Neolithic – so the timing is all wrong for the global destruction of our forgotten race.

Clube and Napier are sometimes ridiculed for attempting to trace the memory of this supposed impact in the texts, art and architecture of our ancient civilisations – as we too will be doing shortly – but their research is generally accepted as scientific in nature. The same cannot be said, unfortunately, of Derek Allan and Bernard Delair's 1995 work *When the Earth Nearly Died*. They follow a similar line, although they suggest the catastrophe was caused by the close passage of a large extraterrestrial body – possibly even a runaway planet – at the earlier date of 11,500 years ago. Their linking of this to the Greek tradition of Phaethon is one thing; but their highly literal translation of the Mesopotamian *Epic of Creation* that we encountered several times in Part 1 is contextually inappropriate in the extreme – yet they use it to determine the supposed path of the extraterrestrial body in question.[27] Not only that but they appear to borrow significantly from Zecharia Sitchin's much earlier and equally misguided work on the subject, without even crediting him in their voluminous footnotes.[28]

An even more serious criticism of Allan and Delair is their suggestion that all supposed evidence of glaciation – boulder deposition, underlying rock striation and so forth – was in fact caused by cascades of water from the massive flooding induced by this one catastrophic event.[29] This denial of ice age theory is simply not tenable, and is compounded by their following Velikovsky and Hapgood in questioning the age of various mountain ranges – another fringe theory that receives little or no orthodox support. So despite the highly detailed and well-referenced appearance of their work, it remains highly questionable at best.

THE CAROLINA BAYS

Probably the best-known physical evidence put forward in support of extraterrestrial disruption at the end of the Pleistocene are the Carolina Bays. These were described by Velikovsky as 'oval craters thickly scattered over the Carolina coast of the United States and more sparsely over the entire Atlantic coastal plain from Southern New Jersey to Northeast Florida'.[30] In fact they had been discovered in aerial photographs taken over South Carolina in the 1930s, but they're now thought to number as many as half a million, the largest being Lake Waccamaw covering around 35 square kilometres. They also display some remarkably consistent features in that most are to some extent oval, have their longest axes more or less oriented northwest to southeast, and have an elevated rim of earth at the southeastern end.[31]

In Velikovsky's day it was commonly accepted that some form of extraterrestrial agent must have been involved in their creation. The first major study by Frank Melton and William Shriever in 1932 concentrated on the evidence in Carolina itself, and concluded that the bays had resulted from the impact of a meteorite shower anywhere from 50,000 to a million years ago.[32] Then in 1952 William Prouty proposed not only a much more recent date of about 11,000 years ago, but also the idea that they were created by shock waves resulting from the aerial explosion of an extraterrestrial body before it hit the ground.[33] At about the same time evidence began to emerge of supposedly similar elliptical bays as far afield as Alaska and the Yukon down to the Beni region of Northeast Bolivia.[34]

As always the key issue is the age of these bays. In the 1950s a team from Duke University found a layer of bluish clay that appeared to have been deposited in some of the Carolina examples shortly after their formation, and the sediments immediately above and below this yielded radiocarbon dates in the range of 11–10,000 years ago.[35] However more recent surveys provide a wide range of dates stretching back tens of thousands of years, suggesting they weren't formed simultaneously by one major catastrophic event.[36] The supposed similarity of other formations away from the Eastern Seaboard is also called into question, as is the supposedly uniform orientation. Indeed it's now commonly accepted amongst geologists that all these formations were created by purely terrestrial processes, although there remains plenty of debate about what these might have been – with wind and subsurface water erosion the preferred candidates.

PURPORTED POLE SHIFTS AND REVERSALS

Several other potential causes of a catastrophe at the end of the Pleistocene have received widespread attention in the alternative world in recent decades. The first is the idea that the *physical* poles marking the axis around which the Earth rotates might have changed their position; the second concerns their *magnetic* counterparts doing likewise, and even reversing. These are quite different concepts, and we'll look at each in turn.

AXIS SHIFTS VERSUS CRUSTAL DISPLACEMENT

If we commence with physical pole shifts, it's the offset of the plane of the equator from that of our ecliptic orbit around the sun – currently about 23.5 degrees – that not only creates the seasons but also, if it changed, would alter the configuration of the tropical, temperate and arctic zones of the Earth. Cuvier certainly supported the concept of pole shifts, and felt that one must have occurred suddenly in a relatively recent epoch in order to account for the apparently flash-frozen mammoths of Siberia and Alaska.[37] Then both Velikovsky and Hapgood argued that an explanation was required for the inconsistent glaciation across the globe, whereby certain northerly regions remained free of ice even at the height of the Pleistocene.[38] They also suggested there are various enigmas in arctic and even Antarctic regions – for example, fossilised trees, forests and coral reefs – indicating that these may once have been temperate zones.[39] These ideas were picked up in the mid-1990s by alternative researchers such as Rand Flem-Ath and Graham Hancock.[40]

There are two main mechanisms by which a pole shift could occur. On the one hand the entire Earth could shift its position relative to the sun, as part of a genuine axis shift. Alternatively the hard outer crust or lithosphere could move relative to the semi-molten mantle underneath it, as part of a crustal displacement. Both would have the same effect in terms of climate change at a particular location on the landmass, but with the latter the angle of the ecliptic would remain unchanged. Needless to say, though, both mechanisms require huge amounts of force.

Hapgood favoured crustal displacement, arguing it would be caused by an asymmetrical build-up of ice at the poles. However he admits that any significant shifting of the crust would take several thousand years at least, because it would encounter huge resistance in trying to move over the mantle – meaning the theory cannot be used to support the idea of a late-Pleistocene catastrophe. By contrast Velikovsky preferred the idea of a genuine axis shift, arguing that the only catalyst capable of causing it would again be the impact of an extraterrestrial body.[41] More recently mathematician Flavio Barbiero has backed up this view with detailed research that 'analyses the behaviour of a gyroscope subjected to a disturbing force, and shows that the torque generated by the impact of a relatively small asteroid is capable of causing almost instantaneous changes of the axis of rotation and therefore instantaneous shifts of the poles in any direction and of any amplitude'.[42]

However there's no credible, physical evidence of either a crustal displacement or an axis shift having occurred at the end of the Pleistocene or at any other time.[43] Not only that but the supposedly anomalous climatic evidence that triggered these theories has more recently been proven to be perfectly explainable via existing, non-catastrophic mechanisms. For example, the supposed fossil enigmas in arctic regions date to remote epochs when there was almost no glaciation at all, while inconsistent glaciation is perfectly well understood.[44]

MAGNETIC POLE REVERSALS

Particles of iron within molten rock align themselves with the magnetic poles as they solidify, thereby keeping a permanent record of the position of the latter at the time.[45] But in the early twentieth century geologists were stunned to find that some rocks were magnetised in a completely different direction to what they expected, and in time further research revealed that the magnetic poles have completely switched round tens of thousands of times in Earth's history. Contrary to many alternative reports such geomagnetic reversals are almost certainly *not* cyclic but entirely sporadic – because at some times in Earth's history the field has remained unchanged for tens of millions of years, while on the other hand two reversals have been known to occur within as little as 50,000 years of each other.

It is also highly unlikely that such reversals are indicative of crustal displacement or axis shifts in the past, although this is what Hapgood suggests. The most commonly held theory about the source of Earth's magnetic field is that convection currents in the molten core act as a dynamo, so that changes in the field would be the result of changes in that flow. What would be the effects of a complete reversal if one were to occur? We cannot say because no one has lived through such an event in recorded history, the last one having occurred around 780,000 years ago. But as far as we know it didn't cause mass extinctions of our distant ancestors or any other species, and there's certainly no time correlation between reversals and mass extinctions. There would, however, be a significant impact on animal species that use the Earth's magnetic field to navigate, such as migrating birds. Related to all this is the question of how rapidly such reversals occur and, although it's clear that the rate of change of the field's strength and direction can vary considerably, it seems highly unlikely they can happen literally 'overnight'.

Popular reports also suggest that we're due for another reversal shortly, but again there's no solid evidence for this. The field has been weakening over the last century and a half and recently this has accelerated, as has the change in direction of polarity. But experts are united that these changes are well within historical parameters, and that fluctuations over time are so unpredictable that to attempt to extrapolate them – especially in any sort of linear fashion – is entirely inappropriate.

All this appears to leave us with precious little reliable evidence for a catastrophe at the end of the Pleistocene. But, fortunately, this is by no means the end of the story.

THE YOUNGER DRYAS IMPACT

The so-called 'Younger Dryas Stadial' was first described around the turn of the twentieth century.[46] Generally the global climate had been entering a warmer interglacial phase after the last glacial maximum around 20,000 years ago – yet from around 12,900 years ago there's evidence of a rapid reversal that lasted around 1200 years. It mainly affected Northern Europe and North America, but more southerly climes may not have been completely exempt. As to what caused it, the most popular theory is that a sudden influx of fresh water into the North Atlantic from a glacial melt or dam-burst in Northeast America caused a change in the thermal currents circulating warm water from the tropics. But there is a great deal of debate about whether this on its own could have caused all the effects that have been noted.

So the key question for our current investigation is whether there was a sudden, catastrophic event at the 'Younger Dryas Boundary', and in particular whether some other event triggered it? Perhaps, because intriguingly the onset of the change is thought to have been extremely swift, taking less than a decade. It also quite clearly coincides with the demise of the Clovis culture in North America, and with the extinction of megafauna discussed earlier.[47] What is more, after this point virtually nothing appears in the archaeological record for the continent until the Folsom and other similar cultures emerge around 11,000 years ago, leaving a gap of as much as two millennia in which it may have seen little human activity.[48]

The most credible hypothesis for this being a sudden, catastrophic event is, again, that it was caused by some sort of extraterrestrial body. The first researcher to promote the idea of a 'Younger Dryas Impact' was Richard Firestone, a nuclear physicist from the Lawrence Berkeley National Laboratory, and the primary author of the 2006 work *The Cycle of Cosmic Catastrophes*. He first became involved in this research via Bill Topping, an archaeologist from Michigan who had stumbled upon an unusual feature of the chert flints from various Clovis sites: many of them had multiple microscopic particles of iron embedded beneath the surface, although always on one side only.[49] Moreover experiments proved they must have been travelling in excess of 1600 kph – in other words probably caused by multiple mid-air explosions as a comet disintegrated after entering our atmosphere. What is more Topping found that the depth of the tiny craters decreased progressively the further a site was from the Great Lakes, suggesting this was the epicentre of the event.

Firestone then visited various Clovis sites himself, collecting and analyzing various samples.[50] He found:

- The same tiny craters with buried magnetic grains, not just in chert but also in mammoth tusks from Siberia as well as Alaska – suggesting the event had impacted the whole northern hemisphere. Again these would only ever be on one side.

- Abundant tiny magnetic grains and spherules just at the end of the Clovis-layer sediment at the Younger Dryas Boundary, but not above or below.

- Markedly increased levels of radioactivity in sediment at the same Boundary, and in chert and tusk samples.

- A widespread 'black mat' of dense, dark, organic material right on the Boundary, thought to have been formed by the decomposition of algae. No Clovis or megafauna remains are ever found above it, only below. This mat corresponds to a similar layer called the 'Usselo Horizon' found at a number of sites in Northern Europe.

- Tiny pieces of molten black glass with holes in it like 'foam' that were not of the normal silica glass composition.[51]

In addition Firestone devotes a chapter to drumlins.[52] These are whale-shaped hills whose formation is known to be associated with glaciation because they're commonly found at the edges of glacial spread in North America and Northern Europe. Although the exact mechanism by which they were formed is unclear, the most widely accepted theory involves a *catastrophic* flooding release of highly pressurised water flowing underneath the glacial ice'.[53] He contends that drumlins have been generally carbon-dated to the end of the Pleistocene, and he also found a high concentration of magnetic particles in the original top level of several examples in Alberta.

Firestone also attempts a thorough reappraisal of the Carolina Bays, noting the following:[54]

- The pure white sand on many of their rims isn't found elsewhere in the region, and is indicative of superheating.

- Ten of them contain concentrations of magnetic particles in their rims.

- The wind and subsurface water theories can't explain why so many bays actually overlap each other, and why wind and water have conspicuously failed to create any more of them in the last 10,000 years.

- The often non-sequential dating of bay layers is due to the blasting of sediment into the air and its jumbled re-deposition, rendering most dating attempts flawed.

- There is evidence of more eroded bays across Nebraska, Kansas and Texas.

- The bays generally show a marked similarity to the shallow craters that litter the surface of the moon and of Mars.

- There are not more of them on Earth purely because we have more wind and surface water action to *erase* them, while those that survive must be relatively recent.

- They are shallow and elliptical, just as on the other planets, because they were created by the low-angle impacts of secondary debris.

- They have several groups of alignments, pointing to several main impact sites. One of these is Lake Michigan, which is itself a main crater because there's no sediment within it dating to before the onset of the Younger Dryas.

- Even main craters such as Lake Michigan are relatively shallow because they were caused by comet rather than asteroid explosions in mid-air, comets being much less dense.

- All of this represents a significant body of argument for a sudden, extraterrestrial cause of widespread bay formation.

Firestone places all this considerable quantity of evidence within the broader context of an original supernova explosion 41.000 years ago. But whether or not that's appropriate, and whether or not his arguments with regard to the Carolina Bays, drumlins and so on stand up, let us concentrate on his base evidence for a Younger Dryas Impact. The first thing to note is that he and his co-authors aren't an isolated group with no support – because in 2007 a total of twenty-four other specialists joined with them to publish an academic paper on the topic in the *Proceedings of the National Academy of Sciences*.[55] Moreover since then they and others who support the idea have continued to collate and publish new evidence – particularly relating to platinum deposits found at the Younger Dryas Boundary in other parts of the world – that suggests it may have had a widespread impact.[56]

It is only fair to report that the impact hypothesis isn't without its critics, some of whom have reported that they weren't able to replicate the team's findings at Clovis sites, while others go as far as to suggest that its main proponents are on something akin to an evangelical mission.[57] However to me at least these criticisms seem selective, and to ignore not only the wide range of different types of evidence now collated, but also the fact that proper, peer-reviewed, academic journals continue to publish papers supportive of the topic. So on balance it does look as if we may have some reasonably credible evidence of a global, late-Pleistocene catastrophe that could easily have wiped out our forgotten race – along with any evidence that they existed.

CORONAL MASS EJECTIONS

We discussed the magnetic poles earlier, but a rather different issue is the fact that Earth's magnetic field interacts with that of the sun and other planets, all of which determines the extent and shape of the magnetosphere.[58] Indeed it's our magnetic field, combined with our atmosphere, that normally protects us from the winds or flares emanating from the sun. However related research into 'sun spots' – areas of intense magnetic activity on its surface – suggests these operate on an 11-year cycle, and that at the high points 'coronal mass ejections' produce geomagnetic storms that can cause serious disruption on Earth.[59] Most recently, the electrical supply to a vast area of Quebec was knocked out in 1989. These cycles have presumably been going on for a very long time – so is there any evidence that they've ever produced ejections major enough to trigger a worldwide catastrophe?

Like me, leading alternative authors Andrew Collins and Graham Hancock both go along with the Younger Dryas Impact hypothesis in their more recent books.[60] By contrast, while he doesn't reject it completely, Robert Schoch goes into some detail about the criticisms thereof in his 2012 work *Forgotten Civilisation*.[61] What he's far more interested in is what caused the relatively abrupt *end* of the Younger Dryas around 11,700 years ago. He argues that it derived from a series of coronal mass ejections that 'unleashed electrical/plasma discharges upon Earth and triggered volcanic activity, earthquakes, fires and massive floods as glaciers melted and lightning strikes released torrential rains from the oceans'.[62] In doing so he is following in the footsteps of the somewhat alternative physicist and cosmologist Paul LaViolette – who he quotes from and properly acknowledges – who first wrote about this possibility in a 2011 paper.[63]

This theory has considerably less academic support than its Younger Dryas Impact counterpart. Yet clearly the two aren't mutually exclusive because they're attempting to explain events at different times and either – or both – could have acted as the agent that wiped out our forgotten race.

MEMORIES

So much for the physical evidence that there was a major catastrophe towards the end of the Pleistocene. But did memories of these terrible events manage to survive orally for thousands of years before being incorporated, sometimes in somewhat distorted form, into the written traditions of the earliest civilisations of the modern epoch? We have already mentioned the abundance of generalised flood traditions from around the world, but some of them appear to contain particularly detailed descriptions of just the sort of mayhem that would follow in the wake of an impact event.

The various world age traditions we discussed in chapter 5 are full of them. If we commence with the Amerindians, we saw how during one destruction in the Hopi version 'the world teetered off balance', 'mountains plunged into seas', 'seas and lakes sloshed over the land' and 'the world froze into solid ice'; while during another 'waves higher than mountains rolled in upon the land', and 'continents broke asunder and sank beneath the seas'. Similarly the Aztecs recorded that the age before ours ended when 'the skies came falling down', and 'all the mountains disappeared'. This is all in addition to the more general descriptions of multiple destructions by flood, fire, volcano, hurricane and earthquake preserved therein. These are backed up by a significant number of detailed descriptions of apparently catastrophic events preserved by indigenous cultures around the world, including those from Africa, Australasia and Oceania too.[64] Meanwhile in the Far East the Taoist *Essays from Huai Nan Tzu* record that as a result of the decadent age 'the four seasons failed', 'thunder-bolts wrought havoc and hailstones fell with violence', while 'noxious miasma and untimely hoarfrosts fell unceasingly'.[65] However, given that these all derive from world age traditions, one could argue that the context is questionable.

By contrast the Mesopotamian texts have nothing to do with world ages, yet they include numerous references to fierce battles conducted by the gods, especially those associated with atmospheric phenomena. They include Ninurta – who is not only the god of war but also of floods, and is further identified with the 'thunderbird' known as Imdugud – and Ishkur the storm god.[66] Furthermore they have weapons with similar associations, such as the *abubu* or flood weapon, and the *kasusu* or wind weapon.[67]

One of the finest examples is the Sumerian *Ninurta Myth* that dates to the beginning of the second millennium BCE and is a composite of three original parts. In the first Ninurta is accompanied by his trusty friend and weapon Sharur, described as 'the one who lays low multitudes' and 'the flood storm of battle', while engaging in a fierce battle with the enigmatic Azag, an object or creature whose main weapon is its 'dreadful aura'. The translator, Thorkild Jacobsen, suggests that Azag is a tree of some sort on the basis that it's described as being the product of 'heaven copulating with verdant earth' – but he would never even have considered the possibility that it might represent an impacting extraterrestrial body. In fact we then find Jacobsen admitting that Azag's description at the end of part one enigmatically changes to *zalag* stone, no translation of which is even attempted.[68] Meanwhile Ninurta's march into battle is described thus:[69]

> The evil wind and the south storm were tethered to him, the flood storm strode at their flanks, and before the warrior went a huge irresistible tempest, it was tearing up the dust, depositing it again, evening out hill and dale, filling in hollows; live coals it rained down, fire burned, flames scorched, tall trees it toppled from their roots, denuding the forests. Earth wrung her hands against the heart, emitting cries of pain... the desert was burnt off as if denuded by locusts, the wave rising in its path was shattering the mountains.

When Ninurta subsequently attacks Azag 'the sun marched no longer, it had turned into a moon... the day was made black like pitch'.[70] Then when Azag retaliates:[71]

> It screamed wrathfully, like a formidable serpent it hissed from among its people, it wiped up the waters in the highland, swept away the tamarisks, it gashed the earth's body, made painful wounds, gave the canebrake over to fire, and bathed the sky in blood, the interior it knocked over, scattered its people, and till today black cinders are in the fields.

Finally, once the battle is over, we're given the following description of the aftermath:[72]

In those days the waters of the ground coming from below did not flow out over the fields. As ice long accumulating they rose in the mountains on the far side... in dire famine nothing was produced.

If any literal rather than symbolic interpretation of this text is appropriate then it's certainly possible to argue that it describes a catastrophe of some sort – which is unlikely to have been merely local, given that Mesopotamia itself hasn't been icebound for many millions of years.[73] What is more, to return briefly to world age traditions, the admittedly somewhat unreliable Greek versions do in general follow the Mesopotamian themes of violent gods associated with severe atmospheric phenomena. For example, in Plato's *Timaeus* Phaethon is described as the child of the sun who 'harnessed his father's chariot but was unable to guide it along his father's course', as a result of which there was 'a widespread destruction by fire of things on the Earth'. Similarly in his relatively short *Theogony* Hesiod's descriptions of Zeus' wars with the giant Titans and with Thyphoeus – the forerunner for Phaethon – are highly comparable to those of Ninurta.[74]

Certain traditions from the Near East even appear to suggest some form of axis shift – albeit that this phenomenon hasn't been associated with, for example, the Younger Dryas Impact. For example, after one brief report of the flood in *The Book of Enoch*, God repents and, swearing that he'll never act in the same way again, says he'll 'place a sign in the heavens' as a token of his covenant.[75] Another passage contains a most intriguing description of how Noah saw that 'the Earth became inclined, and that destruction approached', of how 'the Earth laboured, and was violently shaken', and of how God reports that 'respecting the moons have they [humankind] enquired, and they've known that the Earth will perish'.[76] Nor is this all, as these even more enigmatic passages show: 'In the days of sinners the years shall be shortened... the rain shall be restrained, and heaven shall stand still... the moon shall change its laws, and not be seen at its proper period... many chiefs among the stars of authority shall err, perverting their ways and works.'[77] Similarly in the relatively late Mesopotamian text *Erra and Ishum* the god Marduk, usurping the role originally played by Enlil, recalls sending the flood against humankind:[78] 'A long time ago, when I was angry and rose up from my dwelling and arranged for the flood... the control of heaven and earth was undone. The very heavens I made to tremble, the positions of the stars of heaven changed, and I did not return them to their places.' Is there anything in these traditions that should be taken literally, or are we merely dealing with the general mythical theme of order being overturned by chaos?

Of course we must be ever vigilant for the symbolism in these accounts generally, particularly those describing battles involving gods and their weapons. Nevertheless it seems reasonable to suggest that the significant quantity of reports of catastrophe from all around the world just *may* represent genuine memories of a terrible worldwide destruction, whose survivors were keen to preserve the knowledge of what had happened.

CONCLUSION

Despite the fact that much of the older evidence for a major catastrophe at the end of the Pleistocene has now been comprehensibly rebutted, more recent research arguably presents a renewed case.

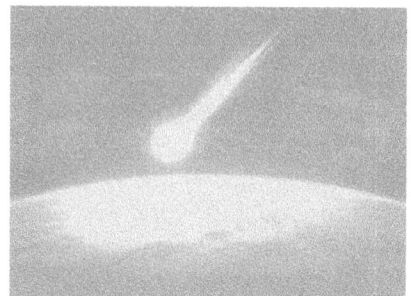

13

THE REAL
ATLANTIS

So far I have deliberately avoided drawing any conclusions about where, when and how our forgotten race lived. The time has come to rectify that omission now all the evidence – textual, archaeological and geological – has been reviewed. We will then close by examining the ways in which their fate may have implications for us in the modern world.

LIKELY LOCALES

We have already seen that our modern human ancestors had moved out of Africa and across Asia and on towards Australia probably around 50,000 to 40,000 years ago at the latest. So our forgotten race would clearly have had a great deal of freedom to travel to any climate and terrain that suited them across a wide geographic area.

So what was the climate like during the late Pleistocene, in particular from around 50,000 years ago? Global temperatures were anything from five to ten degrees Celsius colder at different times, so it would be obvious for them to focus on the equatorial zone stretching as far as the tropics of Cancer and Capricorn – that is, the 23rd parallels north and south respectively of the equator. In fact even the zones just outside this might have been perfectly habitable because, as we saw in Figure 9, even at the *height* of the Pleistocene the ice sheet only reached down to the 50th parallel in Northern Europe and far less in Northern Asia. But generally it's probably sensible to limit our search to the zone between the two tropic lines as shown in Figure 10.

I am also going to factor in the fundamental assumption that our forgotten race were cultured enough to be trading goods over wide areas – and the best way for them to carry heavy and bulky goods would have been by boat rather than dragging them overland. In other words, as I've already briefly suggested a number of times in earlier chapters, they would have chosen to live in *coastal* settlements.

Helpfully, this immediately imposes logistical limitations on their whereabouts. The tropical coastlines of the Americas are extensive, including those of much of Mexico, Columbia, Venezuela, Peru and Brazil, not to mention the islands of the Greater and Lesser Antilles. The same is true of the West African coast from Senegal down to Angola. However, even if our forgotten race were expert sailors, these locations would have been an extremely long voyage away from each other and from anywhere else. By contrast, anywhere on a huge stretch of equatorial coastline from Northern Mozambique up across Arabia and India and on into Southeast Asia and Indonesia could easily have been traversed just by hugging it and keeping land in sight.

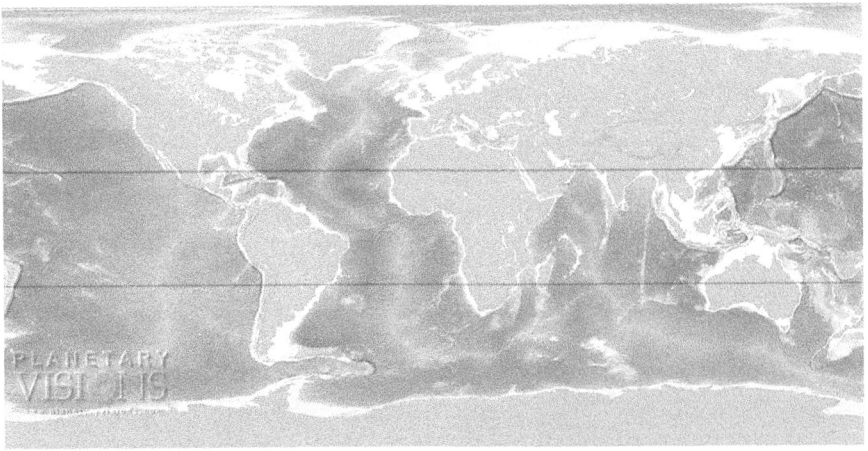

Figure 10: The Continents in the Late Pleistocene [1]

If we now turn to sea levels, around 50,000 years ago they were 75 metres lower, while during the last glacial maximum around 20,000 years ago they were a full 120 metres lower.[2] So, except in those areas where there's little in the way of continental shelf, *all* coastlines have been pushed inwards to a greater or lesser extent. Not only that but if we again look at Figure 10, in which the white areas are less than 200 metres under water, we can see that in the tropical zone the greatest area of now-sunken landmass that was above water during the late Pleistocene is in Southeast Asia. Closer inspection of this area in Figure 11 shows that the bulk of the islands that now make up Indonesia were connected to each other and to the main Asian continent, forming a landmass extension known as the Sunda Shelf or 'Sundaland'.[3] Similarly the Sahul Shelf connected Australia and New Guinea.

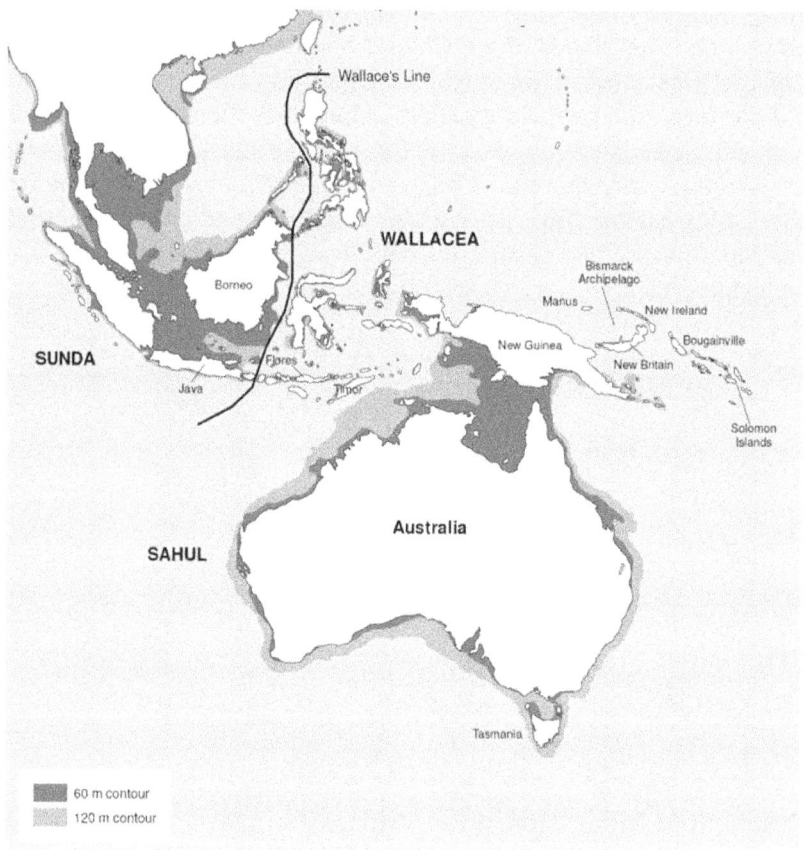

Figure 11: The Sunda and Sahul Shelves

But for us to pinpoint our forgotten race still further we need to appreciate that climate can vary considerably even at any given latitude. For example, if we again refer back to Figure 9 we can see that some parts of Northeast Asia and Alaska were never glaciated even at the last maximum, because weather patterns in these areas remained particularly dry so snow couldn't fall. Similarly the climate and vegetation in different parts of the tropical zone varied considerably during the late Pleistocene, as today. Some areas were mainly desert, others tropical rainforest, others still tropical grassland – which is what we're most interested in because it's where weather patterns, climate and so on would have been most conducive to the cultivation of crops.

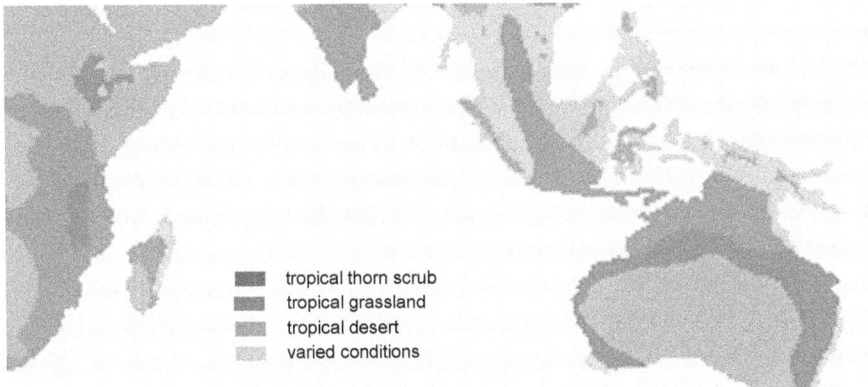

tropical thorn scrub
tropical grassland
tropical desert
varied conditions

Figure 12: Vegetation at the Last Glacial Maximum

Figure 12 shows the vegetation at the last glacial maximum in the coastal regions previously defined as of most interest.[4] The darkest areas represent tropical thorn scrub, but the next darkest are those representing grassland. We can see that these conditions persisted in south and central East Africa, but as we head north along the coast we reach a considerable area of tropical desert – represented by the medium grey shading – that continues all along the Northeast African and Arabian coastline until we reach India. Here we return to grassland across the entire country, conditions also found in central Southeast Asia and Northern Australasia. Meanwhile the lightest shade of grey that surrounds much of this represents a variety of other conditions and, of course, all these conditions would have varied at other times during the late Pleistocene. However, generally speaking, if we're looking for locations conducive to both settled agriculture and trading by sea over reasonable distances, then the now submerged coastal areas of Southern Asia, and possibly Northern Australasia too, are arguably the strongest contenders.

At this point I'd like to reference the work of three other researchers.

The first is British geneticist Stephen Oppenheimer and his 1999 work *Eden in the East*. He uses oceanography, archaeology, linguistics, genetics and what he quaintly refers to as 'folklore' to propose that the world's most ancient known civilisations all originated from a highly cultured population living in Southeast Asia in the late Pleistocene – who were forced to disperse when their homeland was submerged as sea levels rose. The second is the nuclear physicist, climatologist and geologist Arysio Santos, who also focuses on what is now Indonesia in his 2005 work *Atlantis: The Lost Continent Finally Found*. The third is Frank Joseph, who we met in chapter 11, who in his 2013 work *Before Atlantis* 'traces the genesis of modern human civilisation to Indonesia and the Central Pacific 75,000 years ago'. All three of these books are not without their potential problems.[5] But it's nevertheless interesting that all four of us have independently arrived at the same conclusion about the broad whereabouts of any forgotten race.[6]

There is one piece of potential evidence that *could* provide a massive boost to this theory. In the early twentieth century, Dutch colonists became the first Westerners to visit the magnificent site of Gunung Padang on Sumatra, where huge ancient megaliths constructed from volcanic rock are spread across a wide area of man-made terraces.[7] But geophysicist Danny Hilman Natawidjaja had a hunch there was more to the site than met the eye, and in 2012 led a team who used ground-penetrating radar, X-ray tomography, 3D imaging and core drilling alongside more conventional excavation techniques to investigate it further. Sensationally they arrived at the conclusion that underneath the surface lay a massive, irregularly shaped but man-made pyramid built in three stages – commencing before 9000 and possibly as much as 20,000 years ago. The Indonesian president at the time was persuaded by the prospect of his country proving to be the new cradle of civilization and provided funding. However more recent administrations seem to have withdrawn support, not least after 34 Indonesian geologists and archaeologists published a report criticising the methods employed by Natawidjaja's team.[8] The main objection seems to have centred on disagreement about whether supposed cement found on the megaliths is man-made and can therefore be used to date their erection. Updates seem to be thin on the ground, but despite this criticism the team made a presentation to the American Geophysical Union in 2018, which was then reported uncritically in *Scientific American*.[9]

Perhaps most interesting for our purposes, though, was the supposed criticism that came from an archaeologist who wished to remain anonymous – given the political support for the project at the time: 'In the [nearby] Pawon cave we found some human bones and tools made of bones dating to about 9500 years ago... So how could people from 20,000 years ago have the technology to build a pyramid?' He, of course, had no inkling that a forgotten, highly cultured race may have thrived in exactly this area at this time, before being wiped out.

A PLAUSIBLE HYPOTHESIS

Most academics would argue with some justification that missing evidence is no evidence at all, and it's certainly true that as yet no definitive evidence of an Upper Palaeolithic culture of the level of advancement I'm proposing has been uncovered. At least not if we're searching for the sort of large, permanent, stone settlements that we find at the start of the Neolithic from around 11,600 years ago.

But the wealth of textual evidence we've collated in Part 1, *and* the incompleteness of the archaeological record, *and* the fact that dates for cultural firsts are continuously being pushed back – sometimes by a long way – surely gives us a certain degree of licence to make some educated guesses about our forgotten race. Indeed to indulge in a little conjecture about the sorts of lives they might have been leading, and the materials they might have been using. Is it at all feasible they could have been as cultured and widespread as I'm suggesting, yet no significant evidence of their existence has yet been unearthed?

The first issue is that, because of our modern way of living – and in fact the way humans have lived since the Iron Age – we tend to assume that any advanced culture must have used metal and pottery for tools, weapons and utensils, and probably stone for building and sophisticated artwork. Of course all these tend to survive better in the archaeological record too. But are they really *necessary* to achieve a high level of culture?

Starting with metal, what would be technologically possible for a society that *didn't* use it? In fact, if they were sophisticated in their use of flint and bone blades combined with wood for handles, almost anything would be possible – certainly in agricultural terms, and probably in construction terms too. We have already seen, for example, that multiple flint blades were being sunk into probably wooden handles to make sickles for harvesting in the Levant well before the start of the Neolithic in Europe. Moreover, if we forget weapons and concentrate on tools, modern flint-knappers are clearly capable of making not only knives and chisels but also saws and a whole variety of other tools.[10] If they were constructing buildings from mud-bricks or wood, these tools would be more than enough to build sophisticated settlements. Similarly when we come to constructing ocean-going craft for trade, the use of wood and other biodegradable materials surely provides a sufficient level of sophistication? Moreover as with buildings, dowels and other strong joints reinforced with natural resins and glues can be used instead of nails or screws. As for the absence of pottery, again if a culture was experienced in its use of wood it could turn bowls and other items of domestic furniture on a bow-lathe, while utensils could easily be fashioned from wood or even bone, while leather sacks and other materials could be employed for larger scale food and drink storage.

What about the issue of not building in stone: would our forgotten race have been happy to construct their settlements using more perishable materials? Why not? Some countries in Europe, for example, use wooden buildings extensively, but that doesn't make for a society that is any less culturally advanced. An absence of stone might tend to suggest they were less concerned about the risk of attack, yet in the golden age this would have made perfect sense. Meanwhile there's no reason why their subsequent debasement should necessarily have involved warfare, especially if populations were sufficiently widely dispersed, and food production methods efficient enough, that there was no need to compete for resources. Of course it *could* be argued that such an advanced culture would want to make bold statements in stone about their spiritual beliefs or political rulers, as our Neolithic ancestors clearly did with their huge, carved megaliths, and as civilisations have done for millennia with sculptures of their gods, leaders and so on. But what if our golden race was sufficiently spiritually aware and non-egotistical that they really didn't feel the need to make such statements?

Turning to the issue of preservation, of course conditions would have to be incredibly favourable for any trace of wood or other perishable materials to survive in the archaeological record for more than a few thousand years at most, let alone for potentially many times that. To reinforce the point most archaeologists would accept that wooden shafts must have been used for spears for tens of thousands of years, yet we never find them. So the only evidence of even highly cultured activity under such assumptions would still tend to be flint or bone blades and other implements. The only sizeable stone objects we might expect to find might be those used for grinding grain, but even these could have been fashioned from hard wood weighted down with natural stones. The advantages would include them being easier to make to size, easier to attach handles or other apparatus to for motive power, and easier to transport. Of course I'm assuming in all this that our forgotten race had the appropriate stocks of wood but, if they were as advanced as I'm suggesting, they'd either have deliberately settled where they had all the raw materials they needed within easy reach, or they'd have imported what they needed by sea. Remember also that this scenario doesn't have massive worldwide populations all competing for scarce resources, but developing pockets of advanced culture in specific advantageous locations.

To make matters worse in terms of detection of evidence, the selection of archaeological sites is horribly, even though quite understandably, skewed. Permanent stone-built sites to some extent identify themselves unless they're buried under sand, earth, forest or jungle. Caves are an obvious place to excavate, but they were either home to genuinely primitive cultures, or they're only going to provide a glimpse of the level of culture of people who used them for shelter during winters or serious climatic changes – or for ritual purposes, and therefore not as their primary dwelling. In the modern world new construction sites are of course a major source of archaeological finds, as with the dams in Anatolia that also ultimately submerged the evidence – but these sites clearly aren't chosen for their archaeological potential.

The other issue is that in the past artifacts were often discovered by amateurs – for example, labourers engaged in construction, mining or agricultural work. Yet in the modern era well boring, mining, quarrying, foundation digging and ploughing tends to be performed using high technology, providing far less chance for a human operator to detect artifacts. So the possibility of fortuitous and random discoveries is decreasing. A counterbalance to this is the increasing amateur use of metal detectors in the West at least, but if our forgotten race wasn't using this material it's irrelevant. Another is the increasing sophistication of technology such as ground-penetrating radar, but sites still need to be identified before this can be used.

So even *if* archaeologists were looking for evidence of a truly advanced Upper Palaeolithic culture somewhere in the equatorial zone that, despite having sizeable permanent settlements, didn't use metal or pottery or erect stone buildings – which, of course, they're *not* – arguably it would still be like looking for a needle in a haystack. Worse still what if, as suggested earlier, most of our culturally advanced ancestors lived along the Southern Asia coastline so they could travel and trade easily – at a time when sea levels were much lower? Worse even than that, what if these now underwater areas were also massively damaged by huge tsunamis, or submerged under a hail of volcanic debris, or ripped apart by ferocious hurricanes? The odds of finding anything worthwhile soon tend towards zero under this weight of adverse circumstances – which are, nevertheless, not only realistic but, arguably, the most likely to have pertained.

If Richard Firestone and his colleagues are right the catastrophe that wiped out our forgotten race most likely involved some sort of interaction with one or more comets some time around 12,900 years ago. This would have been followed by a transitional period of great hardship and difficult, colder, climatic conditions, during which they may have had to return to a more hunter-gatherer lifestyle – surviving as best they could, all the time waiting for the climate to re-stabilise, and to see where it might be best to settle down again. Finally after some 1200 years the Earth warmed up again – possibly quite suddenly – meaning the equatorial regions they had inhabited now became too tropical. Moving northwards into the newly temperate zones somewhat to the north of the Tropic of Cancer, some would have arrived at the Fertile Crescent and decided this was a good place to re-establish agriculture and permanent settlements.

This means the Neolithic sites uncovered in that area may represent the earliest phase of this rebuilding process. Building in stone for the first time in more remote, inland areas might have become a necessity to protect themselves from marauding nomads still struggling to survive – and one that dovetailed nicely with an understandable desire to avoid repeating the fate of their submerged, coast-based ancestors. Not only that but it seems these generations of survivors preserved the memory of what had befallen their forebears in the more vivid catastrophe traditions that survive all around the globe.

In this context there's one set of tribal traditions I've deliberately omitted until now – those of the Pacific Islands, which seem to retain a strong memory of a time when the sea submerged their ancestors. For example, on Samoa they say:[11] 'The sea... arose, and in a stupendous catastrophe of nature the land sank into the sea... The new earth arose out of the womb of the last earth.' While on Tahiti we find similar ideas:[12] 'In ancient times Taaroa... being angry with men on account of their disobedience to his will, overturned the world into the sea, when the earth sank into the water, excepting a few projecting islands which remained above its surface.' Of course it could be that these are just relatively recent memories of other islands becoming submerged. But what if they're memories of a far more widespread submergence at the end of the Pleistocene that affected that area too?

We might usefully complete this picture by looking at some of the more interesting and less fanciful aspects of the work of two alternative researchers we met in chapters 10 and 11. In *The Lost Continent of Mu* James Churchward records details of a number of impressive megalithic structures still standing on various Pacific Islands, including the Gilbert and Marshall, Kingsmill, Navigator, Cook and Marquesas Islands, and the Caroline and Mariana Groups; and, although it's not clear how many of these he actually visited, he does provide a number of photographs and drawings.[13] More recently David Hatcher Childress has also chronicled them in his *Lost Cities* series.[14] Their assumption that the complexity and distribution of these monuments indicates they must have been erected when all the islands were part of one huge landmass is entirely without foundation – not least because most of them are known to be volcanic atolls created millions of years ago. Moreover the monuments themselves are almost certainly Neolithic at the earliest. Nevertheless it's surely reasonable to suggest that they might add to our understanding of what happened to the survivors of the submersion of Sundaland, and possibly of Sahul too. Although some headed northwest to start the rebuilding process some time later in the Near East, others may have chosen to take their chances at sea by heading southeast – some of them then finding and settling on islands that would be less likely to be found and invaded by nomadic desperados.

COVID-19: A DIFFERENT STYLE OF KARMIC REBOOT?

Coronavirus was pretty much unheard of when I first released this book as *Genesis Unveiled*, although it was the underlying cause of the SARS outbreak in 2003. Nor had the new strain, Covid-19, properly raised its head when I started the rewrite for this new edition. But the timing does somehow seem prescient.

As I write, the pandemic has caused into the hundreds of thousands of deaths globally. The situation may considerably worsen before we have a successful vaccine, or it may not. But what we can say with certainty is that the lockdown effected in most countries to try to combat the virus has caused millions of people to reassess their lives and the way they conduct themselves. Despite the loneliness and mental turmoil faced by some, despite the terrible shock to the global economy, despite the many thousands of businesses who will struggle and even go under and the unemployment that will cause – despite all this, there are surely some silver linings.

During their confinement people have been forced to stop and take stock. Perhaps for the first time in years they have had time to think and reflect. Time to realise that it's a fool's errand to be totally preoccupied with working as many hours as we can just so we can afford bigger houses, more expensive holidays and more and more material possessions – as a symbol of our status in society that in turn supposedly bolsters our self worth. Time to realise that what really matters is friends and family, and spending quality time with them. Time to realise that helping others actually gives us far more pleasure than helping ourselves. Time to realise that walking in nature is far more beneficial to our mental health than any new car, item of clothing, techno gadget or whatever. Time to realise that minutes, even hours spent in meditation and contemplation aren't wasted but gained. Time to realise that, instead of constantly running around chasing our tails, it's wonderful to learn to just be still and in the moment.

Almost everyone will come out of this crisis a changed person, although of course not everyone will change for the better. Some people will have made no constructive use of their confinement at all and will be itching to get back to their bad old ways. Some will be devastated by loss of work and struggling to cope financially – although maybe out of this crisis new, more-enjoyable opportunities for employment will arise. Some will be mourning the loss of loved ones. But huge numbers of people *will* be changed for the better – armed with a new perspective, and a new determination to live in a different way.

I cannot say what proportion of the Earth's population will seize this opportunity for renewal, and whether any change will be temporary or permanent. Only time will tell. Nor can I say for certain that this pandemic was planned at a higher level of our collective consciousness as a chance for a 'karmic reboot' – any more than I can say that for certain about the global catastrophe that wiped out our forgotten race. But I can say that it's a *possibility*.

Having said that, some conspiracy theorists suggest the pandemic was deliberately engineered by a global cabal of powerbrokers to see how much they could strike fear into us all, turn us into real puppets, and thereby control us all the better – crashing the global economy and reducing population into the bargain. But if that *were* the case, it doesn't seem to have been quite the success they'd hoped. Yes a great many people have tragically lost their lives, but it doesn't look likely that it'll put a significant dent in population numbers. In addition, while it's true that a huge number of people who were already that way inclined have become even more like puppets, unquestioningly doing whatever they're told by anyone in authority, perhaps just as many have opened themselves up to the possibility that things may not be quite as they seem in all sorts of areas of life. I sense that increasingly such people will be determined to be powerful, individual human beings who will *not* be pushed around like sheep.

To me this growing sense of people 'waking up' doesn't just have its roots in the pandemic – indeed the virus may have only been a catalyst for change. Rather it seems to me to stem from an undercurrent of growing indignation at greed, inequality, prejudice, the rape and pillage of Mother Earth's resources, the materialistic, throwaway society, global warming – the whole damn melting pot that we've contrived to create. Moreover this is unequivocally a moral movement and, I would argue, in large part a spiritual one too – whether or not this is openly acknowledged.

I hope that in this book I've made a strong case that we should take the ancients' reports about our forgotten ancestors seriously. That is, about their progressive debasement; about their obsession with material possessions and power; about their total lack of respect for the environment and disconnection with nature; and, above all, about their loss of spiritual perspective, awareness and understanding.

Surely no one can read all this and fail to see some sort of connection with our modern world.

SOURCE REFERENCES

Publication details for the books referenced below can be found in the bibliography. All website references were accurate at the time of original publication. Wherever possible the most up-to-date and readily available English translations of ancient texts, as prepared by orthodox scholars, have been used. Biblical references are taken from the Authorised King James Bible unless otherwise stated.

PREFACE

1. For more information on this see Volume 3 of the 'Prehistoric Truth' series, *Mesopotamia: The Truth*, chapter 1, pp. 12–18.

2. A multitude of ancient texts and traditions from nearly every continent on the globe record such an event. We won't examine the detail of *all* of these in the current work because they've been well chronicled by others, but we will meet with many of them in due course. For comprehensive descriptions and discussion see, for example, Oppenheimer, *Eden in the East*, chapters 8–10. In addition a number of websites document flood myths; see, for example, http://en.wikipedia.org/wiki/Flood_myth.

3. Nevertheless I have published the detailed contents of all these king lists, taken from the original sources, on my website, not least because this information is rarely properly recorded. See my paper *Problems with King Lists* at www.ianlawton.com/att1.html.

4. Personal correspondence, 23 February 2001.

5. Campbell, *Primitive Mythology*, Introduction, p. 27.

6. Jung, *Psychology and Alchemy*, prefatory note to the English edition, p. v.

7. The detailed support for these strong allegations is provided in Part 2 thereof. It is worth pointing out that Sitchin never deigned to respond to any of his linguistic critics in any detail at all.

8. At www.ianlawton.com/attchgs.html.

PART 1: REVELATIONS

1 MYTHS IN THE MAKING

1. See Campbell, *Primitive Mythology*, prologue, pp. 14–15 and Eliade, *The Sacred and the Profane*, chronological survey, pp. 229–32.

2. For a full exposition see Campbell, *Primitive Mythology*, Part 1.

3. For a full exposition see ibid., Parts 2 and 3.
4. Ibid., chapter 3, pp. 146–7.
5. Ibid., chapter 10, pp. 403–4.
6. Ibid., Conclusion, p. 462.
7. See http://en.wikipedia.org/wiki/Joseph_Campbell#Comparative_religion.
8. Campbell, *Primitive Mythology*, chapter 4, p. 164.
9. Campbell, *Occidental Mythology*, chapter 3, p. 95.

2 DEBASEMENT AND DESTRUCTION

1. For a discussion of the various texts known to have formed the basis for the Torah see Campbell, *Occidental Mythology*, chapter 3, pp. 100–2.
2. See Note 2 to the Preface.
3. This verse, although not central to the current argument, has caused a great deal of confusion. A similar passage from the Dead Sea Scrolls, however, explains all: 'In the four hundred and eightieth year of Noah's life, he came to the end of them, and God said, "My spirit shall not dwell with man forever, their days shall be determined to be one hundred and twenty years until the waters of the flood come."' This fits in with Noah being 600 years old at the time of the flood, as reported in Genesis 7:6. See Wise et al., *The Dead Sea Scrolls*, Part 2, section 44, p. 275, and also Saint Augustine, *The City of God* 15.24.
4. von Däniken, *Chariots of the Gods*, chapter 4, p. 61.
5. Ibid., plates section.
6. It is worth noting that Sitchin used the '120 years' in Genesis 6:3 to date the arrival of the Nephilim to 432,000 years before the flood, interpreting these years as 'sars' of 3600 years each; see *The Twelfth Planet*, chapter 8, pp. 227–9. See Note 3 above for the proper interpretation that indicates Sitchin's version is a nonsense.
7. The finest example of this is Sitchin's suggestion that Richard Howard Vyse faked the infamous 'Khufu quarry marks' in the Great Pyramid. This appears to be largely a fabrication of his own that some other alternative researchers continue to perpetuate in attempting to justify an older date for the monument. We will discuss this further in chapter 12, although for the full details see Lawton and Ogilvie-Herald, *Giza: The Truth*, chapter 2, pp. 88–107.
8. Again in chapter 12, although for the full details of the arguments surrounding the dating of the Great Pyramid and of the Sphinx see ibid., chapters 2 and 7 respectively.

9. For a summary of Collins' chronology see *From the Ashes of Angels*, chart 3, pp. 345–6. Note that he was to some extent influenced by the research of Christian O'Brien who, in his 1985 work *The Genius Of The Few* and the follow-up *The Shining Ones*, devotes considerable time to reinterpreting the little-known Mesopotamian *Kharsag Epics*, as well as various other better-known Mesopotamian and Judaic texts. From this he suggests that a well-educated group of fair-skinned Atlantean survivors settled in South Lebanon and began the post-catastrophe rebuilding process. While this analysis might suffer from similar chronological and contextual problems to Collins', O'Brien's attempts at retranslation do appear to be of a high scholastic standard. Also, while he tends towards a somewhat technological interpretation of their achievements, unusually he combines this with a high degree of respect for their spirituality. Preservation and continuation of his work is being undertaken by Edmund Marriage; for more information see www.goldenageproject.org.uk.

10. Ancient History of the Jews 2; see Murray, *History of the Jews*, Volume 1, pp. 26–7.

11. *The City of God* 15.22; see www.ccel.org/ccel/schaff/npnf102.toc.html for a full translation.

12. See Laurence's introductory notes to his 1883 translation of *The Book of Enoch*, pp. iv–vi.

13. The Ethiopian and Slavonic versions are normally referred to as '1 Enoch' and '2 Enoch' respectively. There is another related but fragmentary text, the *Enochian Book of Giants*, which forms part of the Dead Sea Scrolls, but this appears to further distort any original message by accusing the fallen angels of bestiality and emphasising the giant stature of their offspring; see Wise et al., *The Dead Sea Scrolls,* Part 2, section 33, pp. 246–50.

14. 1 Enoch 7; see Laurence, *The Book of Enoch*, pp. 5–7.

15. 1 Enoch 8; see ibid., pp. 7–8.

16. It is interesting that the original Hebrew word used for the angels can be translated as 'those who watch', and this correlates with the word used in the Greek versions of these texts that is now translated as 'Watchers'. However the other translation of the Hebrew word is 'those who are *awake*'. See Collins, *From the Ashes of Angels*, chapter 1, p. 3.

17. These are described in Copenhaver, *Hermetica*, Introduction, pp. xxxii–xl.

18. For more information on the various original compilations of source texts see ibid., Introduction, pp. xl–xlv; and on the various commentaries that were then prepared by Arabian and European Hermeticists from the seventh century onward, see pp. xlv–lix. Cophenhaver's 1992 translation is the most

recent available and as such incorporates all the scholarship of his multitude of predecessors. This is important given the problems of interpreting the many different versions of the original texts, and of ensuring that the translation is as faithful to these originals as possible. By contrast the popular translation by Walter Scott in the 1920s is now regarded by most orthodox scholars as distorted and unreliable, even if his extensive commentaries are invaluable; see ibid., Introduction, p. liii. Having said that his is the only modern version that includes the philosophical Stobaeus manuscripts, to which we'll refer on occasion.

19. Corpus Hermeticum 4:7; see ibid., p. 16.

20. Asclepius 25; see ibid., p. 82.

21. For more information see Robinson, *The Nag Hammadi Library*, Introduction, pp. 1–10. This is the most recent compilation of scholars' translations of the various tractates.

22. These are *The Discourse on the Eighth and Ninth*, *The Prayer of Thanksgiving*, *Scribal note* and *Asclepius* 21–9. Three of these were previously unknown but can be identified because they are dialogues in which Hermes Trismegistus takes the lead role.

23. It is interesting to compare this with a passage in the Hermetic *Kore Kosmu*, which suggests that the first incarnations into human form were a karmic punishment for souls that had already erred by 'overstepping the bounds of their own divisions of the atmosphere' and claiming 'nobility equal to the gods in heaven'; the fact that this is so at odds with other Hermetic passages shows how self-contradictory these texts can become after centuries of editing and translation; see Stobaeus Excerpt 23 in Scott, *Hermetica*, p. 184. However for completeness we should also note the similarity between the Gnostic view of the initial fall and that of Islam, in which a 'lesser god' is condemned to incarnation on earth because he 'refused to bow before Adam'; he then pledges to act as a negative influence on humankind's development, which he achieves by making Adam partake of the 'forbidden tree'; see Koran 7:11–25.

24. The main Gnostic texts that contain this message are the *Apocryphon of John*, the *Hypostatis of the Archons*, *On the Origin of the World* and the *Tripartite Tractate*. To a large extent they pick up on and elaborate the themes in Genesis.

25. Robinson, *The Nag Hammadi Library*, pp. 121–2. Although it adds nothing of interest, the only other Gnostic text to directly describe the fallen angels' perversion of humankind is *On the Origin of the World*; see ibid., p. 186.

26. Ibid., p. 121.

27. More details about the background to Ancient Mesopotamia, the excavations, the decipherment of the various scripts and the pantheon of gods are available in Part 1 of *Mesopotamia: The Truth*. Therein I've also prepared summaries of the various Sumerian and Akkadian literary texts, which are too numerous to list here. The main source for translations of the former is Thorkild Jacobsen's *The Harps That Once… Sumerian Poetry in Translation*, and of the latter Stephanie Dalley's *Myths from Mesopotamia*, published in 1987 and 1991 respectively.

28. Dalley, *Myths from Mesopotamia*, p. 229.

29. Ibid., pp. 9–35; see especially pp. 18–24.

30. Jacobsen, *The Harps That Once…*, pp. 145–50.

31. See Note 2 to the Preface for global sources; also for a fuller discussion of the argument against smaller, later, localised floods see my paper *Problems with King Lists* at www.ianlawton.com/att1.html.

32. Dalley, *Myths from Mesopotamia*, pp. 109–16.

33. Ibid., glossary (s.v. Seven Sages), p. 328.

34. Erra and Ishum 1 and 2; see ibid., pp. 291 and 294.

35. Ibid., glossary (s.v. Apsu), p. 318.

36. Erra and Ishum 4; see ibid., p. 306.

37. Erra and Ishum 3; see ibid., pp. 299 and 301.

38. Erra and Ishum 1 and 5; see ibid., pp. 291 and 311.

39. The major breakthrough came when Jean François Champollion managed to decipher the multilingual Rosetta Stone in the early nineteenth century.

40. Translations of all these are readily available. For the first two see Wallis Budge, *The Egyptian Heaven and Hell*, and for the remainder see the translations by Faulkner under the original titles.

41. This can be found in a variety of forms in a variety of sources. The version quoted here comes from www.egyptianmyths.net/mythre.htm, but it is also summarised in the essay on Egypt by Baines and Pinch in Willis, *World Mythology*, p. 41; although the name of the source text is not provided here it is reported as being inscribed on one of the shrines in the tomb of Tutankhamun, and on the walls of later royal tombs.

42. Campbell, *Primitive Mythology*, chapter 10, p. 435 and *Oriental Mythology*, chapter 4, p. 206.

43. Campbell, *Oriental Mythology*, chapter 4, pp. 200–6.

44. See Feuerstein et al., *In Search of the Cradle of Civilisation*; chapter 9 deals with the Aryan invasion theory; chapter 2 emphasises the importance and

antiquity of the *Vedas* and contains a fine introduction to the various categories of Indian text; and chapter 7 discusses the Indus script.

45. Prasad, *The Fountainhead of Religion*, Conclusion, p. 171.

46. Ibid., chapter 5, p. 87, Footnote 1.

47. See, for example, O'Flaherty, *The Rig Veda*, p. 37, Note 11: 'The Asuras are the ancient dark divinities, at first the elder brothers and then the enemies of the gods (Devas).' Also p. 212, Note 9: 'Asura not in its later sense of "demon" but in its earlier sense of sky god.' Finally p. 29, Note 9: 'The two opposed masses are armies, the polarised forces of gods and demons (Asuras).'

48. Prasad, *The Fountainhead of Religion*, chapter 5, p. 87, Footnote 1.

49. Rig Veda 10.124; see O'Flaherty, *The Rig Veda*, pp. 110–2.

50. Satapatha Brahmana 1:8:1:1–6; see Eggeling, *Satapatha Brahmana Part 1* in Müller, *The Sacred Books of the East*, Volume 12, pp. 216–18.

51. Campbell, *Oriental Mythology*, chapter 3, p. 107 and *Occidental Mythology*, chapter 3, pp. 106–9.

52. For a full definition and explanation of my concept of the 'holographic (super)soul' see www.ianlawton.com/holsoul.html.

53. For more details on the worldview underpinning Supersoul Spirituality, especially its 'three precepts', see www.ianlawton.com/suspindex.html, or any of the books listed therein.

54. For more details on the afterlife planes see my book of the same name, or for a simpler version *Death Is An Adventure!!*

3 THE ARTS OF CIVILISATION

1. The various commentaries on Berossus' work were compiled by Isaac Cory in 1832 in *Ancient Fragments,* and are reproduced by Robert Temple in *The Sirius Mystery*, Appendix 3, pp. 548–59. See in particular p. 552.

2. Ibid., Appendix 3, p. 562.

3. Collins and others have suggested that Oannes is the Greek for Enki himself, via his Akkadian name Ea; see *Gods of Eden*, chapter 19, p. 293. But Dalley is quite clear that the name Oannes is the Greek form of Uan, another Akkadian name for Adapa, and that he's to be thought of as Enki's son; see *Myths from Mesopotamia*, Glossary (s.v. Adapa and Oannes), pp. 317 and 326. On a different tack it's a moot point whether or not the fish symbolism associated with Jesus is esoteric and can be attributed to a Mesopotamian source.

4. Dalley, *Myths from Mesopotamia*, pp. 182–8. For more details on any of what follows concerning the Mesopotamian texts, pantheon and so on, see

Lawton, *Mesopotamia: The Truth*, Part 1.

5. Dalley, *Myths from Mesopotamia*, p. 2.

6. Erra and Ishum 2; see ibid., p. 292.

7. Kramer, *The Sumerians*, chapter 4, p. 116. A full list of the translated *me's* is reproduced in Lawton, *Mesopotamia: The Truth*, chapter 4, p. 40.

8. Campbell, *Primitive Mythology*, chapter 10, pp. 454–5.

9. This is discussed in ibid., chapter 10, p. 457.

10. Dalley, *Myths from Mesopotamia*, p. 50.

11. Temple, *The Sirius Mystery*, Appendix 3, p. 551.

12. Ibid., Appendix 3, p. 554.

13. Ancient History of the Jews 2; see Murray, *History of the Jews*, Volume 1, p. 29.

14. Ibid., Volume 1, 'Autobiography of Flavius Josephus', p. 1.

15. Robinson, *The Nag Hammadi Library*, pp. 396–401.

16. 2 Enoch 40; see Morfill and Charles, *The Book of the Secrets of Enoch*, pp. 53–5.

17. Oliver, *Antiquities of Freemasonry*, chapter 4, pp. 81–5; I'm indebted to Jason Colavito's detailed research at www.jasoncolavito.com/the-watchers-and-antediluvian-wisdom.html for providing this lead. In addition Blavatsky has much to say on the topic of Enoch and the knowledge he preserved in *The Secret Doctrine*, Volume 2, Part 2, chapter 21, pp. 529–35.

18. This is described at the beginning of the *Kore Kosmu*; see Scott, *Hermetica*, Stobaeus Excerpt 23, pp. 179–80 and also p. 191.

19. Reymond, *The Mythical Origin of the Egyptian Temple*, chapter 1, p. 9. She also references Boylan, *Thoth: the Hermes of Egypt*, pp. 92–7. The *Edfu Documents* are inscribed on the walls of a Late Period Ptolemaic temple located midway between Luxor and Aswan in Upper Egypt.

20. Lawton and Ogilvie-Herald, *Giza: The Truth*, chapter 1, pp. 17–18. The original translation comes from John Greaves, *Pyramidographia* (London, 1646), pp. 81–3.

21. Again I'm indebted to Jason Colavito's detailed research at www.jasoncolavito.com/the-watchers-and-antediluvian-wisdom.html for providing this lead.

22. For more details on all this see Lawton and Ogilvie-Herald, *Giza: The Truth*, chapter 5.

23. I have personally been into the intrusive, Late Period tombs dug into the

Sphinx's rump; and into the modern, man-made chamber located between its paws behind the Thutmose IV stele; and, for that matter, into the passage to the side of the lowest Relieving Chamber above the King's Chamber in the Great Pyramid, excavated by Caviglia in the early 1800s. There is nothing untoward or exciting in any of them. This evidence is scattered throughout *Giza: The Truth*, including in the plates section.

4 THE GOLDEN AGE

1. 2 Enoch 31:2; see Morfill and Charles, *The Book of the Secrets of Enoch*, p. 44.

2. Ancient History of the Jews 2; see Murray, *History of the Jews*, Volume 1, p. 28.

3. Jacobsen, *The Harps That Once…*, pp. 181–204 and especially pp. 185–6.

4. Rundle Clark, *Myth and Symbol in Ancient Egypt*, chapter 8, pp. 263–4. In the work of most alternative researchers the Egyptian phrase is rendered as *zep tepi* instead of *tep zepi,* and in fact it seems this may be more correct given that the original is apparently supposed to be *zp tpj* (see http://en.wikipedia.org/wiki/Ancient_Egyptian_creation_myths').

5. Especially Bauval and Gilbert in their best-selling 1995 work *The Orion Mystery*, and Bauval and Hancock in the follow-up *Keeper of Genesis*.

6. Reymond, *The Mythical Origin of the Egyptian Temple*, chapter 1, pp. 6–11. The original texts apparently include the *Specification of the Mounds of the Early Primeval Age* and the *Sacred Book of the Early Primeval Age*.

7. Campbell, *Oriental Mythology*, chapter 6, p. 327.

8. Ramayana 1; see Dutt, *The Ramayana and The Mahabharata*, pp. 1–3.

9. See Legge, *Sacred Books of China*, 'Confucian Texts', Parts 1–4 in Müller, *The Sacred Books of the East*, Volumes 3, 16, 27 and 28; and ibid., 'Taoist Texts', Parts 1–2 in ibid., Volumes 39 and 40.

10. Kwang Tze 9 and 12; see ibid., Volume 39, pp. 278 and 325–6.

11. Morgan, *Essays from Huai Nan Tzu*, pp. 35–6.

12. Ibid., pp. 80–2.

13. Works and Days 108–122; see West, *Hesiod: Theogony and Works and Days*, p. 40.

14. Metamorphosis 1:88–111; see Melville, *Ovid: Metamorphosis*, pp. 3–4.

15. Critias 5; see Lee, *Plato: Timaeus and Critias*, p. 145.

5 WORLD AGES AND UNIVERSAL CYCLES

1. Works and Days 123–201; see West, *Hesiod: Theogony and Works and Days*,

pp. 40–2.

2. Metamorphosis 1:112–162; see Melville, *Ovid: Metamorphosis*, pp. 4–6.

3. A related tradition of multiple world ages is found in the *Sibylline Oracles,* a proliferation of texts from the fourth century BCE onwards that originated variously in Egypt, the Near East and Europe, and even held a degree of authority for the early Christian Church. Book 1 of these oracles describes five 'generations' before the flood and several thereafter. See Collins, 'The Sibylline Oracles' in Charlesworth, *The Old Testament Pseudepigrapha*, Volume 1, pp. 335–42.

4. Timaeus 2; see Lee, *Plato: Timaeus and Critias*, pp. 35–6.

5. Critias 2; see Lee, *Plato: Timaeus and Critias*, pp. 131–2.

6. Mackenzie, *Myths of China and Japan*, chapter 15, p. 276.

7. Tao Teh King 18; see Legge, *Sacred Books of China*, 'Taoist Texts', Part 1 in Müller, *The Sacred Books of the East*, Volume 39, pp. 60–1.

8. These extracts are taken from the lengthy description provided in Waters, *Book of the Hopi*, Part 1, pp. 11–21.

9. Leyenda de los Soles 75:1–77:32; see Bierhorst, *History and Mythology of the Aztecs*, pp. 142–7. See also Thompson, *Maya History and Religion*, chapter 9, pp. 331–3. The narrative contains clear influences from across the Atlantic in that a god tells the flood survivors to hide inside a hollowed-out cypress tree, and when they emerge and cook a fish the gods are angry; this idea of the gods smelling the food that the survivors first cook is found in virtually every Near Eastern flood tradition.

10. Anales de Cuauhtitlan 2:24–49; see Bierhorst, *History and Mythology of the Aztecs*, p. 26.

11. Thompson, *Maya Hieroglyphic Writing*, chapter 1, p. 10.

12. No English translation of this text is readily available, so my source is an Italian version published in 1900 that I had translated; see *Il Manoscritto Messicano Vaticano 3738, Detto Il Codice Rios*, Folios 4–7, pp. 24–5. Note also that there appears to be some confusion about these numbers: Thompson quotes a total of 18,028 years in *Maya Hieroglyphic Writing*, chapter 1, p. 10, while Gilbert and Cotterell quote 4081 and 5026 years respectively for the last two ages in *The Mayan Prophecies*, chapter 4, pp. 71–2. All I can say is that I have gone to the source.

13. *Il Manoscritto Messicano Vaticano 3738*, Folio 4, p. 24.

14. Alexander, 'Latin American Mythology', chapter 7, p. 240 in Gray, *The Mythology of All Races*, Volume 11. The sources quoted are: de Molina, 'An Account of the Fables and Rights of the Yncas' translated in Markham, *Rites*

and Laws of the Yncas (London, 1873); Cieza de Leon, 'Segunda parte de la cronica del Peru' (Seville, 1553), translated in Markham, *The Second Part of the Chronicle of Peru* (London, 1883), chapter 5, pp. 5–10; Sarmiento, *History of the Incas,* translated in Markham, *History of the Incas* (Cambridge, 1907), pp. 27–39; and Pietschmann, 'Some Account of the Illustrated Chronicle by the Peruvian Indian, D Felipe Huaman Poma de Ayala', *Comptes Rendus du Congres des Americanistes* 18 (London, 1913), pp. 511–2.

15. Thompson provides a useful summary of these in *Maya Hieroglyphic Writing*, chapter 1, pp. 23–6.

16. See http://en.wikipedia.org/wiki/Mesoamerican_Long_Count_calendar.

17. Mahabharata 3.187; see Ray, *The Mahabharata*, Volume 2, pp. 557–8.

18. Ibid., Volume 2, pp. 558–60.

19. Mahabharata 12.231; see ibid., Volume 7, pp. 235–7.

20. Vishnu Purana 1.3 and 6.3; see Dutt, *Vishnu Purana*, pp. 12–3 and 434–7. See also Dimmitt and van Buitenen, *Classical Hindu Mythology*, chapter 1, pp. 19–24 and 36–43; and Wilkins, *Hindu Mythology*, chapter 10, pp. 353–60.

21. Mahabharata 3.187; see Ray, *The Mahabharata*, Volume 2, pp. 560–2.

22. Keith, 'Indian Mythology', chapter 8, p. 221 in Gray, *The Mythology of All Races*, Volume 6.

23. For more details on the Jain cycle see Campbell, *Oriental Mythology*, chapter 4, pp. 219–23. He suggests that this concept may originally date back to the time of the early Indus civilisation.

24. At the very least this would have occurred while the Jewish people were held in captivity in Babylon in the sixth century BCE. For more information see Collins, *From the Ashes of Angels*, chapter 7.

25. Translated by James Darmesteter in Müller, *The Sacred Books of the East*, Volume 4.

26. See Willis, *World Mythology*, p. 41. Note that this cycle is connected with the traditions surrounding the death and rebirth of the legendary phoenix; for more information see R Van Den Broek, *The Myth of the Phoenix* (EJ Brill, 1972).

27. See http://en.wikipedia.org/wiki/Axial_precession_(astronomy). Note that Plato's precessional 'Great Year' is not the same as, although often confused with, the so-called 'Platonic Year' or 'Perfect Year'. This is something he refers to elsewhere in the *Timaeus*, and it describes the far shorter time it takes for all the planets to return to the same position relative to Earth; see http://en.wikipedia.org/wiki/Great_year.

28. Severin, 'The Paris Codex: Decoding an Astronomical Ephemeris', chapter 5, pp. 68–9 in *Transactions of the American Philosophical Society* 71:5 (1981).

29. See, for example, Stray, *Beyond 2012*, chapter 1, p. 23. In fact the number 26,000 is frequently used even though this is clearly not the product of 5 times 5125.

30. See http://en.wikipedia.org/wiki/Laws_of_Manu.

31. Laws of Manu 1:68–72; see Bühler, *The Laws of Manu* in Müller, *The Sacred Books of the East*, Volume 25, p. 2.

32. See http://en.wikipedia.org/wiki/Yuga.

33. See Campbell, *Oriental Mythology*, chapter 3, pp. 116, 120 and 129 in which he refers to an analysis by Oppert in his paper *The Dates of Genesis*. Integral to his analysis are the numbers used in various versions of the Mesopotamian king lists; see my paper *Problems with King Lists* at www.ianlawton.com/att1.html for more details.

34. Laszlo, *Science and the Akashic Field* (Inner Traditions, 2004), chapter 3, p. 39.

35. Again we can consider these to be the same as the 'afterlife' planes that I write about in the book of the same name. We will examine Madame Blavatsky's view of different 'root races' in chapter 11, but for more on Qabalistic, theosophical and other approaches to all this see www.ianlawton.com.att4.html, and also papers 5 and 6 that follow it.

6 TAKING ON THE EXPERTS

1. Campbell, *Oriental Mythology*, chapter 7, p. 395.

2. Ibid., chapter 3, pp. 127–8. For some reason his figure of 432,000 years is merely the duration of a Kali Yuga rather than an entire Maha Yuga; see our Figure 3.

3. Eliade, *Myth and Reality*, chapter 4, p. 55. In pp. 60–8 he goes on to discuss the various world age theories, and then the Judaeo-Christian apocalyptic traditions, but nowhere do we receive any additional explanation for these themes. His only other relevant comment is on p. 69 when, discussing the golden age, he suggests the Communist and Nazi movements of the twentieth century were attempts to recreate it – and that it's a powerful and natural human trait. He follows the same path in *The Myth of the Eternal Return*.

4. Eliade, *The Sacred and the Profane*, chapter 3, pp. 130–1.

7 THE CREATION OF HUMANKIND

1. For evidence of this we only have to look at the way groups of animals react

similarly and instantaneously without apparent communication, such as flocks of birds changing direction. Perhaps even better, one AF Knudsen conducted some intriguing but little-known research into this in the late nineteenth century. On a stud farm on a South Sea island, he resorted to hypnotic suggestion while attempting to train a difficult horse – and found that another in the same field followed the same instructions; he then followed this up by working with groups of anywhere between three and eighteen horses. He was also able to repeat the experiment although with less elaborations with cattle, who he felt were generally less intelligent and whose group sizes were correspondingly larger at between fifty and a hundred animals. These experiments worked even when the main animal subject was as much as eight kilometres distant from the others. I cannot find any trace of Knudsen's work on the internet, so my source is TenDam, Hans, *Exploring Reincarnation* (Rider, 2003), chapter 12, pp. 259–60; his source is a book by the Swiss parapsychologist Rudolf Passian, *Wiedergeburt: Ein Leben Oder Viele* (Knaur, 1985), p. 145.

2. 1 Enoch 7; see Laurence, *The Book of Enoch*, p. 6.

3. This comes from the descriptions of Enoch's visionary trip to, in particular, the second and fifth 'heavens' in 2 Enoch 7 and 18, and even more from the footnoted commentary that accompanies these passages; see Morfill and Charles, *The Book of the Secrets of Enoch*, especially pp. 20–2.

4. Robinson, *The Nag Hammadi Library*, pp. 182–3. For more on the word *Adam* see http://en.wikipedia.org/wiki/Adam.

5. Corpus Hermeticum 1:14; see Copenhaver, *Hermetica*, p. 3.

6. Jacobsen, *The Harps That Once...*, pp. 151–66; see especially pp. 154 and 157.

7. Atrahasis 1; see Dalley, *Myths from Mesopotamia*, pp. 15–16.

8. Epic of Creation 6; see ibid., p. 261.

9. Berossus fragments recorded by Polyhistor; see Temple, *The Sirius Mystery*, Appendix 3, pp. 553–4.

10. Genesis 1:26–27. Note there's some confusion in the biblical account that derives from combining the original Elohist and Yahwist texts. The first, Elohist-derived chapter simply says 'male and female created he them'; that is, men and women were created together. But the second, Yahwist-derived and more-quoted chapter contradicts this by stating that Adam was created first 'of the dust of the ground', followed by Eve who was fashioned from one of his ribs to act as his 'help-meet' or companion; see Genesis 2:20–2.

11. It is interesting to note that this is followed by a recommendation about the rituals that should be performed 'wherever a woman gives birth', which are

remarkably similar to those followed by the Hopi of North America; see Waters, *Book of the Hopi*, Part 1, pp. 8–9.

12. Epic of Gilgamesh 1; see Dalley, *Myths from Mesopotamia*, pp. 52–3.
13. There are also a number of similar if less detailed accounts of multiple creations or world ages in Mayan tradition; see Thompson, *Maya History and Religion*, chapter 9, pp. 336–73.
14. Popol Vuh 1 and 4; see Tedlock, *Popol Vuh*, pp. 66–73 and 145–8.
15. Waters, *Book of the Hopi*, Part 1, pp. 5–9.
16. Dixon, 'Oceanic Mythology', Part 3, chapter 1, pp. 174–6 in Gray, *The Mythology of All Races*, Volume 9.
17. Ramtha, *The White Book* (JZK Publishing, 2004), chapter 8, p. 122. I am aware of criticism directed at Knight herself, and at Ramtha's messages. Some of this may well be founded, but in my view there are core elements that tie in well with other channelled sources (see another of my books *The Power of You* for proof of this), so it would be wrong to throw the whole lot out.
18. Newton, *Journey of Souls* (Llewellyn, 2002), chapter 11, p. 171. Although I wrote about Newton's research in chapter 2 of the original *Genesis Unveiled*, when I first came up with this idea in the first draft I had never even heard of him. Unfortunately I now see his work as possibly flawed, which is why I no longer use it as evidential support for Supersoul Spirituality, but that doesn't mean odd elements such as this may not have some validity.
19. For Campbell's commentary on the *Birth of Man* see *Oriental Mythology*, chapter 3, pp. 108–11; on the *Epic of Creation* see *Occidental Mythology*, chapter 2, pp. 84–5; and on the *Epic of Gilgamesh* see *Occidental Mythology*, chapter 2, pp. 87–90.
20. Campbell, *Occidental Mythology*, chapter 2, pp. 85–6.
21. Campbell, *Oriental Mythology*, chapter 3, p. 103.

8 THE ORIGINS OF THE WORLD

1. This collation of origin traditions took a great deal of time and effort in the British Library in the days before the internet made research far simpler. I sincerely hope that this spiritual-esoteric reinterpretation thereof may yet receive some recognition in more academic circles, because arguably it is one of the most important contributions made by this work.
2. Corpus Hermeticum 3:1; see Copenhaver, *Hermetica*, p. 13.
3. See West, *Hesiod: Theogony and Works and Days*, Note 116, p. 64; and also Willis, *World Mythology*, p. 128.
4. Corpus Hermeticum 4:10 and 12:20–2; see ibid., pp. 17 and 47–8.

5. Robinson, *The Nag Hammadi Library*, pp. 171–3.
6. Ibid, pp. 61 and 64. Further descriptions of the ultimate deity can be found, for example, in the *Apocryphon of John*; see ibid, pp. 106–7.
7. Dalley, *Myths from Mesopotamia*, p. 233. Note that the opening to the earlier Sumerian text *Eridu Genesis* would probably have contained something relevant, but unfortunately it's missing.
8. Ibid., Glossary, p. 329 (s.v. Tiamat).
9. See, for example, Kramer, *The Sumerians*, chapter 4, pp. 112–13 and Roux, *Ancient Iraq*, chapter 6, p. 93.
10. Taken from www.egyptianmyths.net/mythre.htm.
11. Baines and Pinch in Willis, *World Mythology*, p. 38.
12. Rig Veda 10.129; see O'Flaherty, *The Rig Veda*, pp. 25–6.
13. Morgan, *Essays from Huai Nan Tzu*, 'Beginning and Reality', pp. 31–3.
14. Ibid., 'Life and Soul', p. 58.
15. Nihongi 1; see Aston, *Nihongi*, pp. 1–3.
16. Metamorphosis 1:6–31; see Melville, *Ovid: Metamorphosis*, pp. 1–2.
17. Dixon, 'Oceanic Mythology', Part 1, chapter 1, p. 5 in Gray, *The Mythology of All Races*, Volume 9.
18. Ibid., Part 1, chapter 1, p. 13.
19. Ibid., Part 1, chapter 1, pp. 7–8. The source is Taylor, *New Zealand and Its Inhabitants* (London, 1870), p. 109.
20. Ibid., Part 1, chapter 1, p. 11.
21. Waters, *Book of the Hopi*, Part 1, p. 3.
22. Popol Vuh 1; see Tedlock, *Popol Vuh*, pp. 64–5.
23. Willis, *World Mythology*, p.266.
24. Ibid., p. 267.
25. For example the *World Mythology* compendium and the *Larousse Encyclopaedia of Mythology* are both littered with an emphasis on the more prosaic aspects of cosmogony traditions. In making a distinction between 'creation myths' that involve a supreme creator and those that describe the powers in the void in more metaphysical terms they also ignore the consistent fundamental message in all these traditions, irrespective of the extent to which they anthropomorphise. See, for example, the description of Oceanic cosmogony in *Larousse*, p. 465.
26. Campbell, *Primitive Mythology*, chapter 2, pp. 84–8.

27. Ibid., chapter 6, pp. 232–8.

28. Indian and Chinese mythology are discussed in Campbell, *Oriental Mythology*, Parts 2 and 3. Concerning the latter he even asserts that there are 'no stories of creation, either in these early myths of the Chou period, or in the later Confucian classics'; see chapter 7, p. 380. But surely this is more likely to be due to them not surviving the 'burning of the books' in the third century BCE, as described in chapter 4, than to original absence – and in any case it doesn't justify his failure to discuss later Taoist cosmogony.

29. Ibid., chapter 2, pp. 83–9.

30. Eliade, *Myth and Reality*, chapter 2.

31. Note that in my more specialist spiritual books I tend to avoid the word *physical* because other, for example astral, dimensions can appear just as solid to their inhabitants as this plane does to us. For more on this see Lawton, *Afterlife*, chapter 9.

32. I may be missing a crucial symbolic point here, but I've never been able to associate the idea that, for example, the physical body should be preserved by mummification, and that food and drink should be provided for the afterlife, with a worldview of any true spiritual sophistication.

PART 2: CORROBORATION

9 ARCHAEOLOGY

1. My original source for this data was Richard Klein's 1999 work *The Human Career*, although some dates have now been updated as per http://en.wikipedia.org/wiki/Geological_period.

2. For refutations of their theories see my paper *Problems with Anomalous Human Remains* at www.ianlawton.com/att2.html.

3. Leakey, *The Origin of Humankind*, chapter 2, pp. 29–30. Much of this section and the next is a summary of chapters 1–5. They have been updated to reflect intervening refinements to various dates, new species and so on, but for our nonspecialist purposes the general thrust of Leakey's chapters remains valid.

4. See http://en.wikipedia.org/wiki/Jebel_Irhoud.

5. See http://en.wikipedia.org/wiki/Mitochondrial_Eve.

6. See http://en.wikipedia.org/wiki/Early_human_migrations.

7. Leakey, *The Origin of Humankind*, chapter 5, p. 114.

8. See http://en.wikipedia.org/wiki/Mirror_test.

9. See http://en.wikipedia.org/wiki/Origin_of_language.

10. See https://scienceblogs.com/grrlscientist/2008/10/31/one-of-lifes-tiny-dramas.

11. The work of Lawrence Barham is described by Elizabeth J Himelfarb in 'Prehistoric Body Painting', *Archaeology* 53:4 (2000).

12. See http://en.wikipedia.org/wiki/Qafzeh_cave. It is regularly reported that Neanderthals were ritually burying their dead from around 75,000 years ago, but in fact the evidence for this is sparse and inconclusive. The most cited example is that of the Shanidar Cave. However there are no grave goods, merely unusual pollen remains. While some researchers argue that these indicate flowers had been placed in the grave, others suggest they could easily have been intrusively introduced by small rodents; see http://en.wikipedia.org/wiki/Shanidar.

13. See http://en.wikipedia.org/wiki/Blombos_Cave.

14. Marshack, Alexander, 'A Middle Palaeolithic Symbolic Composition from the Golan Heights: The Earliest Known Depictive Image', *Current Anthropology* 37:2 (1996), pp. 357–65.

15. Bahn, Paul, 'Excavation of a Palaeolithic Plank from Japan', *Nature* 32:9 (1987), p. 110. Finds on some northern Japanese sites are now known to have been faked by the amateur archaeologist Fujimura Shinichi, but he was *not* involved here; see http://en.wikipedia.org/wiki/Japanese_palaeolithic_hoax.

16. See http://en.wikipedia.org/wiki/Behavioral_modernity.

17. For general background seE http://en.wikipedia.org/wiki/Upper_Palaeolithic.

18. Kuhn et al., 'Ornaments of the Earliest Upper Palaeolithic: New Insights from the Levant', *Proceedings of the National Academy of Sciences,* 5 June 2001.

19. The earliest examples so far found come from a site in Moravia; see http://en.wikipedia.org/wiki/Venus_of_Dolni_Vestonice.

20. See http://en.wikipedia.org/wiki/Yuchanyan.

21. See, for example, http://en.wikipedia.org/wiki/Cave_art.

22. For more information on the changes indicated by late Palaeolithic cave art see Leakey, *The Origin of Humankind*, chapter 6 and Campbell, *Primitive Mythology*, chapter 8. For more on the last glacial maximum see http://en.wikipedia.org/wiki/Last_Glacial_Maximum.

23. Experiments conducted by Iegor Reznikoff and Michel Dauvois in the mid-1980s have shown that the acoustics tend to be enhanced in these caves; see Leakey, *The Origin of Humankind*, chapter 6, pp. 139–40.

24. See Leakey, *The Origin of Humankind*, chapter 6, p. 143 and Campbell,

Primitive Mythology, chapter 3, p. 141, chapter 8, p. 328 and chapter 9, p. 376. See also http://en.wikipedia.org/wiki/Rock_art.

25. See http://en.wikipedia.org/wiki/Megalithic_art. Pictures of some of these marks are reproduced in Michael Balfour's beautifully illustrated *Megalithic Mysteries*.

26. For a fine study see Jean Clottes and David Lewis-Williams' 1998 work *The Shamans of Prehistory: Trance and Magic in Painted Caves*. See also Richard Rudgley's *Lost Civilisations of the Stone Age*, published a year later.

27. See http://en.wikipedia.org/wiki/History_of_agriculture.

28. See http://en.wikipedia.org/wiki/Natufian.

29. See, for example, http://en.wikipedia.org/wiki/Qadan_culture; Wendorf, Fred and Schild, Romauld, 'The Earliest Food Producers', *Archaeology* 34:5 (1981); and Unger-Hamilton, Romana, 'Microscopic striations on flint sickle-blades as an indication of plant cultivation: preliminary results', *World Archaeology* 17:1 (1985), pp. 121–6.

30. See www.sciencedaily.com/releases/2015/07/150722144709.htm.

31. There is some debate surrounding Gobekli Tepe, which has been earmarked by some alternative researchers as a site of especial interest – witness, for example, Andy Collins' 2014 offering *Gobekli Tepe: Genesis of the Gods*. For example, it's the only one where there's little evidence of domestic housing, leading Jason Colavito to suggest it was built as a ritual centre by primarily hunter-gatherers. By contrast, in a number of papers published on academia.edu in 2016, Dimitrios Dendrinos of the University of Kansas argues against the radiocarbon dating of the site, suggesting it was based on contaminated in-fill; based on its more advanced monolithic technology, he proposes the earliest buildings are only around 7000 years old. Having said that the use of monolithic T-shaped pillars is clear at the nearby sites of Nevali Cori and Karahan Tepe; for information on the latter see, for example, Celik, Bahattin, 'Karahan Tepe: a new cultural centre in the Urfa area in Turkey', *Documenta Praehistorica* 38 (2011).

32. Details taken from the Wikipedia entries for each site. The date shown is for the first true urbanisation, not the earliest point of settlement.

33. Arnaud, Bernadette, 'First Farmers', *Archaeology* 53:6 (2000). See also www.cnrs.fr/Cnrspresse/Archeo2000/html/archeo11.htm.

34. Mithen et al., 'An 11,600 year-old communal structure from the Neolithic of southern Jordan', *Antiquity* 85 (2011), pp. 350–64.

35. Amended from http://en.wikipedia.org/wiki/Fertile_crescent.

36. See http://en.wikipedia.org/wiki/Hamoukar.

37. Bednarik, *Beads and the Origins of Symbolism* (2000, https://.semioticon.com/frontline/bednarik.htm). The remainder of the information about his work in this section is taken from this paper, unless otherwise stated.

38. These controversial finds were made by the same team that in 2003 discovered the remains of *Homo floresiensis*, nicknamed the 'hobbit' because of its short stature. This latter gained widespread exposure while the potentially much more fascinating earlier tool finds went largely unreported. See http://en.wikipedia.org/wiki/Homo_floresiensis.

39. Bednarik, 'Seafaring in the Pleistocene', *Cambridge Archaeological Journal* 13:1 (2003), pp. 41–66.

40. See www.ifrao.com/first-mariners-national-geographic-project-2004.

41. See http://en.wikipedia.org/wiki/Venus_of_Berekhat_Ram. The evidence for deliberate human working of this figurine is analyzed in detail by Alexander Marshack in *Antiquity* 71:272 (1997), pp. 327–38 (reproduced at www.utexas.edu/courses/classicalarch/readings/Berekhat_Ram.pdf).

42. Belitsky, S, Goren-Inbar, N and Werker, E, 'A Middle Pleistocene Wooden Plank with Man-Made Polish', *Journal of Human Evolution* 20 (1991), pp. 349–53. For more on the dating see 'Mollusc confirms dating of oldest known plank', *New Scientist*, 20 July 1991.

43. For a full analysis see my paper *Problems with Anomalous Artifacts* at www.ianlawton.com/att8.html, and also www.badarchaeology.net; the latter includes some pictures.

44. Although for an excellent rebuttal of this reverse argument see Forrester, Rochelle, *The Discovery of Agriculture* (2002, http://homepages.paradise.net.nz/rochelle.f/The-Discovery-of-Agriculture.html).

45. Rudgley, *Lost Civilisations of the Stone Age*, chapters 4 and 5.

46. See http://en.wikipedia.org/wiki/Damaidi.

10 SUPPOSED LOST CONTINENTS

1. Timaeus 2; see Lee, *Plato: Timaeus and Critias*, p. 36.

2. An excellent listing of various researchers' favoured locations from Plato's time through to 1954 is provided by Sprague de Camp in *Lost Continents*, Appendix C; most of these can be cross-referenced with his extensive bibliography.

3. The location is described in Timaeus 2, and the layout and other aspects in Critias 4; see Lee, *Plato: Timaeus and Critias*, pp. 37–8 and 136–42.

4. Although Plato suggests this metal is 'now unknown' it was actually well

known to all ancient Greeks and to the Romans who referred to it as 'aurichalcum' – more commonly known as brass; see http://en.wikipedia.org/wiki/Brass.

5. The Thera hypothesis is supported by, for example, JV Luce in *The End of Atlantis* and James W Mavor in *Voyage to Atlantis*, both published in 1969, and by Gavin Menzies in his 2013 work *The Lost Empire of Atlantis*.

6. This is based on the enigmatic *Oera Linda Book*, which is alleged to be a thirteenth-century Frisian text from Denmark; see Robert Scrutton's 1979 work *Secrets of Lost Atland*.

7. This idea was first mooted by Charles Hapgood in his 1958 work *Earth's Shifting Crust*, then built on in 1995 by Rand Flem-Ath in *When the Sky Fell*.

8. The main proponent of this theory was Andrew Collins in his 2000 work *Gateway to Atlantis*. Note also that his proposed date for its submergence is rather later then Plato's.

9. The Atlantic continent idea is supported by, for example, Ignatius Donnelly in his 1882 work *Atlantis: The Antediluvian World*, and Otto Muck in his 1979 work *The Secret of Atlantis*. Despite the similarity in name, the consensus is that the ocean was named not after the lost continent but after the Greek god Atlas.

10. See http://en.wikipedia.org/wiki/Mu_(lost_continent). However, while the theory of continental drift relies primarily on *horizontal* plate movement, at least one critic suggests that sediment cores taken from various parts of the Atlantic Ocean bed and other anomalies indicate that significant and rapid *vertical* movements of the crust have occurred; see Pratt, David, 'Plate Tectonics: A Paradigm Under Threat', *Journal of Scientific Exploration* 14:3 (2000), pp. 307–52.

11. See http://en.wikipedia.org/wiki/Sunken_continent, and in particular the links to the two continents mentioned.

12. Sprague de Camp, *Lost Continents*, chapter 1; he also provides an excellent compilation of extracts from these original works in Appendix A.

13. Ibid., chapter 2, pp. 28–35; for more on the translation issue see http://en.wikipedia.org/wiki/Diego_de_Landa.

14. Ibid., chapter 2, pp. 35–6.

15. Ibid., chapter 3, pp. 52–4.

16. Ibid., chapter 2, pp. 43–5.

17. See ibid., chapter 2, pp. 39–43 in which Sprague de Camp provides a sensible critique of a number of aspects of Donnelly's work.

18. For more background see http://en.wikipedia.org/wiki/Helena_Blavatsky.

19. In what follows we'll be concentrating on *The Secret Doctrine* only, and in particular on the second volume entitled 'Anthropogenesis' (the first is 'Cosmogenesis').

20. For more on the book see http://en.wikipedia.org/wiki/Book_of_Dzyan; and on Reigle's work see my paper *The Theosophical Perspective* at www.ianlawton.com/att4.html.

21. All the quoted stanzas from the *Book of Dzyan* can be found in Blavatsky, *The Secret Doctrine*, Volume 2, Part 1, pp. 17–21. Stanzas 1 to 4 have been omitted here as not relevant, while apparently there are others that she has herself omitted.

22. Although Blavatsky suggests in her commentary that the second race were 'the most heterogeneous gigantic semi-human monsters – the first attempts of material nature at building human bodies'; see ibid., Volume 2, Part 1, p. 138.

23. Blavatsky herself may or may not have been a racist, but her undoubted emphasis on the Aryan race was terribly distorted by some of her successors, particularly the occult-inspired Nazi regime in Germany. She does however emphasise that this particular expression 'black with sin' is merely a 'figure of speech' in the stanzas. See ibid., Volume 2, Part 1, p. 408, Footnote. See also Note **Error! Bookmark not defined.** below.

24. Ibid., Volume 2, 'Preliminary Notes', pp. 6–9.

25. Ibid., Volume 2, Part 1, pp. 429 and 432.

26. Ibid., Volume 2, Part 1, pp. 317 and 430.

27. Ibid., Volume 2, Part 1, p. 426.

28. See, for example, his *Histoire des Vierges* (Paris, 1879). Many of the references to these works can be easily traced using the index appended to later publications of *The Secret Doctrine*; although, at least with respect to these two authors, it's by no means exhaustive and a number of references are omitted.

29. Blavatsky, *The Secret Doctrine*, Volume 1, 'Introductory', p. xviii.

30. Scott-Elliot, *The Story of Atlantis and The Lost Lemuria*, p. 34; one wonders if he had come across Arabian tales of King Saurid in the course of his research (refer back to chapter 3).

31. Ibid., pp. 46–9. In mentioning 'personal *vril*' as the early power source he appears to be following Blavatsky's discussions of John Worrell Keely's experiments with 'sympathetic vibratory apparatus' in Philadelphia in the late nineteenth century; see *The Secret Doctrine*, Volume 1, Part 3, p. 563 and

also Lawton and Ogilvie-Herald, *Giza: The Truth*, chapter 4, p. 195.

32. Scott-Elliot, *The Lost Lemuria*, p. 13.

33. The Lemurian maps are reproduced at www.sacred-texts.com/atl/tll/tll01.htm, and the Atlantean at www.sacred-texts.com/atl/soa/soamap.htm.

34. See http://en.wikipedia.org/wiki/William_Scott-Elliot.

35. Scott-Elliot, *The Lost Lemuria*, pp. 19–21.

36. Steiner, *Atlantis and Lemuria*, Introduction, p. 8.

37. Ibid., chapter 1, pp. 13–14 and chapter 3, pp. 51–3.

38. These dates are discussed in Churchward, *The Lost Continent of Mu*, chapter 7; see also chapter 2 for the nature of its inhabitants and history, and chapter 3, p. 36 for a map showing its supposed size and location. Note that Scott-Elliot's maps show Lemuria as occupying not just the Indian Ocean but also considerable portions of the Pacific.

39. Ibid., chapter 1. A page of the 'vignettes' on the Naacal tablets is reproduced on p. 7, revealing many esoteric symbols that are commonly known but with somewhat strange embellishments.

40. Ibid., Addendum, Preface and following pages. Note that the 1994 edition from which our quotes come contains the original 1926 edition, and the 1931 updates to it in the Addendum.

41. Ibid., chapter 4, pp. 51–9.

42. Spence's map of these landmasses can be found in *History of Atlantis*, opposite p. 62. Note that his emphasis on the western island being in the area of the Sargasso Sea is a clear forerunner of the theory that Atlantis lay in the vicinity of the Caribbean.

43. Ibid., chapters 6–7.

44. Spence's map of these landmasses can be found in *The Problem of Lemuria*, opposite p. 160.

45. Spence, *The Occult Sciences in Atlantis*, chapter 1, pp. 7–10.

46. Ibid., chapter 3, pp. 27–31.

47. Background information from Randall-Stevens himself can be found in *From Atlantis to the Latter Days*, Foreword and Part 1, chapters 1–3.

48. This was a common method of channelling in the twentieth century, although it seems to be less so now. For example, many of the communications quoted in my book *Afterlife* were received in this manner.

49. Randall-Stevens, *From Atlantis to the Latter Days*, Part 1, chapters 4–5 and

Part 2, between pp. 108 and 109.

50. Ibid., Part 1, chapter 6, p. 52.

51. Ibid., Part 1, chapter 7, including plates 5–7. For arguments against these specific assertions see Note 23 to chapter 3, or in more detail Lawton and Ogilvie-Herald, *Giza: The Truth*, chapter 5, pp. 232–5 and Figures 20–1.

52. Almost identical drawings appear in Harvey Spencer Lewis' 1936 work *The Symbolic Prophecy of the Great Pyramid*, although it's unclear who was the plagiarist; see Lawton and Ogilvie-Herald, *Giza: The Truth*, chapter 5, p. 222.

53. From the cover copy.

54. See, for example, Kenneth Paul Johnson's excellent *Edgar Cayce in Context*, chapter 1, p. 35.

55. Johnson provides a thorough comparison of Cayce's 'Christian theosophy' with Blavatsky's 'esoteric theosophy' in ibid., chapter 2, pp. 43–8.

56. The oft-touted date of 10,500 BCE is consistently mentioned in a number of readings; see *Edgar Cayce on Atlantis*, chapter 5, pp. 142–3.

57. Johnson, *Edgar Cayce in Context*, Introduction, p. 6.

58. Sugrue, *The Story of Edgar Cayce*, chapter 15, p. 200.

59. Johnson, *Edgar Cayce in Context*, Introduction, p. 7.

60. Much of this originates in the work of quantum physicist and out-of-body explorer Tom Campbell in his lengthy, three-volume, 2007 master work *My Big T.O.E.* – or 'theory of everything'. For a summary of his ideas see Lawton, *Supersoul*, chapter 5, pp. 89–97.

61. Of course my more recent research has led me to question quite how these newer ideas square with the concept of universal cycles, and particularly with my interpretation of global origin traditions that I'm still proposing in chapter 8. It may be that it's completely invalidated. But I still feel that, because these traditions from around the world display so many commonalities, and because they appear to contain some sort of underlying esoteric wisdom, it's well worth laying them out in the way I have – if only as food for further thought. Above all, if I'm wrong on this front, this in no way detracts from my main theme of a forgotten golden race that became debased and was destroyed; nor from my interpretation of the creation-of-humankind traditions in chapter 7.

11 PSEUDOARCHAEOLOGY

1. Two excellent resources for articles debunking many of the non-mysteries covered in this chapter, as well as many others, are www.hallofmaat.com (see articles section) and www.badarchaeology.net.

2. We will specifically return to *The Ninurta Myth*, but he and his impressive array of weapons also figure heavily in *The Epic of Anzu*; see Dalley, *Myths from Mesopotamia*, pp. 203–27.

3. These include, for example, the 'fiery whirlwind' that took Ezekiel away (Ezekiel 1:4–28 and 3:12–4), although to anyone familiar with the Qabalah this passage is replete with esoteric symbolism; and the Lord taking Elijah up to heaven in a 'chariot of fire' (2 Kings 2:11).

4. For detailed discussions of this model, first 'identified' in 1969 by maverick Egyptologist Khalil Messiha, see www.catchpenny.org/model.html and www.badarchaeology.net/data/ooparts/aeroplanes.php.

5. See www.badarchaeology.net/data/ooparts/aeroplanes_2.php.

6. This was first brought to the public's attention by a certain Ruth Hover in 1989. For undoctored pictures of the panel, and an explanation of how recarving gave it its current look, see http://members.tripod.com/a_u_r_a/abydos.html. See also http://en.wikipedia.org/wiki/Abydos,_Egypt.

7. See James and Thorpe's essay on the subject in *Ancient Mysteries*, and also http://en.wikipedia.org/wiki/Dogon_people#Dogon_and_Sirius.

8. Temple, *The Sirius Mystery*, chapter 1, p. 32.

9. The most obvious objection is the fact that the enclosure effectively has only three sides due to the slope of the plateau, so there's no retaining wall at the front (east) end on which the Sphinx Temple stands. It is also beyond question that the latter structure is contemporary with the Sphinx, having been erected using blocks from the quarrying of the enclosure. Aside from any other objections, Temple doesn't explain how water can be retained in a container that only has three sides.

10. For further information see, for example, Welfare and Fairley, *Arthur C Clarke's Mysterious World*, chapter 3, pp. 64–7; De Solla Price, *Gears from the Greeks* (American Philosophical Society, 1974); and www.badarchaeology.net/data/ooparts/antikythera.php.

11. See Welfare and Fairley, *Arthur C Clarke's Mysterious World*, chapter 3, pp. 62–4; and www.badarchaeology.net/data/ooparts/batteries.php.

12. See Heinrich, Paul and Stromberg, Pierre, *The Coso Artifact* (2000, www.hallofmaat.com/modules.php?name=Articles&file=article&sid=77).

13. For reproductions of these two maps see Hapgood, *Maps of the Ancient Sea Kings*, Frontispiece and Figure 49.

14. See http://en.wikipedia.org/wiki/Antarctica.

15. For example on the Oronteus Finaeus map the continent is marked as 'Terra Australis Re'.

16. See the Bibliography for details.

17. I have neither the time nor the inclination to wade through so many similar titles, but once again we can express our gratitude to Jason Colavito, whose insightful reviews of most of the offerings from von Däniken and others are indispensable for anyone who would like to understand why all these books are, in large part, nothing more than entertaining fiction; see www.jasoncolavito.com/book-reviews.html.

18. West, *Serpent in the Sky*, Introduction, pp. 1–2.

19. Lawton and Ogilvie-Herald, *Giza: The Truth*, chapter 2, pp. 76–82.

20. For full details see ibid., chapter 7 and the Epilogue of the latest edition (chapter 16), reproduced at www.ianlawton.com/gttepil.html; also the papers and correspondence at www.ianlawton.com/as.html.

21. This earlier date is used by West in, for example, his 2006 documentary *Magical Egypt*.

22. To appreciate the extent to which Sitchin distorted the evidence for this assertion see *Giza: The Truth*, chapter 2, pp. 88–107. His original arguments were presented in *The Stairway to Heaven*, chapter 13, pp. 253–82.

23. The basic premise of the so-called Orion correlation was the subject of Bauval and Gilbert's 1994 work *The Orion Mystery*. This was subsequently expanded by Bauval and Hancock in *Keeper of Genesis*, particularly with respect to the 10,500 BCE dating, but the basic premise is almost certainly questionable irrespective of its supposed date. For more information on this see *Giza: The Truth*, chapter 9 and the Epilogue of the latest edition (chapter 16), reproduced at www.ianlawton.com/gttepil.html; also the papers and correspondence at www.ianlawton.com/oc.html.

24. Bauval and Hancock, *Keeper of Genesis*, chapter 6, pp. 106–9.

25. Ibid., chapter 3, pp. 27–33.

26. Lawton and Ogilvie-Herald, *Giza: The Truth*, chapter 4.

27. The best of these have come out since the original editions of *Giza: The Truth*, and are included in the Epilogue of the latest edition (chapter 16), reproduced at www.ianlawton.com/gttepil.html; see also the papers and correspondence at www.ianlawton.com/pc.html.

28. Again see the Epilogue of the latest edition.

29. See Doernenburg, Frank, *Baalbek, The Romans Really Did Build It!* (1996, www.ramtops.co.uk/baalbek.html).

30. The extensive experiments have been carried out by Denys Stocks of Manchester University; see his 2010 book *Experiments in Egyptian*

Archaeology. More generally see *Giza: The Truth*, chapter 4, pp. 204–7 and the Epilogue of the latest edition (chapter 16), reproduced at www.ianlawton.com/gttepil.html; also my correspondence with Dunn at www.ianlawton.com/am.html.

31. See *Giza: The Truth*, chapter 3 and Appendices II and III.

32. For my correspondence with Dunn see www.ianlawton.com/gpp.html.

33. See *Giza: The Truth*, chapter 8 (especially Figure 30) and the Epilogue of the latest edition (chapter 16), reproduced at www.ianlawton.com/gttepil.html.

34. See *Giza: The Truth*, Epilogue of the latest edition (chapter 16), reproduced at www.ianlawton.com/gttepil.html.

35. The first reference I can find to this is in a 2013 article by BL Freeborn at https://noahsage.com/2013/07/01/the-odd-little-purse-in-olmec-and-assyrian-art. It was expanded on by Laird Scranton in a 2016 article at http://lost-origins.com/perspectives-on-ancient-handbag-images, although this no longer seems to be available. Considerable numbers of further images and a little commentary can be found at https://rgdn.info/en/chto_nesut_bogi_v_sumochkah.

36. See, for example, his article in *UFO Reality* 3, August–September 1996.

37. See http://en.wikipedia.org/wiki/Chinese_pyramids.

38. See http://en.wikipedia.org/wiki/Bosnian_pyramids.

39. See, for example, http://en.wikipedia.org/wiki/Derinkuyu_underground_city.

40. See www.andrewcollins.com/page/interactive/bahamas.htm for the best account of the circumstances of its discovery.

41. The researcher most recently linked to the site is Greg Little, a senior member of Cayce's ARE who has worked closely with Andrew Collins. After diving there he wrote up his findings in 'The ARE's Search For Atlantis Part 2: Discoveries at Bimini: Columns, Marble Building Ruins, and Possible Building Foundations in 100 Feet of Water', *Alternative Perceptions Magazine* 115 (2007). He continues to be active in arguing the case for a man-made site, date as yet unknown.

42. See http://en.wikipedia.org/wiki/Bimini_Road.

43. See http://en.wikipedia.org/wiki/Yonaguni_Monument.

44. Schoch, *Voices of the Rocks*, chapter 4, pp. 106–13; see also his Plates section.

45. http://en.wikipedia.org/wiki/Marine_archaeology_in_the_Gulf_of_Cambay.

46. Tompkins, *Secrets of the Great Pyramid*, chapter 13, pp. 159–69.

47. See http://en.wikipedia.org/wiki/Angkor_Wat.

48. Although perhaps rather more debatable is their assertion that the template for this 'calendar machine' was part of the wisdom imparted to Enoch by the angel Uriel, which allowed him to anticipate a comet impact in 3150 BCE.

49. See http://en.wikipedia.org/wiki/History_of_Australia.

50. See http://en.wikipedia.org/wiki/Solutrean_hypothesis.

51. See http://en.wikipedia.org/wiki/Crystal_skull. Two skulls that were tested by the British Museum and thought to be recent fakes were one bought from Tiffany's auction house in 1898, which resides in the British Museum itself, and another that was sent to the Smithsonian Institute by an anonymous donor. Two further skulls on which the museum apparently refused to comment are 'Max', owned by JoAnn Parks 'Sha Na Ra' found by Nick Nocerino. See Morton and Thomas, *The Mystery of the Crystal Skulls*, chapter 16 and plates 8–11; and our own Plates 18 and 19.

52. This is confirmed in the original report that appeared in Hewlett-Packard's in-house magazine *Measure*, February 1971, pp. 8–10 (reproduced at www.hparchive.com/measure_magazine/HP-Measure-1971-02.pdf).

53. See http://en.wikipedia.org/wiki/Crystal_skull#Mitchell-Hedges_skull.

54. Watkins, 'How Did the Incas Create such Beautiful Stone Masonry', *Rocks and Minerals* 65 (1990); reproduced at www.ianlawton.com/am10.html.

55. I cannot help but point out that even a cursory glance at the Bibliography will reveal a *huge* proportion of pseudoarchaeological books are published by one house: Inner Traditions/Bear & Company in Rochester, Vermont. I am all for free speech, but we can but hope that one day its editors will become a little more selective about what they publish.

12 GEOLOGY

1. See http://en.wikipedia.org/wiki/Pleistocene, and also the entries for 'last glacial period' and 'last glacial maximum'.

2. Taken from Blyth and de Freitas, *A Geology for Engineers*, Figure 2.1.9, p. 29 (after E. Antevs).

3. See http://en.wikipedia.org/wiki/Sea_level_rise.

4. See http://en.wikipedia.org/wiki/Milankovitch_cycles.

5. The paper was Alvarez et al., 'Extraterrestrial cause for the Cretaceous-Tertiary Extinction', *Science* 208:4448 (1980), pp. 1095–1107; see also http://en.wikipedia.org/wiki/Impact_event#Mass_extinctions_and_impacts.

6. See http://en.wikipedia.org/wiki/Chicxulub_impactor.

7. See http://en.wikipedia.org/wiki/Extinction_event.

8. See the Bibliography for details of their work.

9. See, for example, Martin and Klein's 1984 work *Quaternary Extinctions*, pp. 358–61 and also http://en.wikipedia.org/wiki/Quaternary_extinction_event.

10. Velikovsky, *Earth in Upheaval*, chapter 1; his main source is Whitley, DG, 'The Ivory Islands in the Arctic Ocean', *Journal of the Philosophical Society of Great Britain* 12 (1910).

11. Hapgood, *The Path of the Pole*, chapter 10, pp. 259–64 and 272–5; unfortunately he doesn't provide a source for the dating information.

12. For a fine summary see Bishop, Sue, *Woolly Mammoth Remains: Catastrophic Origins?* (undated, www.talkorigins.org/faqs/mammoths.html).

13. Velikovsky, *Earth in Upheaval*, chapter 1; his main sources are Rainey, F, 'Archaeological Investigation in Central Alaska', *American Antiquity* 5 (1940) and Hibben, FC, 'Evidence of Early Man in Alaska', *American Antiquity* 8 (1943).

14. Hapgood, *The Path of the Pole*, chapter 10, pp. 275–7; the original source is Hibben's 1946 work *The Lost Americans*, pp. 90–2 and 176–8; only a small part of the original quote has been reproduced.

15. I am indebted to geologist Paul Heinrich for pointing me in the direction of this more recent research (personal correspondence, 13 June 2001). A selection of the references he cites regarding the Alaskan muck are as follows: Guthrie, Dale and Guthrie, M Lee, 'Death on the Steppe: The Case of the Frozen Bison', *New Scientist* 127:1727 (1990), pp. 47–51; Westgate, et al., 'A 3 m.y. Record of Pliocene-Pleistocene Loess in Interior Alaska', *Geology* 18:9 (1990), pp. 858–61; and Preece et al., 'Tephrochronology of Late Cenozoic Loess at Fairbanks, Alaska', *Geological Society of America Bulletin* 111:1 (1999), pp. 71–90.

16. Velikovsky, *Earth in Upheaval*, chapter 2; his main source is Buckland's *Reliquiae Diluvianae*. The caves themselves were at Kirkdale, Brentford, Cefn and Bleadon in Britain, and at Breugue and Arcy in France.

17. Ibid., chapter 5; his source for much of the European material is Joseph Prestwich's 1895 work *On Certain Phenomena Belonging to the Close of the Last Geological Period*; Prestwich was a professor of geology at Oxford who investigated many of the sites himself. The British sites were in Plymouth and Pembrokeshire; the European sites were Kesserloch in Switzerland, Neukoln in Germany, and in central and southern France, Gibraltar, Corsica, Sardinia and Sicily; the US sites were Cumberland Cavern in Maryland, La Brea Asphalt Pit near Los Angeles, Agate Spring Quarry in Nebraska, Big Bone Lick in Kentucky, San Pedro Valley in California, John Day Basin in Oregon and Lake Florissant in Colorado; the Asian sites were Choukoutien in Northern China,

the Siwalik foothills in India and the gorges of the Irrawady River in central Burma.

18. See http://en.wikipedia.org/wiki/William_Buckland.

19. For example, no one now seriously considers the La Brea Tar Pit to be anything other than a trap for unsuspecting animals that have strayed into it at their peril for tens of thousands of years. There is no mention of evidence of a catastrophe at http://en.wikipedia.org/wiki/La_Brea_Tar_Pits.

20. Velikovsky, *Earth in Upheaval*, chapter 4, pp. 46–7.

21. One of the few places they are discussed on the internet is at, for example, www.sentex.net/~tcc/michwls.html.

22. See www.lakemichiganwhales.com. Velikovsky reports similar remains in more southerly states such as Alabama, Georgia and Florida in *Earth in Upheaval*, chapter 4, pp. 48–9, but I can find no corroboration of this.

23. Ibid., chapter 16, p. 264.

24. Paine, Michael and Peiser, Benny, *The Frequency and Consequences of Cosmic Impacts Since the Demise of the Dinosaurs* (2002, http://homepage.mac.com/mpaineau/filechute/bioastr2002.pdf).

25. See https://web.stanford.edu/~meehan/donnelly/whiston.html.

26. Napier, 'Cometary Catastrophes, Cosmic Dust and Ecological Disasters in Historical Times: The Astronomical Framework' in Peiser et al., *Natural Catastrophes During Bronze Age Civilisations*, pp. 21–32.

27. Allan and Delair, *When the Earth Nearly Died*, Part 4, chapters 15–17. The *Epic of Creation* continues on from the extract in chapter 8 to describe how Tiamat is cut into pieces to form heaven and earth. The folly of anyone interpreting this as an account of the destruction wrought by a stray planet winding its way through our solar system is demonstrated by the context of the other traditions in which a god's body is broken up for similar purposes – for example, P'an Gu and Ymir in Chinese and Scandinavian traditions respectively; see Dalley, *Myths from Mesopotamia*, p. 19.

28. Some of their diagrams and figures are almost identical to those in Sitchin's *The Twelfth Planet*.

29. Geological engineer Colin Reader points out that the features of relict glaciation that litter northern Europe and North America are directly comparable to those found in modern ice fields; while there are features that usually accompany rock striations – for example, roches moutonnées and drumlin – that are exclusively formed by ice but not water flows (personal correspondence, 4 March 2001).

30. Velikovsky, *Earth in Upheaval*, chapter 7, pp. 98–9.

31. See http://en.wikipedia.org/wiki/Carolina_bays.

32. Melton and Shriever, 'The Carolina Bays: Are They Meteorite Scars?' *Journal of Geology* 41 (1933), pp. 52–66. This and all the following material about the bays is taken from Andrew Collins' compilation of reports in *Gateway to Atlantis*, chapters 21–2.

33. Prouty, 'Carolina Bays and their Origin', *Bulletin of the Geological Society of America* 63 (1952), pp. 167–222.

34. See Carson and Hussey, 'The Oriented Lakes of Arctic Alaska', *Journal of Geology* 70 (1962), pp. 417–39; Kelly, 'The Origin of the Carolina Bays and the Oriented Lakes of Alaska', *Popular Astronomy* 59 (1951), p. 204; and Plafker, 'Oriented Lakes and Lineaments in Northern Bolivia', *Bulletin of the Geological Society of America* 75 (1964), pp. 503–22.

35. Ingram, Robinson and Odum, 'Clay Mineralogy of some Carolina Bay Sediments', *Southeastern Geology* 1 (1959), pp. 1–10.

36. Again see http://en.wikipedia.org/wiki/Carolina_bays.

37. Velikovsky, *Earth in Upheaval*, chapter 8, p. 117.

38. Ibid., chapter 4, pp. 40–4.

39. Ibid., chapter 4, pp. 44–6.

40. The former in *When the Sky Fell* and the latter in *Fingerprints of the Gods*, both published in 1995.

41. Velikovsky, *Earth in Upheaval,* chapter 9.

42. Barbiero, 'On the Possibility of Very Rapid Shifts of the Poles', *Aeon* 4:6 (1997). This paper contains complex mathematics, at least for a nonspecialist, but it certainly appears to be the most in-depth and scholarly study of this subject undertaken to date.

43. For further general references, discussion and analysis see http://en.wikipedia.org/wiki/Cataclysmic_pole_shift_hypothesis.

44. See, for example, the articles by Paul Heinrich at www.hallofmaat.com/topics/wsog concerning Axel Heiberg Island and Antarctica.

45. See http://en.wikipedia.org/wiki/Geomagnetic_reversal.

46. Unless otherwise stated, all the information in this section comes from http://en.wikipedia.org/wiki/Younger_Dryas.

47. See http://en.wikipedia.org/wiki/Clovis_culture.

48. See http://en.wikipedia.org/wiki/Folsom_tradition.

49. Firestone et al., *The Cycle of Cosmic Catastrophes*, chapter 1.

50. Ibid., chapters 2–7, 9, 34 and appendix D.

51. Ibid., chapter 10, pp. 125–8.

52. Ibid., chapter 8.

53. See http://en.wikipedia.org/wiki/Drumlin.

54. Firestone et al., *The Cycle of Cosmic Catastrophes*, chapters 10, 17–20 and 27. One of his arguments is that no Clovis era finds are noted in the literature about the bays, even though if they existed at that time they should have been used as water sources. But they would surely have contained stagnant rather than fresh, flowing water, so this argument may be suspect.

55. Firestone et al., 'Evidence for an extraterrestrial impact 12,900 years ago that contributed to the megafaunal extinctions and the Younger Dryas cooling', *Proceedings of the National Academy of Sciences* 104:41 (2007), pp. 16016–21.

56. For further discussion and analysis see http://en.wikipedia.org/wiki/Younger_Dryas_impact_hypothesis. The academic papers cited include: Kerr, RA, 'Planetary Impacts. Did the mammoth slayer leave a diamond calling card?', *Science* 323 (2009), p. 26; Kennett et al., 'Nanodiamonds in the Younger Dryas boundary sediment layer', *Science* 323 (2009), p. 94; Haynes, G, 'The catastrophic extinction of North American mammoths and mastodonts', *World Archaeology* 33:3 (2010), pp. 391–416; Israde-Alcantara et al., 'Evidence from central Mexico supporting the Younger Dryas extraterrestrial impact hypothesis', *Proceedings of the National Academy of Sciences* 109:13 (2012), pp. 737–47; Bunch et al., 'Very high-temperature impact melt products as evidence for cosmic airbursts and impacts 12,900 years ago', *Proceedings of the National Academy of Sciences* 109:28 (2012), pp. 1903–12; Wittke et al., 'Evidence for deposition of 10 million tonnes of impact spherules across four continents 12,800 years ago', *Proceedings of the National Academy of Sciences* 110:23 (2013), pp. 2088–97; Dalton, R, 'Blast in the past?', *Nature* 447 (2017), pp. 256–7; Moore et al., 'Widespread platinum anomaly documented at the Younger Dryas onset in North American sedimentary sequences', *Scientific Reports* 7:1 (2017); Wolbach et al., 'Extraordinary biomass burning episode and impact winter triggered by the Younger Dryas cosmic impact 12,800 years ago – Parts 1 and 2', *Journal of Geology* 126:2 (2018), pp. 165–205; Moore et al., 'Sediment cores from White Pond, South Carolina, contain a platinum anomaly, pyrogenic carbon peak, and coprophilous spore decline at 12.8 ka', *Scientific Reports* 9:1 (2019); and Pino et al., 'Sedimentary Record from Patagonia, Southern Chile supports cosmic-impact triggering of biomass burning, climate change, and megafaunal extinctions at 12.8 ka', *Scientific Reports* 9:1 (2019).

57. For the lack of replication see Surovell et al., 'An independent evaluation of

the Younger Dryas extraterrestrial impact hypothesis', *Proceedings of the National Academy of Sciences* 106:43 (2009), pp. 18155–8. There have also been severe criticisms of Firestone's co-author on the original book, Allen West, including that he had been convicted of fraud, had changed his name and had no genuine academic qualifications; see Dalton, Rex, 'Comet theory comes crashing to Earth', *Pacific Standard*, 14 May 2011. More generally see http://en.wikipedia.org/wiki/Younger_Dryas_impact_hypothesis, specifically the section headed 'Criticism'.

58. See http://en.wikipedia.org/wiki/Earth's_magnetic_field.

59. See http://en.wikipedia.org/wiki/Coronal_mass_ejection.

60. For example Collins in *Gobekli Tepe*, and Hancock in *Magicians of the Gods* and *America Before*; see the Bibliography for details.

61. Schoch, *Forgotten Civilisation*, Appendix 5.

62. Ibid., back cover.

63. LaViolette, Paul, 'Evidence for a solar flare cause of the Pleistocene mass extinction', *Radiocarbon* 53:2 (2011), pp. 303–23.

64. Despite other problems with their work, Allan and Delair provide a comprehensive review of these traditions; see *When the Earth Nearly Died*, Part 3 and in particular Table 3B, pp. 162–4. It is worth nothing that Firestone et al. provide details of a number of especially Amerindian traditions throughout Part 3 of *The Cycle of Cosmic Catastrophes*; however they're curiously labelled as 'retold from' their source, and close examination of, for example, their 'retelling' of the Indian flood myth of Manu, and of Plato's supposed account of the flood, shows a great deal of poetic license has been taken – especially with modern-style references to 'fires falling from the sun', 'planets whirling through the sky' and 'shaking lose bodies from space' (see chapter 25, p. 263 and chapter 33, p. 328); this is somewhat disappointing given the arguably rather more reliable nature of their physical evidence.

65. Taken from 'Natural Law'; see Morgan, *Essays from Huai Nan Tzu*, p. 82.

66. See, for example, Jacobsen's introduction to the 'Cylinders of Gudea' in *The Harps That Once...*, p. 387.

67. Dalley, *Myths from Mesopotamia*, glossary (s.v. *abubu* and *kasusu*), pp. 317 and 324.

68. Jacobsen, *The Harps That Once...*, Footnotes 7 and 8, p. 237. However we might note that the entire third part of this composite text is comprised of a similarly enigmatic description of Ninurta passing judgment on the various rocks and minerals found on the earth.

69. Ninurta 80–96; see ibid., pp. 240–1.

70. Ninurta 167–8; see ibid., p. 244.

71. Ninurta 174–81; see ibid., p. 245.

72. Ninurta 334–44; see ibid., pp. 251–2. This second part of the text then goes on to describes how Ninurta set up irrigation systems, but that seems to shed little in the way of useful contextual light on the extract under review.

73. Of course the Mesopotamian *Epic of Creation* shares some similarities with this text, and I've rejected literal interpretations of it by Sitchin and by Allan and Delair. Lest I be accused of double standards this is because it's clearly an origin myth that shares much in common with those from other cultures, whereas the *Ninurta Myth* isn't and is arguably more comparable to other catastrophe traditions. As for suggestions by some alternative researchers that the latter describes an aeronautical or even nuclear conflict, we'll return to the issue of supposed advanced technology in chapter 12.

74. Theogony 682–707 and 820–68; see West, *Hesiod: Theogony and Works and Days*, pp. 23–4 and 27–8.

75. 1 Enoch 54:1–3; see Laurence, *The Book of Enoch*, p. 61. In Genesis 9 this is taken to mean a rainbow after the flood, but was there originally some deeper meaning?

76. 1 Enoch 64:1–3 and 9; see ibid., pp. 78–9.

77. 1 Enoch 79:3–7; see ibid., pp. 110–11.

78. Erra and Ishum 1; see Dalley, *Myths from Mesopotamia*, p. 290.

13 THE REAL ATLANTIS

1. Picture adapted from www.planetaryvisions.com.

2. See http://en.wikipedia.org/wiki/Sea_level.

3. See http://en.wikipedia.org/wiki/Sunda_Shelf.

4. See http://en.wikipedia.org/wiki/Last_Glacial_Maximum.

5. For example, Oppenheimer suggests there were three main flood events due to glacial melt, at around 14,000, 11,500 and 8400 years ago (see *Eden in the East*, chapter 1, pp. 29–38); also his detailed review and interpretation of global origin and creation traditions is largely psychological because he connects them to the flood events (see ibid., chapters 11–13). As for Santos, some aspects of his work seem to be somewhat speculative to say the least, while he credits the Atlanteans with a more advanced level of technology than I do. Meanwhile I've critiqued Joseph's work generally in chapter 11.

6. I should point out that in the original of the current work, *Genesis Unveiled*, I merely speculated that substantial areas of the China, Yellow and Java Seas were still dry land connected to the main Asian continent. However by 2010

when I rewrote and republished it as the little-known *History of the Soul* I had fully researched the Sunda and Sahul shelves and identified Indonesia as my main candidate for the location of our forgotten race. Although two of the books mentioned came out before this, I only discovered Oppenheimer's *after* I came to this conclusion, while Santos' (and Joseph's) contributions only came to my attention recently.

7. See   http://en.wikipedia.org/wiki/Gunung_Padang_Megalithic_Site   and related links (although none of these are more recent than 2014).

8. The best English-language source for details of this criticism seems to be Bachelard, Michael and Rompies, Karuni, 'Digging for the truth at controversial megalithic site', *Sydney Morning Herald*, 27 July 2013.

9. See   www.scientificamerican.com/article/long-hidden-pyramid-found-in-indonesia-was-likely-an-ancient-temple.

10. See, for example, www.flintknapperman.com.

11. Williamson, RW, *Religious and Cosmic Beliefs of Central Polynesia* (Cambridge, 1933), Volume 1, p. 8; cited in Allan and Delair, *When the Earth Nearly Died*, Part 3, chapter 5, p. 155.

12. Ellis, W, *Polynesian Researches* (London, 1829), Volume 2, p. 57; cited in ibid., Part 3, chapter 5, pp. 155–6.

13. Churchward, *The Lost Continent of Mu*, chapter 4, pp. 63–79.

14. See the Bibliography for details of his works on Pacific Islands.

BIBLIOGRAPHY

This bibliography is limited to the books specifically referenced in this work. The details given below are for the imprint or edition consulted, although the original date of publication quoted in the main text may have been earlier.

RELEVANT BOOKS BY THE AUTHOR

Lawton, Ian, *Supersoul: A Radical Worldview for a New Consciousness*, Rational Spirituality Press, 2016 (first published 2013).

Lawton, Ian and Ogilvie-Herald, Chris, *Giza: The Truth*, Rational Spirituality Press, 2020 (first published 1999).

Lawton, Ian, *Mesopotamia: The Truth*, Rational Spirituality Press, 2020.

ANCIENT TEXTS, TRADITIONS AND MYTHOLOGY

Aston, WG (trans.), *Nihongi*, Kegan Paul, 1896.

Augustine, Saint, *The City of God* (7 volumes), Heinemann Young, 1958–98.

Baines, John and Malek, Jaromir, *Atlas of Ancient Egypt*, Oxford, 1980.

Best, Robert M, *Noah's Ark and the Ziusudra Epic: Sumerian Origins of the Flood Myth*, Enlil Press, 1999.

Bierhorst, John (trans.), *History and Mythology of the Aztecs: The Codex Chimalpopoca*, University of Arizona Press, 1992.

Budge, EA Wallis (trans.), *The Egyptian Heaven and Hell* (3 volumes in 1), Dover, 1996.

Budge, EA Wallis, *Osiris and the Egyptian Resurrection* (2 volumes), Philip Lee Warner, 1911.

Campbell, Joseph, *The Masks of God* (4 volumes: *Primitive Mythology*, *Oriental Mythology*, *Occidental Mythology* and *Creative Mythology*), Arkana, 1991 (first published 1959–68).

Campbell, Joseph and Musès, Charles, *In All Her Names*, Harper, 1991.

Charlesworth, James H (ed.), *The Old Testament Pseudepigrapha* (2 volumes), Darton, Longman and Todd, 1983.

Coomaraswamy, Ananda K and Sister Nivedita, *Myths of the Hindus and Buddhists*, Dover Publications, 1967 (first published 1916).

Copenhaver, Brian (trans.), *Hermetica: The Greek Corpus Hermeticum and the Latin Asclepius*, Cambridge University Press, 1998.

Cory, Isaac Preston, *Ancient Fragments*, Wizards Bookshelf, 1975 (first published 1832).

Cotterell, Arthur (ed.), *The Penguin Encyclopaedia of Ancient Civilisations*, Penguin, 1988.

Dalley, Stephanie (trans.), *Myths from Mesopotamia: Creation, The Flood, Gilgamesh and Others*, Oxford World's Classics, 1991.

Dimmitt, Cornelia and van Buitenen, JAB, *Classical Hindu Mythology: A Reader in the Sanskrit Puranas*, Temple University Press, 1978.

Dutt, Manmatha Nath (trans.), *Vishnu Purana*, Calcutta, 1894.

Dutt, Romesh C (trans.), [Extracts from] *The Ramayana and The Mahabharata*, Everyman, 1944 (first published 1910).

Eisenman, Robert and Wise, Michael (trans.), *The Dead Sea Scrolls Uncovered*, Penguin, 1993.

Eliade, Mircea, *The Myth of the Eternal Return*, New York, 1954.

Eliade, Mircea, *The Sacred and the Profane: The Nature of Religion*, Harcourt, 1959.

Eliade, Mircea, *Myth and Reality*, Waveland Press, 1998 (first published 1963).

Eliade, Mircea, *Shamanism: Archaic Techniques of Ecstasy*, Arkana, 1989 (first published 1964).

Faulkner, Raymond (trans.), *The Ancient Egyptian Pyramid Texts*, Oxford University Press, 1969.

Faulkner, Raymond (trans.), *The Ancient Egyptian Coffin Texts*, Aris and Phillips, 1978.

Faulkner, Raymond (trans.), *The Ancient Egyptian Book of the Dead*, British Museum Press, 1996.

Feuerstein, Georg, Kak, Subhash and Frawley, David, *In Search of the Cradle of Civilisation*, Quest, 1995.

Fowden, Garth, *The Egyptian Hermes*, Cambridge University Press, 1986.

Frazer, James George, *The Golden Bough: A Study in Magic and Religion*,

Penguin, 1996 (12 volumes, first published 1890–1915).

Graves, Robert, *The White Goddess*, Faber and Faber, 1999 (first published 1948).

Gray, Louis Herbert (ed.), *The Mythology of All Races* (13 volumes), Marshall Jones Co., Boston, 1916–64.

Guirand, Felix (ed.), *The Larousse Encyclopaedia of Mythology*, Paul Hamlyn, 1965.

Heidel, Alexander, *The Gilgamesh Epic and Old Testament Parallels*, University of Chicago Press, 1949.

Heidel, Alexander (trans.), *The Babylonian Genesis*, University of Chicago Press, 1951.

Hodge, Stephen, *The Dead Sea Scrolls*, Piatkus, 2001.

Il Manoscritto Messicano Vaticano 3738, Detto Il Codice Rios, Rome, 1900.

Jacobsen, Thorkild, *The Sumerian King List*, Chicago, 1939.

Jacobsen, Thorkild (trans.), *The Harps That Once... Sumerian Poetry in Translation*, Yale University Press, 1987.

Jung, Carl, *Psychology and Alchemy*, Routledge, 1993 (first published 1953).

Kramer, Samuel N, *Sumerian Mythology*, Harper and Bros., 1961.

Kramer, Samuel N, *Mythologies of the Ancient World*, Anchor, 1961.

Kramer, Samuel N, *The Sumerians, Their History, Culture and Character*, University of Chicago Press, 1971 (first published 1963).

Laurence, Richard (trans.), *The Book of Enoch the Prophet*, Wizards Bookshelf, 1995 (first published 1883).

Lee, Desmond (trans.), *Plato: Timaeus and Critias*, Penguin Classics, 1977.

Lenormant, François and Chevallier, E, *The Ancient History of the East* (3 volumes), Asher and Co, 1870.

Levi-Strauss, Claude, *Myth and Meaning*, Routledge, 1978.

Lewy, Hans, *Chaldaean Oracles and Theurgy*, Études Augustiniennes, 1978.

Mackenzie, Donald A, *Myths of China and Japan*, Gresham, 1923.

Melville, AD (trans.), *Ovid: Metamorphosis*, Oxford World Classics, 1998.

Milik, JT, *The Books of Enoch – Aramaic Fragments of Qumran Cave 4*, Oxford University Press, 1976.

Morfill, WR (trans.) and Charles, RH, *The Book of the Secrets of Enoch*, Oxford, 1896.

Morgan, Evan, Tao, *The Great Luminant: Essays from Huai Nan Tzu*, Kegan Paul, 1933.

Müller, Max (ed.), *The Sacred Books of the East* (50 volumes), Oxford, 1879–91 (see also www.sacred-texts.com/sbe/index.htm).

Murray, Alex (ed.), *History of the Jews* (2 volumes), London, 1874.

O'Flaherty, Wendy Doniger (trans.), *The Rig Veda*, Penguin Classics, 1981.

Oliver, George, *Antiquities of Freemasonry*, Richard Spencer, 1843.

Philippi, Donald L (trans.), *Kojiki*, Princetown University Press, 1969.

Prasad, Ganga, *The Fountainhead of Religion*, Book Tree, 2000 (first published 1927).

Rackham, H, Jones, WHS and Eichholz, DE, *Pliny: Natural History* (10 volumes), William Heinemann, 1938–57.

Ray, Pratapa Chandra (trans.), *The Mahabharata* (9 volumes), Calcutta, 1884–94.

Reymond, Eve, *The Mythical Origin of the Egyptian Temple*, Barnes and Noble, 1969.

Robinson, James M, *The Nag Hammadi Library*, HarperCollins, 1990.

Roux, Georges, *Ancient Iraq*, Penguin, 1992 (first published 1964).

Rundle Clark, RT, *Myth and Symbol in Ancient Egypt*, Thames and Hudson, 1959.

Scott, Walter, *Hermetica*, Solos Press, 1992 (first published in 4 volumes 1924–36).

Smith, George, *The Chaldean Account of Genesis*, London, 1876.

Tedlock, Dennis (trans.), *Popol Vuh: The Mayan Book of the Dawn of Life*, Touchstone, 1996.

Thompson, J Eric S, *Maya Hieroglyphic Writing*, University of Oklahoma, 1960.

Thompson, J Eric S, *Maya History and Religion*, University of Oklahoma Press, 1970.

Thompson, J Eric S, 'The Dresden Codex: A Maya Hieroglyphic Book', *Memoirs of the American Philosophical Society* 93 (1972).

Vermes, Geza, *The Dead Sea Scrolls in English*, Penguin, 1962.

Waters, Frank, *Book of the Hopi*, Penguin, 1977.

Werner, Edward TC, *Myths and Legends of China*, Sinclair Browne, 1984 (first published 1922).

Werner, Edward TC, *A Dictionary of Chinese Mythology*, Kelly and Walsh, 1932.

West, ML (trans.), *Hesiod: Theogony and Works and Days*, Oxford World Classics, 1999.

West, ML, *The Orphic Poems*, Oxford University Press, 1983.

Westcott, W Wynn, *Collectanea Hermetica* (6 volumes), Theosophical Publishing Society, 1895.

Willis, Roy (ed.), *World Mythology*, Duncan Baird, 1993.

Wilkins, WJ, *Hindu Mythology*, Curzon Press, 1900.

Wise, Michael, Abegg, Martin and Cook, Edward, *The Dead Sea Scrolls: A New Translation*, HarperCollins, 1996.

Woolley, Leonard, *The Sumerians*, Oxford, 1929.

Yukteswar, Sri, *The Holy Science*, Self-Realisation Fellowship, 1986 (first published 1894).

ARCHAEOLOGY AND EVOLUTION

Balfour, Michael, *Megalithic Mysteries*, Parkgate Books, 1997.

Behe, Michael, *Darwin's Black Box: The Biochemical Challenge to Evolution*, Free Press, 1996.

Brass, Michael, *The Antiquity of Man: Artifactual, Fossil and Gene Records Explored*, PublishAmerica, 2002.

Breuil, Abbe H, *Four Hundred Centuries of Cave Art*, Centre d'Études et de Documentation Prehistorique, undated.

Chomsky, Noam, *Language and Mind*, Harcourt Brace Jovanovich, 1972.

Chomsky, Noam, *Language and Problems of Knowledge*, MIT Press, 1988.

Clottes, Jean and Lewis-Williams, David, *The Shamans of Prehistory: Trance and Magic in Painted Caves*, Harry N Abrams, 1998.

Crick, Francis HC, *Life Itself: Its Origin and Nature*, Simon and Schuster, 1981.

Darwin, Charles, *On the Origin of Species*, Penguin, 1985 (first published 1859).

Darwin, Charles, *The Descent of Man*, John Murray, 1871.

Dawkins, Richard, *The Selfish Gene*, Oxford University Press, 1989 (first published 1976).

Dawkins, Richard, *The Blind Watchmaker*, Longmans, 1986.

Dawkins, Richard, *River Out of Eden*, Phoenix, 1996.

Deacon, Hillary, *Human Beginnings in South Africa: Uncovering the Secrets of the Stone Age*, David Philip, 1999.

Dennett, Daniel, *Consciousness Explained*, Little Brown, 1991.

Dennett, Daniel, *Darwin's Dangerous Idea*, Penguin, 1995.

Feder, Kenneth L, *Frauds, Myths and Mysteries: Science and Pseudoscience in Archaeology*, Mayfield, 1999.

Gould, Stephen Jay, *The Panda's Thumb*, Norton, 1980.

Gould, Stephen Jay, *The Flamingo's Smile*, Norton, 1985.

Gould, Stephen Jay, *Bully for Brontosaurus*, Norton, 1991.

Gould, Stephen Jay, *The Book of Life*, Norton, 1993.

Klein, Richard, *The Human Career*, University of Chicago Press, 1999.

Leakey, Richard, *The Making of Humankind*, E P Dutton, 1981.

Leakey, Richard, *The Origin of Humankind*, Phoenix, 1995.

Leakey, Richard and Lewin, Roger, *Origins Reconsidered*, Doubleday, 1992.

Lewin, Roger, *Complexity: Life at the Edge of Chaos*, Macmillan, 1992.

Lewin, Roger, *The Origin of Modern Humans*, W H Freeman, 1993.

Morell, Virginia, *Ancestral Passions: The Leakey Family and the Quest for Humankind's Beginnings*, Touchstone, 1996.

Pinker, Steven, *The Language Instinct: The New Science of Language and Mind*, William Morrow, 1994.

Popper, Karl and Eccles, John, *The Self and its Brain*, Springer-Verlag, 1977.

Rudgley, Richard, *Lost Civilisations of the Stone Age*, Arrow, 1999.

Rudgley, Richard, *Secrets of the Stone Age*, Century, 2000.

Stocks, Denys, *Experiments in Egyptian Archaeology: Stoneworking Technology in Ancient Egypt*, Routledge, 2010.

Tudge, Colin, *Neanderthals, Bandits and Farmers: How Agriculture Really Began*, Yale University Press, 1999.

Wesson, Robert, *Beyond Natural Selection*, MIT Press, 1991.

LOST CONTINENTS AND THEOSOPHY

Blavatsky, Helena, *Isis Unveiled* (2 volumes), Theosophical Publishing House, 1972 (first published 1877).

Blavatsky, Helena, *The Secret Doctrine* (2 volumes), Theosophical University Press, 1988 (first published 1888).

Blavatsky, Helena, *The Voice of the Silence*, Quest Books, 1996 (first published 1889).

Blavatsky, Helena, *Collected Writings* (15 volumes), Quest Books, 1960–80.

Cayce, Edgar Evans, *Edgar Cayce on Atlantis*, Howard Baker, 1969.

Childress, David Hatcher, *Ancient Tonga and the Lost City of Mu'a*, Adventures Unlimited Press, 1996.

Childress, David Hatcher, *Ancient Micronesia and the Lost City of Nan Madol*, Adventures Unlimited Press, 1997.

Childress, David Hatcher, *Lost Cities of Ancient Lemuria and the Pacific*, Adventures Unlimited Press, 1998.

Churchward, James, *The Lost Continent of Mu*, BE Books, 1994 (first published 1926).

Churchward, James, *The Sacred Symbols of Mu*, BE Books, 1988 (first published 1933).

Collins, Andrew, *Gateway to Atlantis*, Headline, 2000.

Cranston, Sylvia, *HPB: The Extraordinary Life and Influence of Helena Blavatsky*, Putnam, 1993.

Donnelly, Ignatius, *Atlantis, the Antediluvian World*, Sampson Low and Co, 1882.

Donnelly, Ignatius, *Ragnarok, the Age of Fire and Gravel*, Sampson Low and Co, 1883.

Johnson, K Paul, *The Masters Revealed: Madame Blavatsky and the Myth of the Great White Lodge*, State University of New York Press, 1994.

Johnson, K Paul, *Edgar Cayce in Context*, State University of New York Press, 1998.

Joseph, Frank, *The Destruction of Atlantis*, Bear & Co, 2004.

Joseph, Frank, *Survivors of Atlantis*, Bear & Co, 2004.

Joseph, Frank, *The Lost Civilisation of Lemuria*, Bear & Co, 2006.

Joseph, Frank, *Before Atlantis: 20 Million Years of Human and Pre-Human Cultures*, Bear & Co, 2013.

Leslie, J Ben, *Submerged Atlantis Restored* (2 volumes), Kessinger Publishing Co, 2003 (first published 1911).

Luce, JV, *The End of Atlantis*, Thames and Hudson, 1969.

Mavor, James W, *Voyage to Atlantis*, Souvenir Press, 1969.

Menzies, Gavin, *The Lost Empire of Atlantis*, W&N, 2013.

Muck, Otto, *The Secret of Atlantis*, Fontana, 1979.

Oppenheimer, Stephen, *Eden in the East: The Drowned Continent of Southeast Asia*, Phoenix, 1999.

Randall-Stevens, HC, *From Atlantis to the Latter Days*, Knights Templars, 1981 (first published 1954).

Reigle, David, *The Books of Kiu-te*, Wizards Bookshelf, 1983.

Reigle, David and Nancy, *Blavatsky's Secret Books*, Wizards Bookshelf, 1999.

Santos, Arysio, *Atlantis: The Lost Continent Finally Found*, Atlantis Publications, 2005.

Scott-Elliot, W, *The Story of Atlantis and The Lost Lemuria*, Theosophical Publishing House, 1968 (first published 1925).

Scrutton, Robert, *Secrets of Lost Atland*, Sphere Books, 1979.

Sinnett, Alfred Percy, *Esoteric Buddhism*, Houghton Mifflin, 1884.

Smith, A Robert, *The Lost Memoirs of Edgar Cayce*, ARE Press, 1997.

Spence, Lewis, *History of Atlantis*, Senate, 1995 (first published 1926).

Spence, Lewis, *The Problem of Lemuria, the Sunken Continent of the Pacific*, Rider and Co, 1932.

Spence, Lewis, *The Occult Sciences in Atlantis*, Aquarian Press, 1978 (first published 1943).

Sprague de Camp, Lyon, *Lost Continents: The Atlantis Theme in History, Science and Literature*, Dover, 1970 (first published 1954).

Steiner, Rudolf, *Atlantis and Lemuria*, Anthroposophical Publishing

Company, 1923 (first published 1911).

Sugrue, Thomas, *The Story of Edgar Cayce: There Is a River*, ARE Press, 1997 (first published 1942).

Tomas, Andrew, *Shambhala: Oasis of Light*, Sphere, 1972.

Tomas, Andrew, *Atlantis: From Legend to Discovery*, Sphere, 1973.

MODERN ALTERNATIVE HISTORY

Alford, Alan, *Gods of the New Millennium*, Hodder and Stoughton, 1997.

Arguelles, José, *The Mayan Factor*, Bear & Co, 1987.

Baigent, Michael, *Ancient Traces*, Penguin, 1999.

Bauval, Robert and Gilbert, Adrian, *The Orion Mystery*, Mandarin, 1995.

Bauval, Robert and Hancock, Graham, *Keeper of Genesis*, Mandarin, 1997 (republished in the US under the title *The Message of the Sphinx*).

Childress, David Hatcher, *Vimana Aircraft of Ancient India and Atlantis*, Adventures Unlimited Press, 1991.

Collins, Andrew, *From the Ashes of Angels*, Signet, 1997.

Collins, Andrew, *Gods of Eden*, Headline, 1998.

Collins, Andrew, *The Cygnus Mystery*, Watkins Publishing, 2008.

Collins, Andrew, *Gobekli Tepe: Genesis of the Gods*, Bear & Co, 2014.

Collins, Andrew, and Little, Greg, *Denisovan Origins*, Bear & Co, 2019.

Corliss, William R, *Ancient Man: A Handbook of Puzzling Artifacts*, Sourcebook Project, 1978.

Cremo, Michael A and Thompson, Richard L, *Forbidden Archaeology*, Bhaktivedanta Institute, 1993.

Cremo, Michael A and Thompson, Richard L, *The Hidden History of the Human Race*, Govardhan Hill, 1994 (condensed version of above).

Cremo, Michael, *Forbidden Archaeology's Impact*, Bhaktivedanta Book Publishing, 1998.

Drake, W Raymond, *Gods and Spacemen in the Ancient East*, Sphere, 1973 (first published 1968).

Dunn, Christopher, *The Giza Power Plant*, Bear & Co, 1998.

Elkington, David, Ellson, Paul and Reid, John, *In the Name of the Gods*, Green Man Press, 2001.

Flem-Ath, Rand and Wilson, Colin, *The Atlantis Blueprint*, Little Brown, 2000.

Gardner, Laurence, *Genesis of the Grail Kings*, Bantam, 2000.

Gilbert, Adrian, *Signs in the Sky*, Bantam, 2000.

Gilbert, Adrian and Cotterell, Maurice, *The Mayan Prophecies*, Element, 1995.

Gooch, Stan, *Cities of Dreams: When Women Ruled the World*, Aulis Books, 1995.

Hancock, Graham, *Fingerprints of the Gods*, Mandarin, 1996.

Hancock, Graham and Faiia, Santha, *Heaven's Mirror*, Michael Joseph, 1998.

Hancock, Graham, *Magicians of the Gods: The Forgotten Wisdom of Earth's Lost Civilisation*, Coronet, 2016.

Hancock, Graham, *America Before*, Coronet, 2019.

Hapgood, Charles, *Maps of the Ancient Sea Kings*, Adventures Unlimited Press, 1996 (first published 1966).

James, Peter and Thorpe, Nick, *Ancient Inventions*, Ballantine, 1994.

Jenkins, John Major, *Maya Cosmogenesis 2012*, Bear and Co, 1998.

Joseph, Frank, *Ancient High Tech*, Bear & Co, 2020.

Knight, Christopher and Lomas, Robert, *Uriel's Machine*, Century, 1999.

Kolosimo, Peter, *Not of this World*, Sphere, 1971.

Kolosimo, Peter, *Timeless Earth*, Sphere, 1974.

LaViolette, Paul, *Earth Under Fire*, Starlane Publications, 1997.

Lockyer, Norman, *The Dawn of Astronomy*, Macmillan, 1894.

Miller, Crichton, *The Golden Thread of Time*, Pendulum Publishing, 2001.

Morton, Chris and Thomas, Ceri Louise, *The Mystery of the Crystal Skulls*, Thorsons, 1998.

de Santillana, Giorgio and von Dechend, Hertha, *Hamlet's Mill*, Godine, 1977 (first published 1969).

Schoch, Robert, *Forgotten Civilisation*, Inner Traditions, 2012.

Schoch, Robert and Bauval, Robert, *Origins of the Sphinx*, Inner Traditions, 2017.

Schwaller de Lubicz, René, *Sacred Science*, Inner Traditions, 1988 (first published 1961).

Sigdell, Jan Erik, *Reign of the Anunnaki*, Bear & Co, 2018.

Sitchin, Zecharia, *The Twelfth Planet*, Bear & Co, 1991 (1st Edition, 1976).

Sitchin, Zecharia, The Stairway to Heaven, Avon, 1980.

Sitchin, Zecharia, The Wars of Gods and Men, Avon, 1985.

Sitchin, Zecharia, The Lost Realms, Avon, 1990.

Sitchin, Zecharia, Genesis Revisited, Avon, 1990.

Sitchin, Zecharia, When Time Began, Avon, 1993.

Steiger, Brad, *Worlds Before Our Own*, Berkley, 1979.

Tellinger, Michael, *Slave Species of the Gods*, Bear & Co, 2012.

Temple, Robert, *The Sirius Mystery*, Arrow, 1999 (first published 1976).

Temple, Robert, *The Crystal Sun*, Century, 2000.

Tomas, Andrew, *We Are Not the First*, Souvenir, 1971.

Tomas, Andrew, *On the Shores of Ancient Worlds*, Souvenir, 1974.

Tompkins, Peter, *Secrets of the Great Pyramid*, Galahad, 1997 (first published 1971).

von Däniken, Erich, *Chariots of the Gods*, Souvenir Press, 1969.

von Däniken, Erich, *In Search of Ancient Gods*, Souvenir Press, 1975.

von Däniken, Erich, *The Eyes of the Sphinx*, Berkley, 1996.

von Däniken, Erich, *History Is Wrong*, New Page Books, 2009.

von Däniken, Erich, *Twilight of the Gods*, Career Press, 2010.

von Däniken, Erich, *Odyssey of the Gods*, Career Press, 2011.

von Däniken, Erich, *Evidence of the Gods*, New Page Books, 2012.

von Däniken, Erich, *Astronaut Gods of the Maya*, Bear & Co, 2017.

von Däniken, Erich, *The Gods Never Left Us*, New Page Books, 2017.

von Däniken, Erich, *Impossible Truths*, Watkins, 2018.

Welfare, Simon and Fairley, John, *Arthur C Clarke's Mysterious World*, Collins, 1980.

West, John Anthony, *Serpent in the Sky*, Quest, 1993 (first published 1979).

Wilkins, Harold T, *Mysteries of Ancient South America*, Rider and Co, 1946.

Wilkins, Harold T, *Secret Cities of Old South America: Atlantis Unveiled*, Rider and Co, 1950.

Wickramasinghe, Chandra and Bauval, Robert, *Cosmic Womb: The Seeding of Planet Earth*, Bear & Co, 2018.

Wilson, Colin, *From Atlantis to the Sphinx*, Virgin, 1997.

GEOLOGY AND CATASTROPHE

Allan, Derek and Delair, Bernard, *When the Earth Nearly Died*, Gateway, 1995 (republished in the US under the title *Cataclysm*).

Clube, Victor and Napier, Bill, *The Cosmic Winter*, Basil Blackwell, 1990.

Firestone, Richard, West, Allen and Warwick-Smith, Simon, *The Cycle of Cosmic Catastrophes*, Bear & Co, 2006.

Flem-Ath, Rand and Rose, *When the Sky Fell*, Wiedenfeld and Nicolson, 1995.

Hapgood, Charles, *The Path of the Pole*, Souvenir, 2001 (first published 1958 under the title *Earth's Shifting Crust*).

Hibben, Frank C, *The Lost Americans*, Thomas Y Crowell, 1946.

Hugget, Richard, *Cataclysms and Earth History: The Development of Diluvialism*, Clarendon Press, 1989.

Martin, Paul S and Klein, Richard (eds.), *Quaternary Extinctions: A Prehistoric Revolution*, University of Arizona Press, 1984.

Palmer, Trevor, *Perilous Planet Earth: Catastrophes and Catastrophism through the Ages*, Cambridge University Press, 1999.

Peiser, Benny, Palmer, Trevor and Bailey, Mark (eds.), *Natural Catastrophes During Bronze Age Civilisations*, Archaeopress, 1998.

Schoch, Robert M, *Voices of the Rocks*, Harmony, 1999.

Spedicato, Emilio, *Apollo Objects, Atlantis and the Deluge: A Catastrophist Scenario for the End of the Last Glaciation*, Instituto Universitario di Bergamo, 1990.

Velikovsky, Immanuel, *Worlds in Collision*, Abacus, 1972 (first published 1950).

Velikovsky, Immanuel, *Earth in Upheaval*, Buccaneer, 1955.

White, John, *Pole Shift*, ARE Press, 1997 (first published 1980).

INDEX

Plate 1 One of the deliberate burials in the Qafzeh cave in Israel, dated to 92,000 years ago. Here we see a woman with a child at her feet. (wikepedia.org)

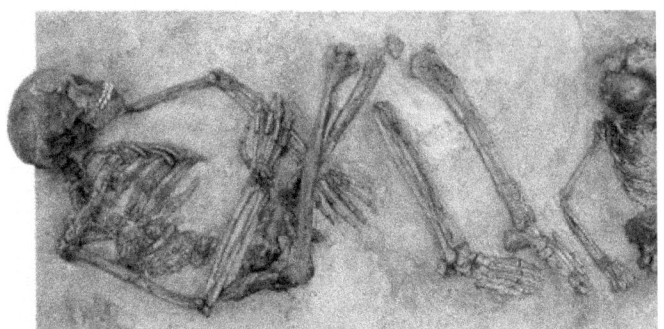

Plate 2 Ochre block found in the Blombos cave in South Africa and dated to-70,000 years ago. Surely these abstract markings suggest a sophisticated level of thought? (wikepedia.org)

Plate 3 The 'Quneitra artifact' found in Israel and dated to 54,000 years ago. Again its patterns of nested semicircles and vertical lines appear to be symbolic and to indicate sophisticated abstract thought. (Alexander Marshack)

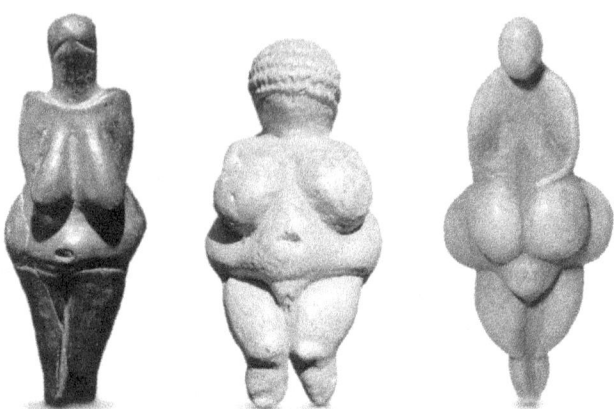

Plate 4 A variety of 'Venus figurines'. These European examples are as much as 40,000 years old and, although stylised, are carefully sculpted. (Ancient Art and Architecture Collection)

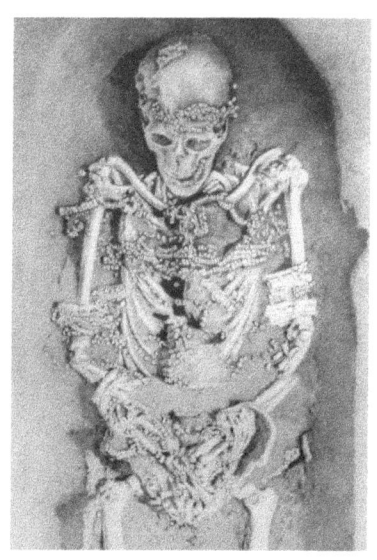

Plate 5 The 'Venus of Brassempouy'. This beautifully sculpted ivory figurine from France is 25,000 years old. Were such fine artists merely subsisting in cold, damp caves? (Agence Photographique de la Réunion des Musées Nationaux)

Plate 6 One of the 'Sungir skeletons'. This adult was buried in Russia 30,000 years ago with full regalia, including clothing adorned with hundreds of drilled ivory beads. Would purely nomadic tribes struggling for survival have time for such luxuries? (Science Photo Library)

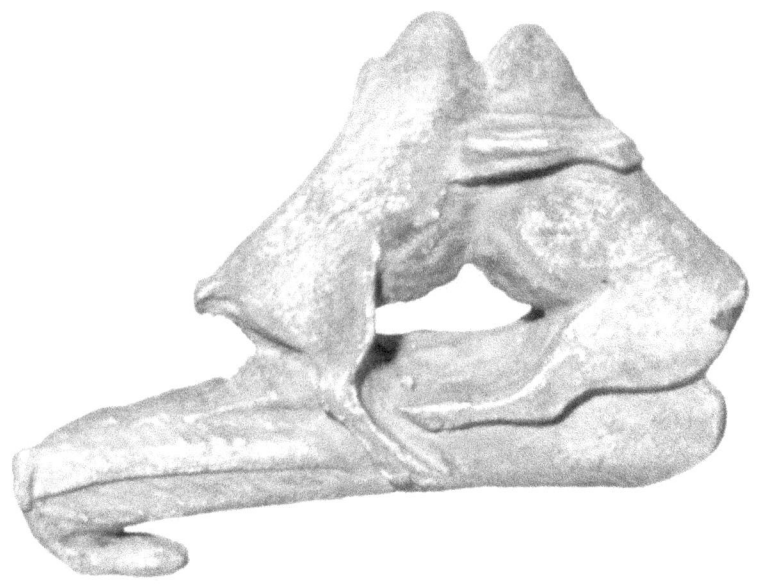

Plate 7 Decorated spear thrower. This beautiful 16,000 year-old example from Le Mas d'Azil in France is carved from bone and shows two fighting bison. (Ancient Art and Architecture Collection)

Plate 8 Bison painting. This is a reproduction of a fine example of Upper Palaeolithic art from the Altamira Caves in Spain that dates to around 15,000 years ago. Is it not the equal of anything produced in the modern era? (StockphotoPro)

Plate 9 Jerf el Ahmar. This sizeable settlement in Syria is around 11,600 years old. Does the fact that it has no precursors prove that it was built by the survivors of a global catastrophe? (Danielle Stordeur/CNRS)

Plate 10 Aerial view of one of the round communal buildings at Jerf el Ahmar, surrounded by individual houses. Stone has been used throughout for construction, and there are clear signs of early agriculture. Were our antediluvian ancestors engaging in settled agriculture long beforehand? (Danielle Stordeur/CNRS)

Plate 11 The site of Jerf el Ahmar about to be flooded by a newly-constructed dam in 1999. It is now buried under 15 meters of water. How much evidence of our coastal-dwelling forgotten race was lost when sea levels rose by as much as 120 meters at the end of the Pleistocene? (Danielle Stordeur/CNRS)

Plate 12 Close up of one of the communal buildings at Jerf el Ahmar. (Danielle Stordeur/CNRS)

Plate 13 Etched terracotta plaquette from Jerf el Ahmar. Are the symbols mnemonics of some sort? (Danielle Stordeur/CNRS)

Plate 14 Drawings of more etched plaquettes from Jerf el Ahmar, showing a variety of symbolism. (Danielle Stordeur/CNRS)

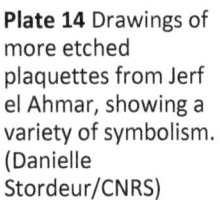

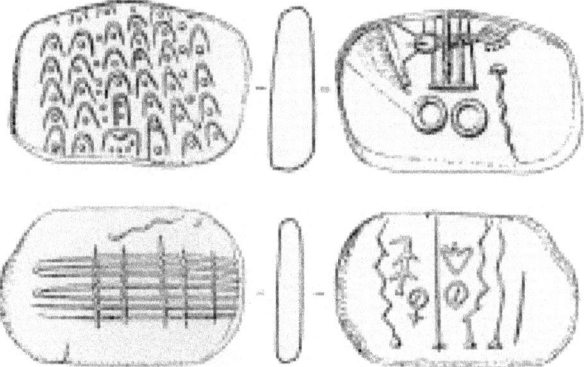

Plate 15 Example of late Sumerian pictographic script, which first emerged some 5000 years ago. Is this merely a development of the etchings from Jerf el Ahmar many millennia before? (Ancient Art and Architecture Collection)

Plate 16 Hand-held model of the 'Celtic cross'. Note how the bob-weighted dial revolves and is read through holes in the upright. Were our antediluvian ancestors using such a simple but effective device to navigate the oceans? (Crichton Miller)

Plate 17 Full-sized model of the 'Celtic cross' being used by its 'reinventor' to measure the angle of the sun. (Crichton Miller)

THE PREHISTORIC TRUTH SERIES

all published by Rational Spirituality Press *www.rspress.org*
see also *www.ianlawton.com*

[Volume 1] GIZA: THE TRUTH (2020) is the 20th anniversary edition of this celebrated book, which thoroughly investigates how, why and when the most famous archaeological monuments in the world were built... in the process placing grave doubt on the multitude of alternative theories that surround them.

[Volume 2] ATLANTIS: THE TRUTH (2020) is a reinterpretation of the most revered ancient texts and traditions from all around the world that postulates a forgotten, highly cultured but not technologically advanced 'golden race' who were wiped out in a global catastrophe around 13,000 years ago... with supporting geological and other evidence suggesting where, when and how this 'Atlantean' race most likely lived.

[Volume 3] MESOPOTAMIA: THE TRUTH (2020) is an investigation into what was really going on in what is perhaps the definitive cradle of civilisation, and what elements of modern living were introduced for the first time... coupled with a thorough rebuttal of alternative interpretations of its texts concerning supposed extraterrestrial visitors who genetically created humankind.

THE SUPERSOUL SERIES

all published by Rational Spirituality Press *www.rspress.org*
see also *www.ianlawton.com*

RESEARCH BOOKS

[Volume 1] SUPERSOUL (2013) is the main reference book for Supersoul Spirituality, containing out-of-body and channelled evidence that each and every one of us is a holographic reflection of a supersoul that has power way beyond our wildest imaginings.

[Volume 2] THE POWER OF YOU (2014) compares modern channelled wisdom from a variety of well-known sources, all emphasising that each of us is consciously or unconsciously creating every aspect of our own reality, and that this is what the current consciousness shift is all about.

[Volume 3] AFTERLIFE (2019) is a state-of-the-art, clear, reliable guide to the afterlife based on the underlying consistencies in traditional channelled material and modern out-of-body research.

SIMPLE BOOKS

SH*T DOESN'T JUST HAPPEN!! (2016) introduces Supersoul Spirituality by explaining how and why we ourselves create or attract everything we experience in our adult lives... so that we are never victims of chance, God's will, our karma or our life plans.

WHAT JESUS WAS REALLY SAYING (2016) is a fundamental reinterpretation of the Christian message that uses excerpts from the Gospels to propose that, through his supposed miracles, Jesus was trying to show us that each of us is a creator god of the highest order and can manipulate the illusion we call reality at will.

THE GOD WHO SOMETIMES SCREWED UP (2018) charts the author's progression from motorcycle and car racer, to pyramid explorer and researcher of ancient civilisations, to spiritual philosopher... with analysis and examples of how he has created or manifested all the various aspects of his life, both good and bad.

DEATH IS AN ADVENTURE!! (2019) is a simple yet essential guide to the afterlife, which answers all your questions such as why you will continue to exist, what to expect and how best to prepare. Based on evidence not belief, it describes the unlimited possibilities we have to create wondrous new experiences... as long as we have a reliable map of the territory.

IAN LAWTON was born in 1959. Formerly an accountant, sales exec, business and IT consultant and avid bike and car racer, in his mid-thirties he changed tack completely to become a writer-researcher specialising in ancient history. His first two books, *Giza: The Truth* and *Genesis Unveiled*, sold over 30,000 copies worldwide.

After this he turned to spiritual philosophy, and in his *Books of the Soul Series* he originated the ideas of Rational Spirituality and of the holographic soul. But since 2013 he has been developing the more radical worldview of Supersoul Spirituality in the *Supersoul Series*. A short film clip discussing the latter can be found at *www.ianlawton.com* and on YouTube.

Lightning Source UK Ltd.
Milton Keynes UK
UKHW021043050321
379837UK00016B/2258